Charles Rennie Mackintosh and Co.

1854 to 2004

A book plate designed by Charles Rennie Mackintosh for John Keppie.

Charles Rennie Mackintosh and Co.

1854 to 2004

David Stark

UNIVERSITY of GLASGOW MEDICAL QUEEN MARGARET COLLEGE DERRTT JOHN HONEYMAN AND KEPPIE ARCHITECTS

Stenlake Publishing Ltd.
2004

ISBN 1 84033 323 5

**The publishers regret that they cannot supply
copies of any pictures featured in this book.**

Plans [are] prepared by the eminent architects, Messrs Honeyman & Keppie, whose
names are sufficient guarantee of the excellence and good taste of all the arrangements
and details of the building.

Bridge of Allan Reporter, 27 April 1895.

Acknowledgements

A great many people have helped with the production of this book over the past four years. Special mention is due to the many current and former staff of the Keppie practice who gave me their recollections and supplied me with information; my researcher Morag Cross, without whom a lot of flesh would have been missing from bones; and the numerous people who let me into their homes and buildings. Thanks are also due to: Morag Baker, St Serf's Church, Dysart; Andrew Bethune, Edinburgh Central Library; Roger Billcliffe for his advice on Mackintosh drawings; Mike Davis, Helensburgh Library; Chris Fleet and Diana Webster, the National Library of Scotland; Carol Fleming and Kate Parker, the Royal Scottish National Orchestra; Margaret Harrison, Jordanhill College Library; Graham Hopner, West Dunbartonshire Libraries; Alan Lamont; Dr E. Mairi MacArthur, New Iona Press; James MacAulay and Theo van Asperen, Glasgow Art Club; Murdo MacDonald, Argyll and Bute Libraries; Dr Irene O'Brien and staff, Glasgow City Archives; Matthew Pease; George Rawson and Sarah Hepworth, Glasgow School of Art Archives; David Roberts, Paisley Library; Pamela Robertson, Hunterian Art Gallery; Stuart Robertson, Charles Rennie Mackintosh Society; Jane Smith, Glasgow City Council Cultural and Leisure Services; Peter Trowles, Glasgow School of Art; Gordon Urquhart; Dr David Walker, who checked various facts and supplied information on architect biographies; Kristina Watson and her colleagues at RCAHMS; Friends of Govan Old; Friends of Kilfinan Church; the National Library of Scotland Map Library; the Scottish Record Office; numerous churches that provided details of their histories; and staff at the following institutions: Ardrossan Library; A. K. Bell Library, Perth; Ayrshire Archives, Ayr; the Glasgow Room at the Mitchell Library; Glasgow University Archives.

Picture credits

t – top, m – middle, b – bottom, l – left, r – right

Aerofilms: 24b; Tom Affleck: 189; T. and R. Annan and Sons: 11ml, 28, 74b, 138, 141, 143, 183; Paul Bell (Devis Ltd.): 312; Brechin Cathedral: 164; George Cairns, University of Essex: 207; Charles Babbage Institute, University of Minnesota: 247; David Crocker: 30b, 242; E3DI: 309t; Bill Early: 303; Edinburgh City Libraries: 122; Eric Eunson: 48l, 140b; Glasgow Art Club: 139; Glasgow Caledonian University, Heatherbank Museum of Social Work: 88; Glasgow City Council Development and Regeneration Services: 48r, 213t; Glasgow Museums and Art Galleries: 142; Glasgow School of Art: 11tl, 11tr, 13, 68, 97, 98, 108, 118l, 140t, 146ml, 146bl, 146tr, 146br, 147, 148, 154, 156, 158, 168, 179, 184, 186, 187t, 188, 191, 192, 193, 195, 197, 202/203, 208, 209, 212, 213b, 219tl, 220, 223, 230b, 319; Keith Hunter: 244, 250, 284, 286, 296, 298, 300t, 300b, 301, 302t, 302b, 304/305, 306t, 307t, 308t, 308b, 310, 311; Hunterian Art Gallery, University of Glasgow, Mackintosh Collection: 3, 32, 100, 117, 137, 144/145, 155, 174, 180, 181, 214/215, 218; Guthrie Hutton: 55, 93; Bruce Jamieson: 163t; David Jamieson: 238l; Ken Bear Illustrations: 309b; David Kidd: 227b; Kilfinan Church: 157; A. Graham Lappin: 243; Dr E. M. MacArthur: 160; Stuart Marshall: 228; Margeorie Mekie: 124; Mitchell Library, Glasgow City Libraries & Archives: 21t, 40b, 47, 66t, 66m, 66b, 87b, 103, 104t, 172t, 172b, 185, 269, 271; Trustees of the National Library of Scotland: 90; Ozturk Modelmakers: 194; Paisley Library and Museum: 82, 83, 84, 85t; Royal Commission on the Ancient and Historical Monuments of Scotland: 18, 35, 49, 50; Royal Scottish National Orchestra: 36, 37; St Serf's Church, Dysart: 150r; Skelmorlie Church: 120b; the late Andrew Stuart: 44; Peter Stewart: 273l; University of Glasgow Archives: 22, 23, 41, 266; University of Strathclyde: 261b; Victoria and Albert Museum: 146tl; David Walker: 77b.

Contents

Paisley Library and Museum. The extension on the right was probably designed by Mackintosh.

Introduction

The title of this book seeks shamelessly to capitalise on the fame of Charles Rennie Mackintosh, one of Scotland's most eminent architects. He was the third principal of an architectural practice founded in Glasgow in 1854 by John Honeyman, and which today retains the name of its second principal, John Keppie. At the beginning of the twenty-first century it is one of Scotland's largest ever architectural practices.

Mackintosh's talents were not widely recognised during the period he worked with Honeyman and Keppie from 1889 to 1913. In Victorian and Edwardian Britain, the style he promoted when he was given his artistic freedom was regarded as peripheral to mainstream design. Those who wrote books about him in the second half of the twentieth century (none of whom incidentally were practising architects) constructed a vision of Mackintosh to suit their theses. One of his first biographers, Thomas Howarth, portrayed Mackintosh as a modernist, ahead of his time and a significant influence on twentieth-century architecture. Subsequent scholars have questioned this, and many have been more interested in his position within artistic movements of the nineteenth century.

Most architectural books on Mackintosh concentrate on a relatively small number of buildings where architectural historians can identify the development of a style which will fit into context. Academics are comfortable with such an approach, and inconsistencies, compromises and apparent lapses of stylistic integrity are blamed on commercial pressures brought to bear by others. In Mackintosh's case these might have been imposed by his boss John Keppie, until he became a partner himself.

The aura of Mackintosh relies on a romantic idea of a past era in which an artistic genius was tragically misunderstood. It is bolstered by references to modern artefacts such as the jewellery on sale in all good Glasgow jewellers and tourist shops, 'inspired by Rennie Mackintosh', even though he did not design much jewellery (but does it matter if they are in themselves attractive objects to the beholder?). The truth is that Mackintosh was not an independent architect working alone, an impression given by some books on his work, which barely mention that he was part of an architectural practice for 24 years, nor hint at the fact that he was almost certainly involved in the design of dozens more buildings than they give him credit for.

Clients pay for buildings. While architects will try to persuade them as to the merits of a particular architectural approach, they will usually prefer compromise to resignation from a commission. Architects who promote a single or house style seldom have much work or longevity. Honeyman might have designed a Free church in a Gothic style or a Catholic one with Italian references because that was felt appropriate. A public building such as Paisley Library and Museum was designed in Grecian Ionic because Victorians admired classical society and architecture. Alexander 'Greek' Thomson exploited this for various building types. Scots baronial was deemed correct for a town hall in Helensburgh or Gothic revival for a Highland hotel at Ballachulish. Most buildings were modest in nature and style because their clients worked to small budgets or did not wish to appear ostentatious.

The Ballachulish Hotel.

This story of an architectural practice over a 150 year period is as much a social history as an architectural one. Architecture is a product of the society which spawns it; it is more than an abstract art form. This book is not an architectural catalogue or record. While ruins may have a romantic charm, buildings without use are sterile. I am more interested in their value to society – why they were built, why their occupants loved them and how they continue to perform a useful role when their original function comes to an end.

I also hope that the book will give an insight into what architects are and what they do. I met the then Secretary of State for Scotland, Donald Dewar, three times in 1998, twice being interviewed with Richard Meier of New York for the chance to design the Scottish Parliament Building, and the third time at the commencement of construction of the Royal Infirmary of Edinburgh and the University of Edinburgh Medical School.

Dewar looked at the schematic hospital drawings on the wall of the site hut and remarked that the architect's role on the project must be nearly complete since the visual form of the hospital had been defined. I informed him that there would be an architectural team of 30 working on the project for the next year, reducing to five over the following three years of construction. He did not understand that architects were carrying out an extensive consultation exercise with clinical staff representatives to ensure that every detail of the 5,000 rooms in the hospital reflected their requirements. With the advice he had been given, Dewar assumed that architects worked on the conceptual, artistic aspects of building design and that engineers, builders or someone else dealt with more practical aspects.

Above all, I hope that the reader will enjoy wallowing in nostalgia for the places illustrated. Most people in Scotland will either have lived in, been born in, been educated in, worked in, received medical treatment in, shopped in, flown from or at least have visited several of the buildings mentioned in this book. They, their parents and grandparents have been part of the society which spawned them. The buildings which remain today are more than the bricks and mortar, or the architectural facade. They echo with the voices of the people who inhabited them, and are our permanent reminder of them. From the most modest to the most celebrated, they are part of our heritage. Most of the buildings are still there to be seen, and many are worth a visit.

The story of the architectural practice is also the story of its people, especially in the first 90 years when four principals shaped the direction it took: John Honeyman as its founder who took John Keppie into partnership in 1888, and passed on his share of the business to Charles Rennie Mackintosh between 1902 and 1904. Honeyman and

John Honeyman (1830–1914), illustrated in the Bailie, *26 August 1896.*

John Keppie (1862–1945).

Charles Rennie Mackintosh (1868–1928).

Graham Henderson (1882–1963).

Alex Smellie.

Keppie were from wealthy families. Mackintosh, a police superintendent's son, needed time to buy his way into the partnership. Graham Henderson took the position vacated by Mackintosh at the end of the First World War.

Having Mackintosh in the practice has been fortuitous, with extensive research resources available in a multitude of books and articles. The inevitable comparative brevity in this book on the subject of Mackintosh is countered by a list of references at the end, and brief notes as to their content. A few people have written academic dissertations on Honeyman, and these have been useful sources.

John Keppie has received less attention, perhaps by being under the shadow of Mackintosh to architectural scholars; but most of the designers over the last 150 years have been happy to serve their clients and society without making a fuss. They have been ordinary people with the everyday pressures of making a living, developing personal relationships and raising families.

Honeyman married three times and was widowed twice, his first wife dying from childbirth complications and his second from tuberculosis. Two of his four sons also died from TB. One of his sons was a lifelong friend of artist and designer Herbert MacNair, who became Charles Rennie Mackintosh's brother-in-law. Mackintosh's girlfriend in the early 1890s, Jessie Keppie, was his boss's sister, but he transferred his affections to Margaret Macdonald and married her. John Keppie also lost out to one of the artistic community, his sweetheart Helen Law choosing to marry 'Glasgow Boy' E.A. Walton. He may also have had a romantic attachment with 'Glasgow Girl' artist Bessie MacNicol in 1897. John and Jessie Keppie never married and lived together in Prestwick to their dying days.

Graham Henderson came back from the First World War with a badly injured right arm and had to learn to draw with his left hand. In the pre-war recession from 1910 to 1913, he was more resilient than Mackintosh, who often became morose with the consequent lack of artistic challenge. Keppie, and increasingly Henderson, kept the practice alive during the fallow years between the two world wars.

There was a fifth principal during this period, Alex Smellie, who started as an apprentice in 1906 (there is evidence that he gained unpaid experience in the office before this) but was not made a partner until 1930. Structural engineering did not exist as a separate discipline until around the 1920s when building structures became more complex, and Smellie was the technical specialist who made sure the designs produced in the studio were technically competent. Although more behind the scenes, apart from in the more mundane, industrial projects, his contribution must have been sufficiently valued to merit partnership as Keppie neared retirement age. He never became a qualified architect, but joined the Royal Institute of British Architects, obtaining the initials LRIBA after his name as a licentiate, which one could do in those days if one could demonstrate at least eighteen years in architectural practice.

If there were five principals up to the Second World War, there have been over 30 since, as the world and the architectural profession changed dramatically. There had been no more than half a dozen staff in the office at any time during the first 90 years. In the 1980s there were 80 before Keppie Henderson was taken over by Scott Brownrigg and Turner in 1989, and at the beginning of 2004 Keppie Design had 157 people working in design studios in Glasgow, Edinburgh, Perth and Belfast. An Inverness office opened in November 2004.

It is less easy to objectively chronicle the last 50 years, as a large number of us who contributed to them are still alive. To us the period still seems mundane and it is not appropriate for us to validate our own contributions; only posterity can do this.

Knowing this has not stopped me occasionally commenting on recent times, and I came to the conclusion that I had to write this book in the first person since the history is seen through my eyes, with my interpretation of events. Perhaps the person who updates it for the 200th anniversary of the practice will cover these years more objectively.

This 1911 Graham Henderson sketch of Le Vieux Saint-Etienne Church in Caen, Normandy, illustrates his proficiency as a draftsman prior to his right arm being injured during the First World War.

The Keppie Practice Corporate Lineage

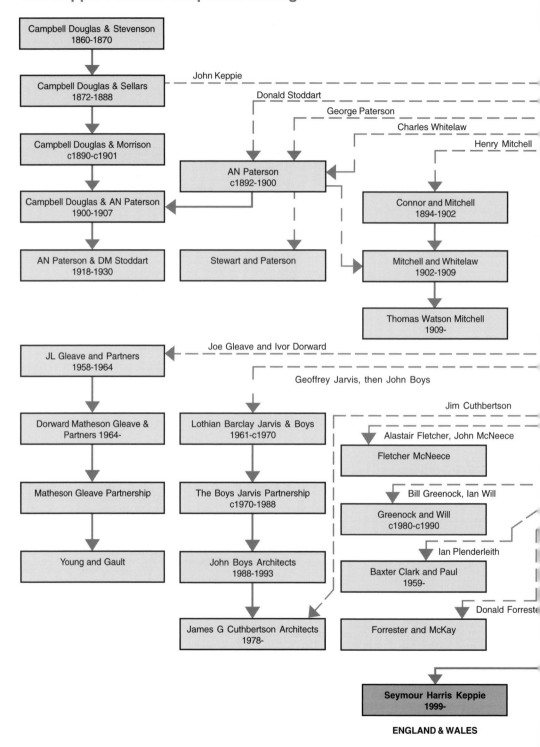

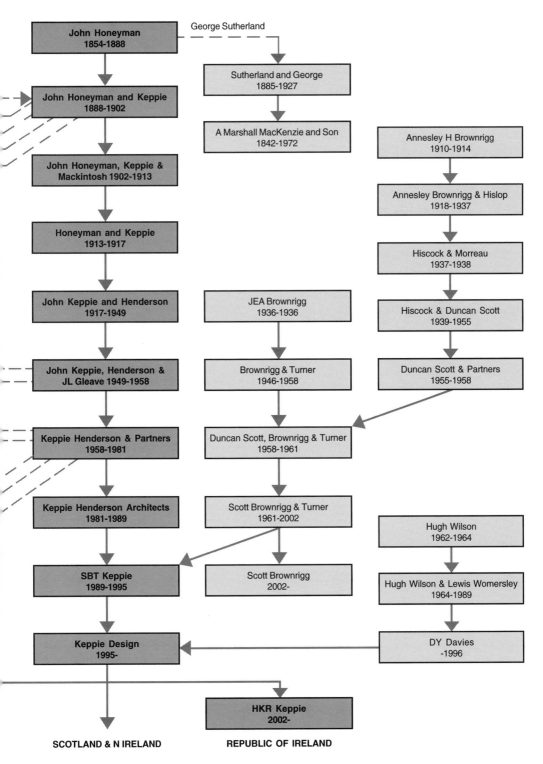

John Honeyman
1854-1888

George Sutherland

Sutherland and George
1885-1927

A Marshall MacKenzie and Son
1842-1972

John Honeyman and Keppie
1888-1902

Annesley H Brownrigg
1910-1914

John Honeyman, Keppie &
Mackintosh 1902-1913

Annesley Brownrigg & Hislop
1918-1937

Honeyman and Keppie
1913-1917

Hiscock & Morreau
1937-1938

John Keppie and Henderson
1917-1949

JEA Brownrigg
1936-1936

Hiscock & Duncan Scott
1939-1955

John Keppie, Henderson &
JL Gleave 1949-1958

Brownrigg & Turner
1946-1958

Duncan Scott & Partners
1955-1958

Keppie Henderson & Partners
1958-1981

Duncan Scott, Brownrigg & Turner
1958-1961

Keppie Henderson Architects
1981-1989

Scott Brownrigg & Turner
1961-2002

Hugh Wilson
1962-1964

SBT Keppie
1989-1995

Scott Brownrigg
2002-

Hugh Wilson & Lewis Womersley
1964-1989

Keppie Design
1995-

DY Davies
-1996

HKR Keppie
2002-

SCOTLAND & N IRELAND

REPUBLIC OF IRELAND

15

*The Fairfield Shipyard in Govan was founded by John Elder and Charles Randolph in 1852.
John Honeyman and Keppie were commissioned to design its new offices (left) in 1890.*

CHAPTER 1

The Napiers and the Elders

In business terms, Central Scotland, and the Glasgow area in particular, is somewhat like a village. People develop relationships which may last much of their working lives, and it is foolish to fall out since paths will almost inevitably cross sometime in the future. Woe betide anyone who fails to deliver on a promise, for it will soon circulate around the marketplace. The Keppie practice has always obtained a large proportion of its workload by word of mouth or by repeat business from the same clients. On many occasions alterations are made to buildings in different eras, sometimes because of a long-standing relationship, sometimes just by luck. This chapter demonstrates how a relationship with two families led to the commissioning of projects over more than a century.

John Honeyman's merchant father probably introduced him to one of his first clients, the shipbuilder and engineer James R. Napier. Honeyman carried out works to his Glasgow house at 16 Newton Place in 1856 and to Saughfield House, Hillhead, in 1858 and 1865. The latter has since been demolished and is the site of the University of Glasgow's Queen Margaret Students' Union. In 1866 additions were made to the boiler shed at the Vulcan Foundry, Govan, for R. Napier and Sons, and in 1873 works took place to their new yard, at Highland Lane in Govan. None of these Honeyman buildings remain today.

The Napier family was prominent in the development of British shipbuilding. In 1812, David Napier built the boilers for the *Comet*, the first commercial steamship, designed by Henry Bell of Helensburgh. In 1827 Napier launched one of the first iron steamships, *Aglaia*. His cousin James introduced the haystack tubular boiler in 1830, which cut coal consumption by 25 per cent. When David Napier moved to London in 1836, his cousins Robert and James continued to develop new ideas on the Clyde. Robert met Samuel Cunard from Halifax, Nova Scotia in London in 1839. The Cunard family were American loyalists who fled to Canada around 1780 during the War of Independence, and were favoured by the British Admiralty. With the help of George Burns of the City of Glasgow Steam Packet Company, they quickly raised £270,000 to set up the Cunard Line. This would probably equate to a few hundred million pounds today. With their first bid, they won the mail contract from Liverpool to Halifax and Boston. In less than a year they had built four wooden paddle steamers for the service, *Britannia*, *Acadia*, *Caledonia* and *Columbia*. *Britannia* set off from Liverpool on 4 July 1840, and arrived in Boston fourteen days later, exactly on schedule. Incidentally, David MacBrayne, through marriage, inherited part of the Burns family shipping empire, and his name is still seen on west of Scotland passenger craft today. John Honeyman even designed Roundelwood, Crieff (1883) where MacBrayne later lived, the practice carrying out further work for his family there in 1931.

In 1864 Honeyman designed offices for Burns's company at 30 Jamaica Street in Glasgow. At a cost of £11,000 it was Honeyman's most expensive project to date. The *Building News* in June 1867 was complimentary about his design:

> It is in the Italian style, by an architect who had hitherto been known almost exclusively as a Goth of the Goths – Mr Honeyman – and sufficiently proves that he is no less at home among the soft and rounded mouldings of the sunny south, than among the hard and angular forms that are perhaps so telling and so more fitting in our mirky [*sic*] atmosphere.

The offices of George Burns, co-founder of the Cunard shipping line.

Unfortunately, the category 'A' listed building burned down in 1999.

Many aspiring young men were apprenticed to the Napiers. Two of these were John Ure and John Elder, the former a son of a lawyer, and the latter the third son of David Elder, who had built Robert Napier's first marine engine in 1822 for a boat named the *Leven*. It is unlikely that they met as apprentices, but in 1852, the year John Ure became resident engineer to the Clyde Navigation Trust, John Elder went into partnership with Charles Randolph. They expanded his millwright business into the manufacture of marine engines and formed the shipbuilding company that became Fairfield's, later Upper Clyde Shipbuilders and then Kvaerner Govan. 1852 was the same year that John Honeyman started practising architecture.

As early as 1853, Randolph and Elder patented a marine compound expansion engine, cutting coal consumption by up to 40 per cent, and allowing ships from their home ports to reach the Pacific. This was such a success that by 1875 three quarters of all steam engines relied on this invention. Their shipbuilding company was also highly successful, winning many contracts at home and abroad, including orders from the American Confederates for ships to break the blockade during the American Civil War (1861–65). During the 1850s and 1860s Clyde shipbuilders produced 70 per cent of the iron ship tonnage in Britain.

John Ure introduced his sister Isabella to John Elder, and in March 1857 they were married. If Elder at the age of 33 was already a wealthy man, Isabella had her own family inheritance which she protected in a prenuptial agreement. Prior to the Married Woman's Property (Scotland) Act of 1877, all the property of a woman belonged to her husband. The agreement meant that she could control her own estate, obtain

The grave of the Elder family at the Necropolis, Glasgow.

Isabella Elder.

£100 a year from her husband for personal use and receive all of his estate after he died. She did, when John Elder passed away on 17 September 1869 aged 45, while seeking medical help in London for a liver complaint. In his memory, the Pacific Steam Navigation Company named its next ship *John Elder*. In 1870, Honeyman designed the funeral monument for John Elder at the Necropolis on the hill opposite Glasgow Cathedral. Isabella and John Ure are also commemorated there, as are David Elder and his wife. Many of their friends are buried around them, marked by a variety of graveyard edifices. The cream of Victorian society and entrepreneurship lie together on a hilltop overlooking the Second City of the Empire.

Isabella might not have had personal financial worries, but since John had been the sole owner of the shipyard, his widow inherited responsibility for one of the largest shipbuilding companies in the world, employing almost 5,000 men. The social consequences of its failure for the new Burgh of Govan would have been catastrophic. This was in the days when women did not receive the vote and were denied further education. It is an indication of women's status at the time that, unlike her brother, little is known about Isabella prior to her marriage. She bore sole responsibility for the yard for a period of nine months until she was joined on the board by John Jamieson, the residing general manager, and by William Pearce, later Sir William and MP for Govan from 1885. Honeyman received work from both of them: from Jamieson, some ten years earlier for his house at Shandon, near Helensburgh, and from Pearce in 1890/91 (or rather his son who took over in 1888) for new shipyard offices on Govan Road at a cost of £15,562. It was the largest project that the practice had carried out.

John Ure also answered the call to help his sister, but could not join the company until November 1870 due to commitments as resident engineer on the Tyne. He was busy deepening the river so that ships could sail up to Newcastle, and was also devising a swing bridge which opened in 1876 and is still operational today. Ure was a partner in the Fairfield Shipbuilding and Engineering Company until he retired in 1879. He went to live in the south of France where he died in 1883.

As she reached her 50s, Isabella Elder turned her attention away from making money towards philanthropic ventures. In 1883 she made three major charitable

*When Elder Park opened,
the population of Govan had risen from
around 9,000 to over 55,000.*

awards: the endowment of £12,500 to create the John Elder Chair of Naval Architecture at the University of Glasgow, the purchase of the 37 acres of Fairfield's Farm to form Elder Park at a cost of £50,000, and the purchase of North Park House for £12,000 to house the Queen Margaret Medical College. The first of these was important as it raised the status of engineering at the university, the professors in the theology, arts, law and medicine faculties previously ensuring that it was a minor subject, even when a BSc degree was introduced in 1872. The other two philanthropic ventures led to commissions for Honeyman.

Honeyman was responsible for laying out Elder Park. It was a much-needed social facility with a boating pond and children's play areas, although many of the original features are no longer there. A huge crowd took part in the opening celebrations on 27 June 1885. The official party had lunch before the opening ceremony at Isabella Elder's home, Claremont House (remodelled by Honeyman in 1871 while she was wintering on the Continent – it is now part of Claremont Terrace). Those present included Lord Rosebery, James and Jessie Campbell of Tullichewan, Dumbarton, and Sir Charles Tennant and Edward Tennant from Edinburgh. Surprisingly, John Honeyman did not attend, although the possible reason, relating to his new wife, his third, is explained in a later chapter.

Between 1864, when Govan became a burgh, and 1885, the local population rose from 9,058 to 55,463 with four shipbuilding and engineering yards established there. The park became the centre of an industrial community, which saw the ships it produced as 'the active pioneers of civilisation and commerce, the intermediaries of human intercourse, and messengers of peace and goodwill throughout the world'.

During this period of growth Honeyman carried out a number of projects in the Govan area in addition to the work for the Napiers. Accommodation for 350 people at Govan Free Church was built in 1862, although the building was converted into a theatre and music hall in 1873 and was later demolished. The foundation stone of Dean Park Parish Church was laid on 27 September 1872, the building being large enough to accommodate 990 people. Honeyman also designed the adjacent Dean Park Baptist Church in 1877. St Anthony's Roman Catholic Church was opened on 26 October 1879, demonstrating that Honeyman's talents were much in demand by several denominations. It is the only one of Honeyman's six churches in the area still standing. The others were Oatlands Trinity and Elder Park Church. Fairfield Public School housed 1,775 children and was opened in 1875.

Isabella's friend Jessie Campbell was the wife of prominent Glasgow businessman James Campbell, who was the nephew of a former Lord Provost of Glasgow and cousin of the future Liberal prime minister, Sir Henry Campbell-Bannerman. She instigated 'Lectures for Ladies' in the McLellan Galleries from 1868, and campaigned for formal further education for women. In 1877, the Association for the Higher Education of Women in Glasgow and the West of Scotland was formed, with Queen Victoria's daughter, Princess Louise, nominated as president. Legislation passed in 1889 permitted Scottish universities to admit and graduate women students. Isabella and Jessie were soulmates with a common cause.

However, medical students were having difficulty obtaining practical instruction, the Glasgow Western Infirmary refusing a request to allow clinical instruction of women in case it reduced the opportunities for men. Potential female medical students faced much prejudice from male doctors. At a debate on the subject on 4 October 1877, Glasgow Southern Medical Society president Ebenezer Duncan expressed the view that 'exceptional women of better brain power than the average man might be allowed, and certainly ought not to be hindered from practising'. Others had different views: 'They cannot attend their duty properly and they want strength of character'; 'the physical difficulties are insuperable, they would fail utterly and completely'; 'medical women would be very useful in obstetric cases, and men would be relieved of much irksome and poorly paid work'.

John Honeyman inherited North Park House, Glasgow, from John Thomas Rochead when the latter became ill.

The Royal Infirmary of Glasgow finally accepted women in 1890 and Isabella Elder agreed to meet all associated costs for the first few years. She also purchased North Park House for the ladies' Queen Margaret Medical College. John Honeyman had been involved in the original design of North Park House. In 1869 John Thomas Rochead started designing it for John and Matthew Bell, who owned the Glasgow Pottery. Due to illness, Honeyman took over, with construction taking place between 1872 and 1874. Some Bell brothers' pottery is still on display in the building. They were also keen – but gullible – art collectors,

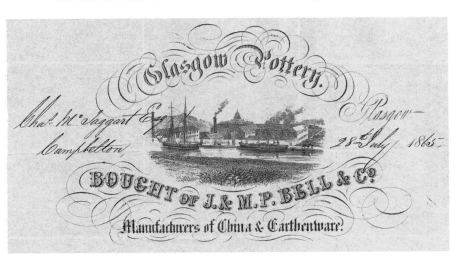

A billhead from the Bell brothers' Glasgow Pottery.

The Queen Margaret Medical College opening ceremony.
Isabella Elder and Jessie Campbell are at the top of the steps.

having the interiors designed to house a collection which they thought included ten Titians, eleven Rembrandts and twenty Rubens. When the two brothers died intestate, 25 executors were appointed to deal with their effects, and some of the paintings were found to be fakes. Others were sold off extremely cheaply.

Queen Victoria was in Glasgow to open the new City Chambers on 22 August 1888, and probably at the request of her daughter, agreed to officially open Queen Margaret College on 24 August. This was a rare occasion as the queen had not been in Glasgow since 1849, when she complained about the appalling slums and bad weather. Princess Alix of Hesse, who later became the Tsarina of Russia and was executed after the revolution in July 1918, accompanied her. The *Govan Press* reported the events:

> The company pulled themselves together to receive Her Majesty. Mrs Campbell had the address all ready in its glittering casket, Miss Galloway carried a beautifully bound copy of the Calendar and a young lady who had been nursing a lovely bouquet of orchids handed it over to Mrs Elder. The prancing of horses' hooves was heard outside, the cheering got more enthusiastic, when to the undisguised horror – no other word can express the feelings which were reflected in the faces of the company inside the College

grounds – the whole cavalcade swept past the gateway without stopping, and the great crowd, breaking through the barriers, swarmed down the road after it. A mistake had been made, the gate had simply been missed, and after making a detour to turn the carriage, the Royal party retraced its steps.

After 1892, mixed classes took place at the main University of Glasgow campus at Gilmorehill, but it was felt that it would be unseemly for women to attend mixed medical classes, and Queen Margaret Medical School soon required to be extended. Isabella Elder insisted that the budget should allow for a handsome building in stone, and Honeyman and Keppie were employed as designers in 1894. John Keppie was in charge of the project, although his assistant, Charles Rennie Mackintosh, contributed largely to it.

Women's lessons were fully integrated with the main university by 1935. The BBC took over the former Queen Margaret College buildings and broadcast from them from 1938. Subsequent development of the site resulted in the classroom wing of the medical school being demolished and the rest of the building being engulfed in new construction. An accommodation study of the Queen Margaret Drive site by SBT Keppie in 1994 confirmed that it was too limiting for future development of the BBC, and it is moving from there to Pacific Quay, Glasgow, the site of the 1988 Garden Festival. London architect David Chipperfield was selected to design the new headquarters of BBC Scotland, and is being assisted by Keppie Design to deliver the project.

To provide boarding accommodation for Queen Margaret College students in 1894, Lilybank House was purchased. Since 1857 it had been the home of John Blackie, co-founder of the Blackie publishing empire, elected Lord Provost of Glasgow in 1863 and one of the driving forces behind the City Improvement Trust that reshaped the old town of Glasgow (Honeyman was one of its consultants). Alexander Thomson's south

In common with many Mackintosh buildings, the importance of Queen Margaret College was not appreciated when it was radically altered and consumed by the expanding BBC Scotland headquarters. An opportunity exists for amends to be made when the BBC moves to Pacific Quay.

23

Although Alexander Elder left money to build a hospital when he died in 1915, the David Elder Infirmary was not completed until 1928. The layout of this small hospital could not have been simpler: an administration block at the entrance (left), followed by outpatients and x-ray departments, two wards, and an operating theatre and mortuary at the rear.

wing extension was built for Blackie to entertain the likes of Gladstone, and the north wing bedroom block was added by Honeyman and Keppie in 1894 for Queen Margaret College. This may have been the only building on which both 'Greek' Thomson and Charles Rennie Mackintosh worked, albeit at different times. Lilybank House remains the property of the University of Glasgow, and for many years acted as the elegant backdrop for portraits of girls from Laurel Bank School, whose premises were adjacent in Lilybank Terrace.

However this was not the end of the Keppie practice's connection with the Elders. Isabella's estate was worth £159,404 and one of the beneficiaries was her husband's younger brother, Alexander Elder. He was already a rich man, and when he died in 1915, he left £100,000 for a hospital to be built near Elder Park, to be known as the David Elder Infirmary, after his father. The First World War intervened, and building costs in the years following it rose enormously because of shortages of labour and materials. So it was not until 1925 that John Keppie and Henderson Architects started on the project, which was completed early in 1928. The medical consultant for the project was Colonel D.J. Mackintosh CB, MVO, MB, LLD. The hospital was run by the Western Infirmary of Glasgow since it was situated in the Parish of Govan (which spanned the Clyde in those days), and already provided hospital services for Govan folk.

A dedication service took place on 16 December 1927, and a further ward was added in 1930. David Elder was interested in music and invented a steam organ. This passed to his son Alexander, and it ended up as a memorial to both of them in the nurses' dining room. In the entrance hall were placed a bronze tablet and bas-relief by Benno Schotz, an artist whom John Keppie supported on many occasions. His statues adorn John Keppie and Henderson's Bank of Scotland building on the corner of Sauchiehall Street and Blythswood Street, and the Mercat Building at Glasgow Cross.

In 1993, SBT Keppie was interviewed by the Health Board which was considering refurbishment and reuse of the David Elder Infirmary buildings. Many of the original drawings were still retained in the practice archives. The project fell through, however, and sometime later the buildings were demolished to make way for housing.

The name was perpetuated in the David Elder Wing in Keppie Henderson's Department of Obstetrics and Gynaecology at the Southern General Hospital, just across the Clyde Tunnel approach road from the David Elder Infirmary site. The maternity unit comprised 115 maternity beds, a 24-bed GP unit, twelve labour rooms and two operating theatres. It was completed in December 1969, 113 years after John Honeyman started working for the Napier and Elder families.

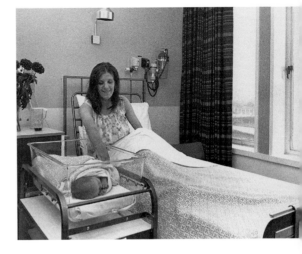

In David Elder's time child mortality rates were almost 20 per cent, and in the 1960s the figure was still around 3 per cent. New specialist maternity units such as this one at Glasgow's Southern General Hospital sought to reduce the figure further.

Knockderry Castle, Cove.

CHAPTER 2

Beginnings

John Honeyman was a Victorian. Born on 11 August 1830 in Glasgow, he was seven years old when Victoria became queen and retired soon after she died. While Victorians did not invent the Industrial Revolution and the British Empire, each reached new peaks under them. They were inventors, industrialists, merchants, philanthropists and social reformers. Urbanisation followed industrialisation, and local industry supported local communities, such as Govan, as they grew.

To understand the challenges John Honeyman faced, we must understand something about Victorian Scotland. Its resonances appear in various chapters of this book: the formation of the Free Church leading to ecclesiastical commissions; industrialists of the Second City of the Empire requiring factories, shipyards and homes to show off their wealth; the burgeoning urban population requiring schools; the less socially fortunate being consigned to poorhouses and Magdalene Institutions.

The hundred years before Honeyman founded the practice set the scene for Victorian prosperity and growth. It was Scotland's golden age, the Scottish Enlightenment, and so important that American historian Arthur Herman entitled a book describing it *How the Scots Invented the Modern World*.

Adam Smith, who lectured at the University of Glasgow, is known today for his economic theories which championed free trade and the freedom of the individual. He said:

> The natural effort of every individual to better his own condition is so powerful a principle that it is not only capable of carrying on the society to wealth and prosperity, but of surmounting a hundred impertinent obstructions with which the folly of human laws too often encumbers its operation.

Smith's disciple, David Hume, turned religious and secular dictates on their heads by saying, 'reason is, and ought to be, the slave of the passions'. He argued that human beings have never been governed by their rational capacities:

> Reason's role is purely instrumental; it teaches us how to get what we want. We are, in the end, creatures of habit, and of the physical and social environment within which our emotions and passions must operate. We learn to avoid the passions which destroy, and pursue the ones that succeed. Society has to devise strategies to channel our passions in constructive directions.

Hume invented the secular golden rule: I won't disturb your self-interest, if you don't disturb mine. 'Commerce and liberty, liberty and refinement, refinement and the progress of the human spirit are all interrelated.' He believed that society required authority to preserve it, but the liberty of the individual should still be as great as possible. Some taxation was necessary for authorities to effect the infrastructure for society to function, for example roads and a safe water supply, but private individuals should have maximum control of their wealth to advance themselves.

It was believed that education for all would channel an individual's passions to constructive ends, since cultured people would be honourable and responsible. Robert Burns, a poor farmer's son, received an education worthy of any English gentleman, including Latin and French. At the University of Glasgow, the tuition fee of £5 per year was one tenth the cost of attending Cambridge or Oxford, and within the reach of most middle class people. Consequently, Scotland in the eighteenth and nineteenth centuries produced a wealth of writers, poets, philosophers, inventors, doctors, businessmen and politicians.

The counter to personal selfishness and greed was a moral code. Hume may have been an atheist, and in a liberal society could be open about it, but the vast majority of middle class people were churchgoing. Disease and affliction were constant reminders of one's own mortality. Without the control of a central authority like that of the Catholic Church in Rome, Presbyterianism could express itself in a variety of forms, depending on an individual's views on the place of religion in society, or one's interpretation of the Bible. However, there was a common belief in charity for the deserving poor. The Victorian concept of philanthropy stemmed from this.

Prominent theologians like Thomas Chalmers attempted to bring the parish system to town life. He was against civic charity, stating that, 'legal charity is injurious'. Pauperism was 'a thing not to be regulated, but destroyed'. Private charity from the better-off in the parish brought personal contact between rich and poor, lessened class division, and prompted a tranquil society. Victorians directed their theories towards succour of the victims of a harsh society, while leaving unquestioned the principles on which that society was constructed.

It is not clear why John Honeyman decided to practice architecture. After attending Merchiston Castle School in Edinburgh from 1841 to 1846, he enrolled on an arts course at the University of Glasgow, originally intending to enter the ministry. He seems to have left university without a degree (although the Merchiston

Honeyman attended the University of Glasgow at its old site to the east of High Street.

register credited him with an MA), which was not uncommon, and some years less than 10 per cent of students bothered to obtain one. Perhaps the method of examination had an effect, since before written examinations started in 1858, candidates sat in the Blackstone Chair and were verbally questioned as long as the sand ran in the hourglass. Honeyman worked in his brother's accountancy firm before obtaining an apprenticeship with Glasgow architect Alexander Munro. For a short time he worked in London with an eminent Scottish architect, William Burn. He took advantage of his London base to travel in the south of England and study church design.

John Honeyman returned to Glasgow in 1854 and set up a practice of his own at 13 Moore Place. Family contacts probably led to some early commissions which were not large or exciting, but established a financial base. His father was a successful Glasgow corn merchant, and in addition to a house off Glasgow Green, by the 1850s he owned one on the Gare Loch, close to Helensburgh. The extension of the railway from Dumbarton in 1858 put Helensburgh within commuting distance of Glasgow.

In 1854, Honeyman's job book notes a project to put roofs on sheds in Dublin Harbour. This could well have been for a business contact of his father. The repeal of the Corn Laws in 1846 ended protectionism and allowed cheap foreign imports of food, on which John Honeyman senior prospered. The recent famine in Ireland created a market among those who had not emigrated. Honeyman's father may also have known James and Robert Napier through his shipping connections.

A number of small domestic projects at Helensburgh are noted in Honeyman's job book in the 1850s, and at nearby Cove, Garelochhead and Rhu (see chapter 12). However, the first large commission was for a new house at Cove, Knockderry Castle, sitting on a promontory overlooking the Firth of Clyde. It was designed around 1856 for John Campbell, his family being historic owners of the Rosneath Peninsula. One of Alexander 'Greek' Thomson's biographers claims that this Scots baronial castle was designed by him, although it is not in a style Thomson happily promoted, and Honeyman went on to design additions in the 1870s and 80s for the second owner, Bailie William Miller. Honeyman also carried out alterations to a house in Busby, Glasgow, in 1857, which Alexander Thomson had remodelled for Durham Kippen in 1856. Perhaps Honeyman had an early link with the great Glasgow architect, with whom he certainly came into contact in architectural societies in later years. The Historic Scotland category 'A' listing states that Thomson carried out designs for Knockderry Castle from 1851 to 1854, so Honeyman may have adapted these.

One link to Thomson could have been through his partner, John Baird. Honeyman, Baird, J.T. Rochead, Alex Galloway, John Buchanan, William Church and a few others were founding members of the Glasgow Archaeological Society in 1856. The group was sufficiently well-connected to obtain the services of Sir Andrew Orr, Lord Provost of Glasgow, as chairman. Shipbuilder and merchant Michael Connal, a later client of Honeyman's for his house at Parkhall, Killearn, in 1879, gave a talk at the launch. As Honeyman told in his reminiscences:

> The Society was fairly launched with my friend William Church as honorary treasurer and myself as honorary, and indeed only, secretary, a post which I held for many years and which I reluctantly gave up only on account of the excessive pressure of ordinary work.

Honeyman's first job book kept records of construction work, and it is not clear whether he designed some of the buildings described above or merely attended to site inspections and building contract administration. Even where there are sketches of building details, it is not clear whether they are explaining to the builder how his design, or someone else's, worked. The methodical nature in which he kept financial records probably contributed to his reputation for looking after his clients' money well, a habit he would have learned in his brother's accountancy firm.

By 1858, Honeyman was definitely gaining work on his own accord. Around this time he was a founding member of the 1st Dumbartonshire (Helensburgh) Artillery, a group of volunteers set up as a reserve force in the event of French invasion. Honeyman was first lieutenant in the volunteers, and he designed Towerville at the corner of George Street and Montrose Street, Helensburgh for Captain James Galbraith. Honeyman later designed the Drill Hall in Cardross (1889), called Geilston Hall, for the volunteers, which is now the village hall.

The Volunteer Force was founded in 1859, a cross between a territorial army and a 'Dad's Army'. While Britain had been an ally of France in the Crimean War, which ended in 1856, Napoleon III's aspirations for reshaping the continent of Europe led to suspicions about his intentions. Victorian anxiety about a French invasion was enhanced due to the efficiency of the very steamships that the British had invented. For the first time, a modern French armada could reach most parts of Britain within a few hours, largely irrespective of prevailing weather conditions. The volunteers offered a chance for Britons to come together to celebrate their patriotism. Volunteering 'made men less idle and dissipated, and more respectful to authority'. Members had an alternative to dancing saloons and billiard rooms to 'give their days to shoot and evenings to drill and find pleasure in music and chorus singing'. For the middle classes it also provided a pleasant and gratifying way of passing their increased leisure time. The social side of the volunteers brought Honeyman into contact with potential clients.

The life of Honeyman's client James Galbraith epitomised the enterprise of the Victorians. He was born in the small Lanarkshire town of Strathaven in 1818. As a boy he wished to emulate his uncle who was a ship's surgeon in the Royal Navy, and who settled in Brussels to practice medicine, but he could only obtain work as a clerk. He left one company because the sons of the owner barred his prospects, and another went into financial difficulties. Finally he entered the employment of ship and insurance brokers P. Henderson and Co. During the Napoleonic Wars, Mr

Towerville, Helensburgh, home of Captain James Galbraith.

John Honeyman helped found the 1st Dumbartonshire Artillery Volunteers. He designed Cardross Drill Hall, known as Geilston Hall, for them.

Henderson had been press-ganged to serve in the Royal Navy from his home in the fishing village of Pittenweem, but on the basis that the king had not consulted him when his services were required, there was no great sin in not consulting the king when he wished to bring these to an end, and he took 'French leave', moving to Glasgow with his brother to start up their business. The two brothers died a few years after Galbraith joined them, and he took over the company.

Galbraith set up trade between the Clyde and Rangoon using sailing ships that went round the Cape. When the Suez Canal opened he realised that steamships were the future and he set up the British and Burmese Steam Navigation Co. Ltd. His steamships could sail 1,000 miles up the River Irrawaddy above Rangoon, close to the Chinese frontier. He also set up the Albion Shipping Company, which transported 50,000 people to New Zealand without losing a single life through loss or wreckage of any of the ships. In 1860 he was appointed Austrian vice-consul in Glasgow. He moved to Wemyss Bay in 1874, not far from Honeyman's house in Skelmorlie. Both were keen yachtsmen, Galbraith experimenting with steam power in his yachts, which he sailed throughout the west coast of Scotland, to Norway and to the Mediterranean. This was the social circle Honeyman entered during his twelve years at Skelmorlie from 1869, and it was fertile ground for obtaining work.

Some of Honeyman's early work included projects gained from the misfortunes of others. Keeping an architectural practice together for several years, never mind 150, is no mean feat. Most practices, like most small businesses, are formed by one or a few individuals with a good idea or knowledge of their subject, but with little business sense. This is especially so for design organisations, which often become absorbed in the creative process and neglect basic business matters; success and expansion can be as big a threat to business stability as contraction and an insufficient workload.

Honeyman completed Wynd Free Church in Glasgow from a design by the Hay brothers of Liverpool, and two churches by J.T. Emmet were completed after the latter retired due to ill health and his practice dissolved. He had obviously not put a succession strategy in place, but regarded his practice as a personal affair and not a corporate body to be passed on (or sold on) to colleagues or outsiders. A design practice is a people business. It has little or no value when its principal retires, and Honeyman probably obtained the remnants of the practice without cost. Sandyford Church, 13 Kelvinhaugh Street, Glasgow, still exists, as does St Thomas's, Brougham Street, Greenock, although the latter is now a carpet warehouse. Finishing off other people's designs was not ideal, but it allowed Honeyman to build up a portfolio of church projects.

The Hay brothers' problems arose from their inability to control expansion of workload. They were originally from Coldstream, but found a seam of work in the Liverpool area and based their practice there. It did not stop them designing churches in Scotland, twelve of them from 1848 to 1857. Honeyman's involvement in the Wynd Free Church in Glasgow probably stemmed from the Hays overstretching themselves on projects some distance from their office. Their workload in north-west England was also heavy and travel to projects was not as easy as it is today. Bad publicity from a mishap on Stirling High School (more recently the Stirling Highland Hotel) led to a sharp and irreversible decline in the practice's fortunes. The Hay brothers allowed the builder to draw down money in advance of work completed, and Stirling Town Council had to step in to guarantee the men's wages when the builder failed to complete. The school opened in May 1856 at a cost of £5,081 against a budget of £4,136, and only half of the originally planned school was built. Completion was not accomplished until 1889, when a former pupil, James MacLaren, was the designer.

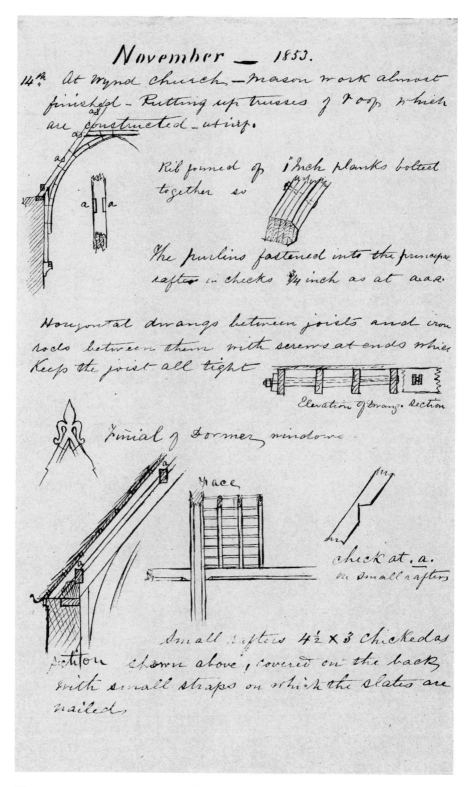

November — 1853.

14th At Wynd Church — mason work almost
finished — Putting up trusses of roof which
are constructed as inp.

Rib formed of 1 inch planks bolted
together so

The purlins fastened into the principal
rafters in checks ¾ inch as at a.a.a.

Horizontal drrangs between joists and iron
rods between them with screws at ends which
keeps the joist all tight

Elevation of drrang. Section

Finial of dormer windows

brace

check at a.
on small rafters

section

Small rafters 4½ × 3 chicked as
shewn above, covered on the back
with small straps on which the slates are
nailed

Like the Hay brothers, Honeyman's practice was built on the expansion of church-building. Some of his biographers have suggested that he obtained commissions from fellow students at the University of Glasgow who continued on to qualify and take up positions in parishes. There is in fact little evidence of this, although he had a lot of clergymen friends. A bigger factor in the increase in opportunities for church commissions was the creation of the Free Church.

The headmaster of Honeyman's secondary school, Merchiston Castle in Edinburgh, was Charles Chalmers, the brother of Thomas Chalmers. When Honeyman was an impressionable twelve year old, Thomas Chalmers led 478 ministers out from the General Assembly of the Church of Scotland to set up the Free Church. As one of the foremost churchmen of his time, Thomas Chalmers would have been a great influence on Honeyman, and perhaps inspired him to study divinity at the University of Glasgow. Chalmers died in 1847, and reports of the time suggested that half of the population of Edinburgh lined the streets to watch his funeral procession.

Honeyman benefited from the legacy of Thomas Chalmers and the establishment of the Free Church as he obtained commissions for 22 Free churches from 1854 to 1881. Immediately prior to the formation of the Free Church, Chalmers had been convenor of the Church Extension Committee, a body set up to raise funds for new churches and parishes. During a seven-year period his committee had raised £300,000 to build 220 new churches, without any government aid. No doubt some of this money transferred from the supporters of the Established Church as they switched allegiance to the Free Church.

The Disruption was such a large upheaval for Scottish society of the time that it is worthwhile understanding why it happened and what its consequences were. Family history researchers will be well aware of its effects, since parochial records of baptisms, marriages and deaths for the third of the Scottish population which left the Established Church were non-existent or at best incomplete from 1843 to 1855.

Thomas Chalmers was born in 1780, was educated at the parish school in Anstruther and went to the University of St Andrews when he was twelve. Although more interested in mathematics and chemistry, he began studying for the ministry from the age of fifteen. He was licensed at the age of nineteen and gave his first sermon on 25 August 1799 at Wigan. In November 1814 he was appointed minister to the Tron Parish in Glasgow. Chalmers was a very popular preacher, drawing crowds to hear about contemporary problems and issues. This was in contrast to many other ministers who confined themselves to strictly evangelical messages. There was much suitable subject matter at hand due to bad harvests and unemployment following the end of the Napoleonic Wars. Glasgow was also suffering the problems of industrialisation. After touring England to study poor law, Chalmers returned to St Andrews in 1823 to take up the Chair of Moral Philosophy, moving to Edinburgh in 1828 to become Professor of Divinity at the university where he campaigned for the emancipation of Roman Catholics.

By this time, the conflict between moderates and dissenting evangelists in the Church of Scotland was increasing, and Chalmers was to be transformed from a leading establishment figure to the leader of a revolt. Members of the moderate party in the Church of Scotland were seen as the agents of the Whig government, and aligned with landowners. They had a tendency towards Anglicanism in an attempt to be part of

*Opposite: **Honeyman kept records in his notebook of explanations to builders of construction details.***

the elite British ruling class. During the French Wars from 1793 to 1814, they portrayed dissenting evangelists as 'democrats' and 'revolutionaries', with evangelist Sunday schools 'calculated to produce discontent, to foster an aversion to the present order of things'.

The schism between evangelists and moderates finally came after the 'Auchterarder case' which highlighted the social differences between the two. An Act of 1711 gave a lay patron (usually the local aristocratic landlord) the right to present the minister of his choice regardless of the wishes of the rest of the congregation. The General Assembly of the Church of Scotland passed the Veto Act in 1834, counteracting this and giving parishioners the ability to reject a minister they did not want. That year, Robert Young was presented to the Parish of Auchterarder by the local landowner and was rejected by the congregation. He appealed to the Court of Session which ruled that the Parliament Act of 1711 prevailed. An appeal by the General Assembly in May 1839 was turned down by the House of Lords, and Young was confirmed as minister.

The split eventually came on 18 May 1843, when the evangelical party walked out, Thomas Chalmers taking away 38 per cent of the clergy. The 1851 census showed that only 32.2 per cent of the population adhered to the Established Church, 31.7 per cent were members of the Free Church and 27.3 per cent were other dissenters. Above the Highland Line, the Free Church was closely identified with the Gaelic-speaking lower orders, and in the Lowlands it appealed to the growing middle classes. The Free Church initially used any premises it could find to hold services, or erected cheap and temporary church buildings until money was available to build better ones. The peak in construction therefore coincided with Honeyman's early years in practice.

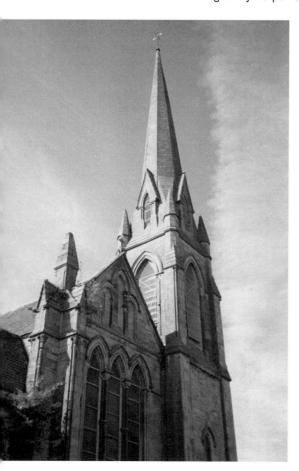

Park Free Church, Helensburgh. John Honeyman's sister Christina was a member of the church.

The middle classes were full of benefactors like Richard Kidson, who funded £1,284 worth of alterations at Helensburgh Free Church Manse in 1859, and provided £4,600 for a new church in the town in 1862, Park Free Church in Charlotte Street. Honeyman was now designing whole churches, having won a design competition in 1861 for the Free West Church in Greenock, later called St Mark's. The commission for Lansdowne Church on Great Western Road, Glasgow, followed in 1862. In Glasgow one commission would lead to another, since one congregation would set up a mission church in another part of the city where one did not exist. The Wynd Free Church sponsored a remarkable 73 other churches, including the ones Honeyman obtained – the Barony Free in Cathedral Square, St Andrew's at Glasgow Green, Stonefield Free on Rutherglen Road, and Candlish Memorial at the corner of Cathcart Road and Calder Street. Thank goodness the Hay brothers had fouled up and given Honeyman a chance to work for the Wynd Free Church. After only eight years in practice, business was booming.

Barony Free Church stood at the north-west corner of Cathedral Square.

The completed Henry Wood Hall with the orchestra testing the acoustics.

CHAPTER 3

Glasgow churches

Early churches

Sir Archibald Campbell and other breakaway members of St Jude's Episcopal Church founded St Silas Episcopal Church in 1863 at the corner of Park Road and Eldon Street, just off Woodlands Road in Glasgow. It was designed by Honeyman. Campbell is commemorated by a mural on the north-west wall. Construction was complete by 1865. Honeyman was invited by the congregation to design St Silas Episcopal Mission Church at 14 Hayburn Street, Partick in 1874. It became derelict in the late 1980s and was later used as an electrical retail warehouse.

The original Cathcart Free Church that Honeyman designed in 1864 is now the church hall of Battlefield East Church, a larger church having been designed by John Galt in 1912. The congregation had to submit Honeyman's plans to Sir John Maxwell of Pollok for approval as he was the feu superior. The foundation stone was laid in September 1864 and the church, seating 500, was opened in May 1865. The timber fleche on the roof has long since been lost to the ravages of wind and rain.

Trinity Congregational Church on Claremont Street was opened on 30 April 1865. It seated 970 people plus another 300 in a basement hall. Its spire is a landmark on Berkeley Street as one approaches it from the west end of Bath Street. Much of the stonework detailing was by sculptor John Mossman. The last service was held in 1974, and the building fell into disrepair. It was rescued in 1980 by the Scottish National Orchestra, which appointed conservation specialist Jack Notman to convert it for rehearsal facilities. They had looked at a number of redundant churches, but concluded that the acoustics in the Claremont Street church were good, while it was close to the city centre but did not suffer badly from traffic noise outside. The

The Trinity Congregational Church on Claremont Street was purchased by the Scottish National Orchestra in 1980. Having been converted for use as a rehearsal and concert venue it was renamed the Henry Wood Hall.

large basement was filled with changing rooms, a practice room, a recording control room, cafeteria, music library and instrument store. Although primarily for rehearsal, the church can be used for an orchestra of up to 120 players with an audience of 500.

Lansdowne Church, 1863

Honeyman won the commission for Lansdowne Church on Great Western Road (below) from a limited competition. When it opened on 6 December 1863, it marked the western boundary of the city, with its slender spire rising 67 metres from the ground. It was founded by wealthy breakaway members of the Cambridge Street United Presbyterian Church, four elders and 68 members taking part in the inaugural service. The collection on that Sunday amounted to the enormous sum of £1,234. The cost of the church was £12,563, and the debt was fully paid off by 1876.

The first minister, the Rev. John Eadie, was a colourful character, as the caricature of the time suggests. The following poem was found on the door of the church on the opening Sunday, and summed up the feelings of those who for one reason or another were excluded:

The church is not for the poor and needy
But for the rich and Dr Eadie,
The rich step up and take their seat
But the poor walk down to Cambridge Street. '

Dr Eadie was also Professor of Biblical Literature to the United Presbyterian Church and from 1870 to 1875 edited a revision of the English Bible, a copy of which is in the church. He died in 1876 and the sculptor John Mossman carved his head above the internal doorway to the church.

The technology behind the tallest, slimmest spire in Scotland should not be underestimated. The last material one would build it with today would be stone, one like brick or concrete which does not perform well when bent by the wind. That is, it is strong when being compressed by a load that acts vertically, but cracks or breaks when it bends and suffers tension. To ensure that a spire such as this does not bend in the wind, there is a cast-iron rod running through its centre which is tensioned to continually pull downwards like a tent guy. The rod continues to keep the stone in compression, despite the high winds that have threatened to blow it over for the last 140 years.

Dr John Eadie, first minister of Lansdowne Church, as depicted in the Bailie.

Honeyman developed the layout he had used in 1861 for the Free West Church in Greenock, but introduced a semicircular barrel vault in the nave to improve the acoustics, and enlarged the design to seat 1,200 people. At this time organs were disapproved of, being regarded as 'music hall' entertainment. Singing was led by a precentor appointed by the Kirk Session, and acoustics had to be good to hear him properly.

Honeyman relied a lot on the help of sculptor John Mossman and his assistant James Shanks for the stone detailing. At the south door from Great Western Road there are carved gargoyle heads, known as the 'Lansdowne Devils'. Apparently, a workman, after being sacked, cursed on his way out: 'I'll leave the de'il in this Kirk', and gave Mossman the inspiration for the carved devils' heads.

The stained glass windows were installed later and were dedicated as a memorial to victims of the First World War, the artist, Alfred Webster, himself losing his life in the conflict. The right-hand side of one of the windows shows Jesus entering the Holy City, but the city depicted is Glasgow. The other shows St Paul preaching to the licentious Romans, but Rome is identified as London. The artist had a sense of humour.

The original chancel has been altered over the years, the marble base for the polished pine pulpit now being used as the communion table. Church attendance peaked in Glasgow after the Second World War, but has rapidly decreased since. To retain a viable congregation, the church merged with Cambridge Street from which it originally spilt, as well as Woodside Parish (formerly St Oswald's) and Burnbank.

North Woodside Mission, 1879, and William Smith

Just around the corner from Lansdowne Church is a much more modest building on North Woodside Road. It was designed by Honeyman to fit in with the neighbouring tenement blocks, although today the adjacent building to the east is the only remaining tenement in the street. One is still inclined to drive past it and not notice the small plaque on the wall. This intimates that in this building were sowed the seeds of one of the major western world youth organisations of the twentieth century.

North Woodside Mission Hall,
where the Boys' Brigade was founded.

In 1878, Honeyman was commissioned to design a mission church for the Free College. It was completed in 1879 with the first minister being George Reith, father of the first Director General of the BBC, Lord Reith. Sunday school teachers William Smith and brothers James R. Hill and John B. Hill were given the unenviable task of looking after the teenage boys, who were not the least interested in bible studies. Boys could leave school at the age of twelve, and half of the Sabbath school class were apprentice joiners, cabinetmakers, blacksmiths, clerks or engine fitters. They had to come up with something new, so they invented the Boys' Brigade.

William Alexander Smith was born near Thurso in 1854, the year Honeyman started his architectural practice. His father died of fever in China in 1868, and to relieve his family of a mouth to feed he accepted the offer of a job from his uncle in Glasgow.

William Smith, founder of the Boys' Brigade,
as illustrated in the Bailie.

Alexander Fraser was an evangelical Free Church man and a wholesale dealer in clothing and shawls, trading principally with the South African market. His business was in Princes Square in the city centre, and he had a summer home in Callander, where members of the extended family were welcome.

William Smith joined the Lanarkshire Volunteers in 1874, much against the wishes of his pacifist uncle. The 1st Lanarkshire Volunteers drew its membership from the prosperous West End of Glasgow. It was sponsored by shipping companies and businesses such as Wylie and Lochhead and J. and W. Campbell, and had members who were lawyers, accountants, stockbrokers, actuaries and bankers. To pay for the

An illustration showing the Boys' Brigade parade at Burnbank in 1886.

organisation, the annual subscription was ten shillings and the purchase of the uniform 30 shillings. Only the better-off could afford this. Two future prime ministers were members, Henry Campbell-Bannerman and Andrew Bonar Law, as well as the future chairman of the Independent Labour Party, Jimmy Maxton.

William Smith's solution to his problem was to create a junior version of the volunteers called the Boys' Brigade. The initial meeting of the 1st Glasgow Company was held on Thursday 4 October 1883, with 59 boys between the ages of twelve and sixteen attending. With a motto of 'Sure and Steadfast', the object was 'the advancement of Christ's Kingdom among Boys and the promotion of habits of Reverence, Discipline, Self-Respect, and all that tends towards a true Christian Manliness'.

Allied to this was Sunday Bible Class. Half of the boys had left school, and Victorians worked hard. Factories and offices opened at 7.00 a.m. and closed at 6.00 p.m., with many shops opening until nine or ten in the evening. Sundays were different. While only about 20 per cent of the population were regular churchgoers, ministers and magistrates made sure that the Sabbath was kept calm and quiet. This left teenage boys with a lot of free time on their hands, and the movement quickly spread throughout Britain and beyond. The only place where it proved difficult to set up a company was Belfast, where even the use of wooden rifles for drill practice by religious groups was deemed confrontational.

At the Glasgow Fair holiday in July 1886, boys set off from Broomielaw Pier in the middle of Glasgow on the *Columba* for the first camp near Tighnabruaich. For the first few years the camp was held in a local hall at Auchenlochan, as some mothers who had migrated to the city did not wish their country cousins to think they could not afford to put a roof over their sons' heads. Eventually the camp was held under canvas at nearby Portavadie.

Scouting was developed from within the Boys' Brigade by Boer War hero, Robert Baden-Powell, one of Smith's vice-presidents in 1902. Smith helped him convert his army manual *Aids to Scouting* into *Scouting for Boys*, which was published in the *BB Gazette* in June 1906. There were proficiency tests in open-air observation, camping and orienteering which led to the award of a 'fleur-de-lys' badge.

Baden-Powell's emphasis was more on the secular ideas of Empire and citizenship, rather than those on which Smith had founded the organisation, and the rift between the two men grew. Baden-Powell's ideas were even attracting girls, so much so that, when the Girl Guides organisation was eventually formed, it instantly attracted 8,000 members.

In a last-ditch attempt to keep the two strands of the organisation together, Baden-Powell wrote to Smith on Christmas Day 1909:

> if leagued as a 'combine' we might tackle the whole mass effectively and really make a nation of God-fearing virile citizens in the next generation. We all naturally look to you as the leader of the Boy movement. If you decide to help in directing the policy of the Scout movement the other heads will follow suit . . . the possibilities are then enormous . . . the Prince of Wales is in favour of such an amalgamation of aims and would I believe become the president of such a council if formed.

He probably knew that the old puritan could not be persuaded. The Boy Scouts moved forward independently and soon dwarfed other youth organisations, with over 150,000 members in the UK by 1914.

St Anthony's, Govan, 1879

St Anthony's Parish Church in Govan is the only Roman Catholic church by Honeyman, although he designed various churches and schools in the area.

The name Govan, or Gowan, means 'the land of the blacksmith'. Although consumed

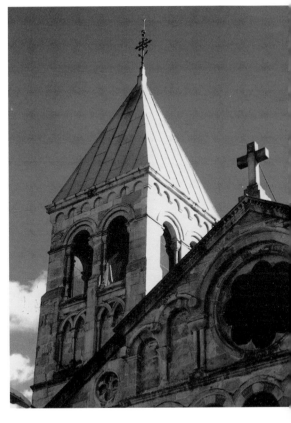

St Anthony's Church opened in 1879, more than 300 years after there had last been a place of worship for Roman Catholics in Govan.

by the growth of Glasgow in the late nineteenth century, from the early Christian period when there was a monastery founded by St Constantine, to the beginnings of shipbuilding, it was a thriving community in its own right.

On 19 July 1560, the priest in Govan, Stephen Betoun, was charged with 'treasonable offences' in common with all those not succumbing to the dictates of the Reformation. However, it was not until Betoun died in 1567 that Govan got its first Presbyterian minister. For the next 300 years there was no place of worship for Roman Catholics. Eventually the influx of shipyard workers from Ireland led to the establishment of a new parish in 1861.

By 1862 there were 1,449 Catholics in the area who worshipped in a small hall which they leased. Each Saturday night, seats were wheeled in barrows from the nearest Catholic church in Glasgow, much to the entertainment of ridiculing Protestant bigots, and taken back on a Sunday evening. The hall was a former stable and storehouse, near where Govan underground station is today. It was constructed of tin, had whitewashed walls and a clay floor. In dry weather the congregation came out white with lime from the walls and dust from the floor; in wet weather the floor became muddy.

Efforts were made to purchase a site for a new church, but when landowners learned what the use was to be they found a reason not to sell. Eventually, John Galt, a local builder and a Protestant, obtained the site on which St Anthony's now stands. He was unpopular locally for 'showing favour to the Papists', and in the light of threats from Protestants men guarded the new church at night during its construction.

With the growing population it soon became too small, but the church was unable to obtain additional land to construct a new building. Honeyman was appointed architect, and his solution was to erect a larger church around the existing one. Work on the Byzantine style building commenced around 1872, and once the walls were complete there was a period when the church could not be used while the old walls were demolished and the roof built. In 1878 the church was complete. A primary school for 400 pupils was erected alongside at the same time. The new church was officially opened on 26 October 1879.

The choice of Honeyman as architect may have arisen from his work on Govan Poorhouse. In 1872 it had come under the care of St Anthony's Parish, which retained an interest when the poorhouse moved to buildings that are now part of the Southern General Hospital. In 1877 Honeyman received a further commission from the Catholic

Church, making alterations to Dalbeth Convent for the trustees of the Convent of the Good Shepherd. A chapel, school, convent and a priest's house were all linked by corridors. All but the priest's house were demolished in 1996.

The Mother Anti-Burgher Church of Glasgow, 1880

This is the title of the history of the United Presbyterian Church (Barony North) in Cathedral Square, Glasgow, written by the Rev. James Primrose and published by Blackie and Son in 1896. It was written to celebrate the 'Ter-Jubilee' of the Congregation in 1897, that is, it had been 150 years since this particular branch of Protestantism had broken away from the Established Church. Honeyman designed the church they took possession of in 1880. The congregation was proud of its location in Cathedral Square:

> It was about this very spot, thirteen centuries ago, that Kentigern, that holy man of God, met Columba, the Great Apostle of the North. It was here, too, Kentigern proclaimed the story of Jesus and his love to our semi-savage Celtic forefathers, sitting listening on the green braes under drooping birches or sombre pines, amid the murmurings of the Molendinar flowing fast by the oracle of God.
>
> Our church, then, is built upon historic – upon holy ground – upon what for Glasgow is emphatically the hill of God. And as we further ponder over this – the square in which we are situated has representatives in each of its corners of the grand old historic Church of Scotland – the Established, the Free, and the United Presbyterian – along with the Cathedral itself, which is the 'Mother of us all'. So that in these four churches we have what may be not inaptly termed 'a veritable Quadrilateral of Presbyterianism'.

Honeyman had an interest in all four churches. A later chapter describes his work on Glasgow Cathedral while the Free Church referred to above was probably the Barony Free designed by Honeyman in 1867 when over half of the Wynd Free Church (see chapter 2) congregation split away to what was to be their mission church. It fell into disrepair in the 1950s and was demolished around 1972. It seated 1,100 people in the main church and over 500 in large side rooms. The £10,000 building (including the cost of the site) had a 130-foot tower and was a prominent landmark at the corner of Castle Street and Mason Street.

In 1886, Honeyman entered the design competition for the Established Church's Barony Church (now owned by the University of Strathclyde) opposite his UP Barony North. John James Burnet won, but his design exceeded the budget, much to Honeyman's disgust. He was supported by James Sellars in having a motion passed

Barony North Church, originally called the Mother Anti-Burgher Church of Glasgow.

by the Glasgow Institute of Architects that, in future, competition entries exceeding 10 per cent of the budget should be disregarded. I wonder what Honeyman would have said about the 1998 Scottish Parliament architect selection process where the winning design will cost in excess of £400 million (albeit including various client changes), while other competitors were showing what they could achieve for £50–£60 million.

It is worthwhile explaining why there were such divisions in the Protestant Church, which, even in the 1880s, were widely regarded as prosaic and irrelevant. In 1745, after Bonnie Prince Charlie's Stuart rebellion, there was concern about a resurgence of Roman Catholicism, and it was resolved that all men wishing to be ordained as burgesses in Edinburgh, Glasgow and Perth would take the Burgess Oath:

> Here I protest before God, and your Lordships, that I profess and allow with all
> my heart, the true religion presently professed within this realm, and
> authorised by the laws thereof: I shall abide thereat, and defend the same to
> my life's end; renouncing the Roman religion called Papistry.

An oath that one is taking for a cause one is willing to die for is a serious thing, and there was much debate as to what it meant. Was 'the true religion' merely Protestantism or did one need to subscribe in all respects to the tenets of the Established Church of Scotland? The United Presbyterian Church had split from the Established Church in 1733, and there was subsequently a further split between those who held one interpretation or the other. The ones who were willing to take the oath were known as 'Burghers', while those opposed, the 'Anti-Burghers', risked being excluded from civic position to protect their religious beliefs. The Anti-Burghers formed the congregation in 1747 that later appointed Honeyman for Barony North, hence the name for the church 'The Mother Anti-Burgher Church of Glasgow'.

The congregation first met in Cow Lane, later renamed Queen Street, then at Havannah Street close to the old university off High Street. In 1871 they moved into a new church on Duke Street by Hugh Barclay with a Venetian Romanesque facade. However, in 1878 the North British Railway obtained a Bill from Parliament to increase the size of College station (now High Street station) and the church had to sell its premises for £19,146. The congregation purchased the site in Cathedral Square from the City Improvement Trust for £5,300, and a memorial stone was laid by Lord Provost William Collins on 17 May 1879. It is recorded that the time capsule under it contained a photograph of the session and manager, the constitution of the church, copies of the *Herald*, *Mail*, *Scotsman*, *News*, *Daily Review*, *Evening News*, *Evening Citizen* and *Evening Times*, a map of Glasgow and silver coins.

Situated on the corner of Cathedral Square, the Barony Free Church was later overwhelmed by the mammoth Royal Infirmary building, which replaced a much more elegant Adam-designed infirmary, much to the anger of the architectural community of the time. John James Burnet's Barony Established Church is at the left-hand edge of the picture, the commission for it having been won in controversy.

Honeyman was asked to design the new church in Italian style. He had had a chance to study Italian architecture at first hand on visits to Italy in 1876 and 1877 to supervise construction of the Scots Church in Genoa he designed there for the Free Church (unfortunately it was bombed during the Second World War). The original design of the facade facing Cathedral Square was symmetrical, with a tower at either end. Only the one facing the Cathedral was built. Statues of the Evangelists Matthew, Mark, Luke and John were placed on pedestals, with St Peter and St Paul located in niches over doorways. The six statues cost £300 from McCulloch of London.

The interior was no less grand, with a sculpted marble font, large stained glass windows, expensive black marble columns in the apse, an elaborately patterned cast-iron stair balustrade, and rich, colourful plasterwork throughout. When the church opened on 30 May 1880, the ministers of Belhaven, Westbourne and Lansdowne Churches preached at the ceremony. With seating for almost 1,000 people, it cost £20,000. The organ was built by Forster and Andrews of Hull and installed in 1887. It has 1,800 pipes and is driven by a 400 volt, two-horsepower motor. The original motor was water-driven and a special main was brought in to serve it.

In 1978 the Evangelic Assembly purchased the building. The Glasgow Evangelical Church was formed in 1972 by members of various churches who 'became discontented with the continuous flirting of the Protestant churches with the Church of Rome'. Restoration work to the church was carried out in the early 1990s in conjunction with improvements to the Cathedral Square area. The building is now associated with the Orange Order, and perhaps not inappropriately it is watched over by nearby statues of John Knox and King William III ('King Billy').

Westbourne Church, 1881

For expediency, the Free Church erected an iron church on Great Western Road in 1875. One of Honeyman's iron churches on Loch Goil at Carrick Castle is still worshipped in today, and consists of corrugated iron walls and roof. Erected in 1892, it celebrated its centenary by having a new profiled metal sheet roof installed. The valley can still only be accessed by a single-track road from the main Strachur road,

Located at Carrick Castle on Loch Goil, this prefabricated iron church is still in use in 2004. It was designed by John Honeyman in 1892.

through Hell's Glen and down the loch, and when the church was built it would have been easier to reach by boat. Prefabricated iron churches were also regularly shipped out to the colonies to start parishes, and the *Building News* of 18 July 1890 stated that Honeyman had designed such churches in Australia just before he entered the design competition for the Sydney Houses of Parliament.

The Free Church in the prosperous West End of Glasgow did not have long to wait for much more suitable accommodation. John Honeyman was chosen 'as being . . . likely to secure internal comfort and good acoustics'. The neo-classical style building, with Ionic columns below Corinthian ones,

*Westbourne Church, located in Westbourne Gardens,
is now called the Struthers Memorial Church.*

was formally opened on 20 October 1881. An industrialist client of Honeyman's and church supporter, James Mirrlees, had laid a memorial stone in April 1881. There was seating for 750 people, and a carved walnut pulpit and communion table. John Keppie returned in 1892 to install a new organ.

In 1898/99, John Honeyman and Keppie carried out extensive alterations to Belhaven Church in Dundonald Road, and to the beadle's house in 1904. John Keppie's ex-boss, James Sellars, designed the original church, a commission won in a design competition in 1875 in which John Honeyman also competed. In 1960 the congregation from Belhaven Church moved into the church in Westbourne Gardens following a merger of the congregations. The redundant building was then purchased by the Glasgow restaurateur Reo Stakis to be used by the Greek Orthodox Church, and was renamed St Luke's.

Westbourne Church is now called the Struthers Memorial Church, its congregation being part of an independent Pentecostal fellowship founded in Greenock in the early 1950s.

Lost churches

Church attendances dropped dramatically after the 1950s, and congregations combined to survive as the cost of repairing and restoring old churches became too heavy a burden for church authorities to bear. Churches in inner suburban areas were often swept away in 'comprehensive redevelopment', a term that effectively meant wholesale demolition of vast areas, since it took decades to find the resources to build the infrastructure back up again. Many of Honeyman's churches have been lost, with

47

*Between 1947 and 1953 the former Buchanan Memorial Free Church was in secular use.
Its spire was removed during its 1953 conversion to St Bonaventure's RC Church.*

those in Govan already noted in chapter 1 and Barony Free mentioned under Barony North above.

St Andrew's Parish Free Church on Charlotte Street, Glasgow Green, was sanctioned by the Wynd Free Church in 1862 and completed in June 1864 with accommodation for 1,100 persons. It changed its name to the Charlotte Street Free Gospel Church, St Andrew's Free Church, Trinity Free Church and the Central Church of Scotland before it was demolished in the 1990s.

The foundation stone of Partick Free High Church in Hamilton Crescent was laid in June 1868 and it was formally opened on 28 March 1869. The first minister Robert Sandeman preached to around 700 of a congregation. Complaints about the acoustics were remedied when galleries were installed. Partick High united with Partick Downvale in 1936, and when this congregation then joined with St Mary's Partick South in 1977 the Hamilton Crescent building was sold to the City Temple. It was destroyed around 1983.

The Buchanan Memorial Free Church was designed for minister Alexander Cook Fullarton in 1877 and built on the north side of Caledonia Road, close to the gushet with Rutherglen Road, opposite the Southern Necropolis. Alterations and repairs were carried out by the practice in 1887 and 1894, but in 1947 the congregation united with the nearby Augustine Church on Rutherglen Road, another Honeyman church. For a few years after 1947 the building was used as a carpet factory until the Catholic Church purchased it and Gillespie Kidd and Coia converted it back to religious use, it being consecrated in 1953 as St Bonaventure's RC Church. The spire was removed and the resulting tower capped with a copper lid. It was eventually demolished in 1992 after a number of arson attacks.

The Augustine Free Church at 281 Rutherglen Road was originally built as Stonefield Free Church in 1872, changing its name in 1900. It was a mission church jointly sanctioned by the Wynd Free Church, Barony Free Church and the Trinity Free Church, the ministers of all three being Honeyman's clients. On the merging of congregations in 1947 it changed its name again to the Augustine Buchanan Church, and with another merger with Oatlands Trinity (another Honeyman church from 1882/83) it became Rutherglen Road Church. The Baptist Church occupied it before it was demolished.

The Wynd Church initially sponsored a mission church in what became the church hall of the Candlish Memorial Church (Candlish Polmadie) in 1874. The permanent church followed soon after (opened 1877) on the corner of Cathcart Road and Calder Street, taking its name from a former minister. It united with Polmadie Church in 1968 and was demolished in the late 1990s. Having passed it many times when I lived in the south side suburbs several years ago, sensing it as a grand landmark but taking it for granted, it was sad to go back to witness an empty space, having only missed its demolition by months.

The Wesleyan Chapel at 20 Admiral Street, Kingston (later Great Wellington Street) was built as part of the city's second Methodist revival, and was formally opened on 6 August 1871. It was a classical Greek design with Corinthian columns externally and cast-iron ones inside with lotus leaf capitals. Latterly called the Admiral Street Methodist Church, it was converted to an auction house in 1981 but it burned down in 1985.

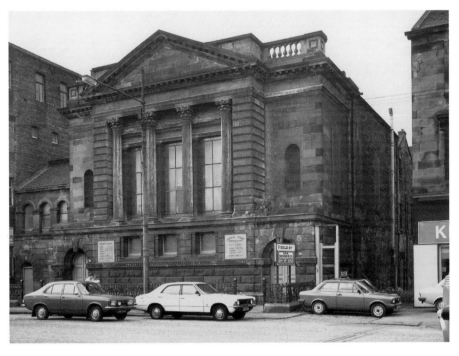

The Admiral Street Wesleyan Chapel, Glasgow,
latterly the Admiral Street Methodist Church.

The Free West Church, Greenock, was originally intended to feature a spire on the corner seen here to the right obscured by trees.

50

CHAPTER 4

Town and country churches

St Thomas's and the Free West Church (St Mark's Greenbank) Greenock, 1862

In 1856 Honeyman inherited the commission for St Thomas's in Brougham Street, Greenock, from architect J.T. Emmet who had retired due to ill health. It still exists at the corner of Patrick Street and Gray Place although it is now a carpet warehouse.

The Free West Church was won in a design competition in 1861 and was Honeyman's first major church project in his own right. At a cost of £2,938, it was prestigious enough for him to make his first appearance in an architectural journal, the *Builder*, the same year. The foundation stone was laid on 12 June 1861 and the church opened on 13 November 1862. It had a tower at its south-west corner on which it was intended to build a spire, 220 feet high, but funds never became available. The congregation was unhappy about the acoustics, and an independent report by Campbell Douglas and Sellars in 1875 resulted in Honeyman returning to install a lowered ceiling.

In 1929, when the United Free Church combined with the Church of Scotland, the church, situated at the corner of Ardgowan Street and Kelly Street, became known as St Mark's. It combined with the congregation of Greenbank in 1955 but numbers continued to fall until it closed in 1987. It was demolished around 1992.

Dumbarton Free Church, 1864

The foundation stone for this was laid on 13 July 1863, and when completed the church could seat about 850 people. The site is quite close to the River Leven and its silted banks, and this probably explains why the tower and spire is off plumb. Honeyman had taken precautions against this, sitting the tower on four sandstone blocks, each three metres square.

The church was later known as Dumbarton High Parish Church, but became surplus to requirements in 1972

Bridge Street, Lockerbie, with the spire of Lockerbie Free Church on the left.

51

when the North and Old Parish Churches combined. In 1981 it reopened as a licensed leisure complex. When I visited it in 2001, it was in use as a market and snooker hall.

Lockerbie Free Church, 1867

The existing church was almost completely rebuilt in 1867, and the modified building bore similarities to that at Dumbarton. However, there Honeyman had £3,890 to spend whereas at Lockerbie the budget was only £1,600. Consequently the detailing is much simpler. Honeyman had not ventured into this part of the country before, and it is possible that the Rev. Campbell was a former fellow student. Strangely, the project is not contained in Honeyman's job books, but the *Dumfries and Galloway Standard* of 14 March 1867 attributed it to him, albeit saying that he came from Edinburgh.

The roof was removed, the walls were raised to allow the insertion of a gallery and the whole front elevation was rebuilt with red sandstone, featuring Honeyman's favourite wheel window. To save money, the columns supporting the galleries were painted red to look like good sandstone.

The church became St Cuthbert's Church of Scotland in 1929 when most of the United Free Church rejoined the Established Church. The final service was held in December 1986, and the building was last used as a chapel of rest.

Aberfoyle, 1870; Port of Menteith, 1878

Since 1983 Aberfoyle Parish has been linked with that of Port of Menteith, sharing a minister. The churches also share the architect of the original buildings, John Honeyman. The double parish spans 20 miles of some of the finest scenery in Scotland, starting just above sea level in the east and extending almost as far as Loch Katrine in the west, with adjacent mountains such as Ben Lomond rising to over 3,000 feet. Its churches are also among the prettiest in the country.

Aberfoyle Church has as its backdrop the bare and rocky face of Craigmore and is set on its own mound, surrounded by trees. Honeyman inherited the project from J.T. Rochead when he retired in 1869 due to ill health. The cost of construction was met by Robert Hampson and Mary Hampson (née Joynson) in memory of their brother and husband respectively, Richard Hampson. It was built in 1870. All windows were fitted with blinds for worship on long summer evenings, but there was initially no heating in the building for cold winter mornings. The Italian alabaster pulpit and font, and the communion table were gifted by the Hampsons, and the east gable has a window in memory of Robert and Mary Hampson. A modern set of windows in the north transept, designed by Gordon Webster in 1974, is dedicated to Major and Mrs Will Joynson of The Glassert.

The church started off as a plain rectangular building, but in 1883/84 the

Aberfoyle Parish Church.

porch was moved to the west and transepts were added to provide extra seating, giving it a cruciform shape. A vestry was added at the same time, and a pipe organ was installed in 1887. Before electricity was introduced, its bellows were operated by boys who relieved the tedium between hymns by carving their names on the woodwork at the back of the organ. The old paraffin wall lamps on either side of the nave are still in place, albeit having been converted to electricity some time ago.

Other commissions were associated with the church. Adjacent to it is Aberfoyle School, today serving primary pupils, although in 1870 it was all that was required for a community where the school leaving age was unlikely to extend beyond thirteen. The church and school cost £2,558 in 1870, and the alterations to the church £1,100 in 1884. Honeyman returned in 1890 to build a £420 extension to the school. The benefactors for this building were also the Hampsons, and Mrs Hampson's family, the Joynsons, had Honeyman make alterations to their house, The Glassert, the following year. In 1898 J. Walter Joynson had £1,470 worth of alterations carried out to his house, Altskeith, Kinlochard, Aberfoyle. Today it is the second oldest house in the district. It was formerly called the Lochard Lodge and is now the Altskeith Hotel.

Honeyman designed Port of Menteith Church in 1876, replacing an earlier church of 1771. It cost £2,878 and was completed in 1878. Its location beside Scotland's only lake (the rest are lochs) is even more picturesque than Aberfoyle's. The largest of the lake's islands contains the ruins of Inchmahome Priory, which was founded in 1238. Mary, Queen of Scots was taken here after the Battle of Pinkie in 1547. The Burgh of Port of Menteith was established as early as 1467. The peacefulness of the lake belies its historic importance and its proximity to Glasgow and Edinburgh, both of which are less than an hour away by car.

Port of Menteith Church.

St Mary's, Kirkcudbright, 1874, 1887 and 1894

On 25 November 1871, the following circular was issued by the Free Church authorities:

Proposed new Free Church at Kirkcudbright. The present church was built in 1843, in the midst of all the haste and excitement of Disruption times, and, like most of the country churches of that period, it is now found, in the changed circumstances produced by the lapse of thirty years, to be inadequate to the wants of the congregation . . . . Within the last ten days . . . a generous Edinburgh friend – who, to use his own words, regards the present church as 'unworthy of the position of the Free Church in Kirkcudbright, and unbefitting of the requirements of the times' [has] spontaneously and unexpectedly sent to the Rev. Dr McMillan the munificent sum of five hundred pounds towards the erection of a new building. Stimulated by this handsome gift, the congregation have unanimously and heartily resolved that . . . it is manifestly their duty to accept the gift, and take steps to raise such an additional sum –

say three thousand pounds – as will enable them to erect a handsome, commodious and suitable church.

To obtain the church of their aspirations, a lot more than £3,000 was required. The Ferguson Bequest Fund donated £150, but only on condition that the total cost would exceed £4,300. Honeyman's job book records the cost at £4,390. Funds came from families with Kirkcudbright connections, some as far away as America. Thomas Cochrane of New York represented these people at the laying of the foundation stone on 20

St Mary's Free Church Kirkcudbright, whose spire is a local landmark, was converted into flats in 1987.

August 1872, and had a silver trowel presented to him by the Rev. Dr McMillan. The usual documents and journals were placed in a bottle under the stone. 'The stone having been placed and laid, Mr Cochrane took the mallet and gave the customary knocks, declaring it to have been well and truly laid.'

The church opened on 26 March 1874, with the local newspaper stating: 'that altogether the building has an air of comfort which will be duly appreciated by the congregation, especially during the winter season'. The congregation could obviously afford more commodious surroundings than those at Aberfoyle, where only the heritor, that is the landlord, was responsible for the funding. Although Honeyman obtained all other tradesmen and contractors from Glasgow, Kirkcudbright and Castle Douglas, he had to go to Coventry to find Richard and Co. to provide the gas-fitting service.

In April 1884, at the request of Isabella Johnston, daughter of the founder of the education trust that ran the Free Church school in the town, the church obtained ground to the east to build a church hall. There was a concern that the new school board would take over Johnston's Free School and not allow its use for the Free Church's Sunday school. Honeyman designed the hall extension in 1887 at a cost of £1,278. The practice came back in 1894 to make further modifications. If John Keppie had represented it, he would have had the welcome opportunity to call in on friends of his in the Glasgow artist community which flocked to the pretty town, especially E.A. Hornel whose studio Keppie designed.

The Kirkcudbright congregation has gone through many changes over the years. With the union of the Free and United Presbyterian Churches in 1900, the church changed its name to St Mary's United Free Church of Scotland. In 1914 St Mary's combined with St Cuthbert's. By 1987 the church was no longer required for religious use and was converted into flats by Paul Ansbro.

St Matthew's, Perth, 1871

The Free West Church, as it was originally called, commands a prominent position on a bend of the River Tay in the middle of Perth. Before W.S. Turnbull of Huntingtowerfield purchased the site for a new church, a street did not run along the banks of the Tay, the town turning its back on the river. Indeed the initial proposals for Tay Street drawn

This view from downriver shows how the view of St Matthew's Church, Perth, is obscured by the adjacent building. This was due to an error by the builder when the latter was laid out.

up by the police commissioners envisaged the bend in the river being taken out by forming a straight line for the road between the post office and the county buildings. A campaign then ensued, headed by two Perth men who were members of the Royal Scottish Academy, John M. Barclay and RSA secretary Mr D.O. Hill. They also enlisted the help of eminent Edinburgh architect David Bryce, designer of Fettes College, the Assembly Hall on the Mound, the Bank of Scotland headquarters, and Edinburgh Royal Infirmary. He argued that the new church required the setting of the bend in the river, and the straightening of the road would reduce the available site depth below that suitable for a building of the size necessary to accommodate three congregations.

The congregations which W.S. Turnbull envisaged sharing the same roof were the three Free churches in the town, St Leonard's, the Middle and the West Churches. After initial agreement between them, St Leonard's broke rank first, stating: 'It appears that the site proposed is specially defective, as being in an obscure and hidden location, besides being too close to the river, and probably objectionable in a sanitary point of view'. Perhaps the river smelled somewhat in those days. On 5 February 1867 the joint committee of both remaining congregations met to review a design in 'Early Gothic, of about the middle of the thirteenth century' by John Honeyman, which although 'highly approved of' had to wait until 6 May 1867 for the politics of the two churches to be resolved to allow Honeyman to be officially appointed. By 12 October 1868, it was clear that the Free Middle Church would be unable to raise its share of the building funds, and the West Church went forward on its own, instructing Honeyman to change the design accordingly.

Sadly, W.S. Turnbull died on 26 January 1869 and did not see Honeyman's final design of April of that year. The estimate for the building at that time was £6,000. After further design work the cost rose to £7,600, although a saving of £1,859 might have been made if the upper part of the tower and spire were omitted. Building work started in September 1869 and the memorial stone was laid by the Earl of Dalhousie on 18 May 1870, the 27th anniversary of the Disruption. A procession made its way from the town hall, all local dignitaries attending except Lord Provost Pullar who was 'unavoidably absent'. A glass time capsule with various documents and copper and silver coins was laid under the memorial stone.

One other problem occurred with respect to the site. The building committee asked Honeyman to set out the building two feet back from the proposed pavement line on Tay Street. This he did, but when the adjacent building was set out to the south (downriver) the next year, it was not two feet in front of the wall of the church, but four feet. The church considered legal action against the owners of the building, but were too short of funds to risk losing. The south view of the tower is therefore now more restricted than Honeyman had intended. He quickly thereafter pegged out the frontage line of the empty site to the north of the church, and the Savings Bank next door complied with this when it was built.

As construction progressed, the foundations had to be reinforced in the riverside alluvial soil, and in March 1871 the decision was taken to complete the spire, which would cost an extra £220 if delayed until a later date. The Deacons' Court would have realised that if this were delayed, it would probably never be finished. The final building cost was £9,384. 17s. 1d., but with various other items of expenditure, including Honeyman's fee of £652. 7s. 9d., the total cost was £12,273. 4s. 7d. On 23 November 1871 the church was opened for public worship.

In 1874 sufficient funds had been

Perth had previously turned its back on the river, but with the building of Honeyman's St Matthew's Church and subsequent developments adjacent to it the city acquired a view to be proud of.

The spectacular scenery in which the Ballachulish slate quarries and John Curry's oat fields were located, with the Ballachulish Hotel on the right.

The tower and gallery of St Munda's Church, Ballachulish, were added by Honeyman.

raised to add some finishing touches, including a stained glass window at the pulpit end of the church in memory of W.S. Turnbull. His widow witnessed completion of the building, and was guest of honour when the memorial stone was laid for a church hall extension in 1895.

Turnbull's vision of a combined church did come to pass, but in a different form on 1 May 1965, when the congregations of the Middle Church (on Tay Street next to the Royal George Hotel), Bridgend Church (now the site of a special housing area) and Wilson Church in Scott Street combined with the West Church, which was renamed St Matthew's.

Ballachulish, 1881

John Honeyman was appointed to add a tower and gallery to St Munda's Church, Ballachulish, at the recommendation of its treasurer John Curry. The foundation stone was laid by the Duke of Argyll in September 1880, and the extended church was dedicated by the Rev. Robert Blair of St Columba Church, Glasgow, on 23 July 1881.

The building had been opened as a mission church in 1845 and was named after St Munda, who founded a church early in the seventh century on the island in Loch Leven that still bears his name (the burial island of the Macdonalds, Camerons and Stewarts). The last service was held there in 1653. There is a display of historical items in Honeyman's gallery in the church, and newspaper articles of the time that refer to the local hotel owner, John Curry.

Honeyman designed the Ballachulish Hotel for Curry in 1877 at a cost of £2,769 to serve the ferry crossing. It was in Gothic revival style. In the valuation roll for the County of Argyll, Lismore and Appin Parish, 1890/91, Curry is recorded as occupying two farms, a farmhouse, house and hotel. He held these buildings under the trust of the late Sir George de la Poer Beresford of Ballachulish.

John Curry was a pillar of the community and he hosted dinners for local worthies including Hugh MacColl, manager of the Ballachulish slate quarry, and John Anderson, secretary of the Callander and Oban Railway. He was also a notable farmer. In September 1890 the *Oban Times* reported that: 'an oat stalk from one of his fields which has been taken as a fuse for use in the quarry was found to have 240 grains and to be seven feet in length'. It was quite common for oat stalks to be used as fuses in the quarry. Three lines of holes were bored into the rock face and bunged with explosives. Those setting the fuses and running for it before the dynamite blew would have been obliged to John Curry for his expertise in growing long oat stalks.

Lochgilphead, 1885 and 1891

The Lochgilphead Parish congregation was not wealthy, but was forced to consider building a new church since the one it had been occupying since 1820 was suffering badly from dry rot, probably because the foundations were not constructed properly to stop rising damp. During 1881 and 1882 a sum of £1,870 had been promised, but architects Baldie and Tennant estimated the cost at £2,300. Hoping that a competitive tender might be less than this, bids were sought, but the cheapest was £2,500. Baldie and Tennant were paid off for £20 and John Honeyman commissioned instead.

The current church records contain all the correspondence of the time. Honeyman wrote from 140 Bath Street, Glasgow, on 24 October 1883:

Rev'd and dear Sir,
I regret that I was not able to send you the designs for the proposed church last week as I hoped to do. I send them today. I have shewn two totally different arrangements – one a modification of the sketch which I showd to the Committee and the other having an end gallery. The latter would be rather cheaper than the first and would suit either the old site or the new. I think if Concrete were used for the corners and for the spire (to which I see no objection) it might be erected including the spire for the sum you mentioned. I may say that I prefer the other design and if not more than two or three feet of under building is required it would cost very little more – in short on a new site there would be very little difference between them.

I send a small perspective view that gives a better idea of the group. The spires would be very much alike.

I remain, Yours very truly
John Honeyman

Since the most difficult element to estimate in a budget is often the underground works and foundations, a six-foot trial hole was dug, and Honeyman was asked for recommendations to ensure that dry rot would not be a problem in the future. His letter of 16 November stated that all existing soil should be removed from the site, the area drained, the walls built on concrete foundations and made of Portland cement up to ground floor level, and asphalt used to cover the whole area to stop rising damp. With these reassurances, the site of the existing church was chosen.

Honeyman ended his letter with a discussion about the position of the steeple, arguing against the minister's suggestion that it be in the centre of the gable rather than at the side. The site lies at the top of Argyll Street and a symmetrical composition might have been expected. He drew a marvellously simple sketch at the side of the page to explain how an asymmetrical arrangement would look better and make the short steeple look higher. His next letter of 21 November estimated that, apart from the spire at a cost of £300 to £400, the church could be built for less than £2,000.

The foundation stone was laid on 21 August 1884, but in November of that year the builders, W. and J. Robertson, asked for payment in advance, threatening to stop work if this was not approved. Honeyman advised against this, suspecting that Robertsons' was heading for bankruptcy. The church decided to arrange the work itself using the suppliers and tradesmen already chosen for the project. This involved activities such as negotiating with shipbroker J.M. Paton to deliver 35 tons of stone by boat to Lochgilphead at four shillings per ton. Inevitably the disruption to the process caused delays, and the project ended up costing £2,412 by the time it was completed in September 1885.

Finishing touches took place later, such as railings whose decorative tops were ordered from Belgium. A bell was purchased for £44, and Honeyman is believed to have designed the communion table in 1891.

The nature of the surrounding townscape and the small size of Lochgilphead Parish Church led Honeyman to reject a formal, symmetrical building for the site at the head of Argyll Street.

Although it once had a population of 50, today only two houses remain at Port Allen from where crops from the Carse of Gowrie were shipped out. The Tennent family owned several farms in the area. Until fairly recently one of these houses was the home of John Anderson, athletics coach to Liz McColgan and star of the TV show 'Gladiators'.

CHAPTER 5

Industry in the second city of the Empire

Chapter 1 tells how John Honeyman gained work from the shipbuilding and engineering industries which were burgeoning in the Glasgow area in the second half of the nineteenth century. As the urban population grew, a number of other industries developed and spawned commissions.

In 1856 Honeyman designed alterations to the Tradeston warehouse of G.L. Walker and Company, powerloom and cloth manufacturers. This is thought to have been the Falfield Cotton Mills, which closed in 1901, although parts of the building still survive. Frederick Grosvenor, earthenware manufacturer, commissioned Honeyman to carry out a number of alterations to his pottery in Boden Street, Bridgeton, between 1869 and 1881. This is still in existence today, and the quality of the 130-year-old brickwork on this simple building would put modern brickies to shame. Industrial businesses also need offices, Honeyman designing those for the Great Canal Brewery at 28 Gordon Street for Hugh Baird in 1866 and 1870.

The Mirrlees dynasty

One of Honeyman's most interesting industrial clients was James Buchanan Mirrlees, part of a Glasgow business dynasty that lasted from the mid-1750s to the end of the nineteenth century. Among those who married into the family to seek or consolidate their financial and social positions was James Lumsden, whose son James was a passenger aboard the *Comet*'s maiden voyage, a founder of the Clydesdale Bank, Lord Provost of Glasgow from 1843 to 1846, and treasurer of the Royal Infirmary of Glasgow from 1831 to 1850, his statue standing in Cathedral Square today. Another up-and-coming businessman, Richard Kidson, married James Buchanan Mirrlees' aunt Isabella. He was a benefactor of Honeyman's Helensburgh Free Church Manse (1859), Park Free Church, Helensburgh (1862), and of houses by Honeyman for his sons William (Ferniegair, Helensburgh, 1867), and Charles (Glenoran, Rhu, 1869).

The first step in the family's social and financial rise occurred when Charles Mirrlees (James Buchanan Mirrlees' great grandfather) was admitted as a Burgess and Guild Brother of Glasgow in 1756 having married the daughter of John Ewing, a weaver who was already a burgess. An old regulation of the Merchants' and Trades' Houses urged apprentices 'to take their master's daughter in marriage before any other, which will be a great comfort and support to freemen'. Their eldest son William also became a burgess and was admitted to the Incorporation of Hammermen, the largest of the trades in Glasgow, encompassing a number of metalworking specialists such as smiths, toolmakers, armourers and cutlers. William was a saddler, no doubt obtaining much work, as it is recorded in James Cleland's *Annals of Glasgow 1816* that there were 1,679 horses in the city. He was officially defined as a saddle-tree maker.

James Buchanan Mirrlees was born on 19 August 1822. With the development of the railway network in the 1840s, he could see that horses and saddlemaking might have a limited future, and looked for another direction for the family business. His father, William Mirrlees II, had married the daughter of a sugar plantation owner, James Buchanan, who had estates and businesses in Grenada, Jamaica and Rio de Janeiro.

In September 1848, James established a relationship with Peter McOnie, whose family repaired sugar production machinery. The abolition of slavery in the early decades of the nineteenth century had made plantation ownership uneconomic, with more money to be made in the processing of sugar than its primary production. Peter died in 1850, and James recruited William Tait from the Hyde Park Locomotive Works in Springburn to form the sugar machinery company Mirrlees and Tait. He obtained a loan of £12,000 from the Clydesdale Bank (courtesy of his uncle James Lumsden), and for good measure married Williamina Nicol Fleming, daughter of a leading East India merchant, John Fleming of Claremont. This marriage was carefully arranged, since James Lumsden and John Fleming were close friends, founding the Custom House in Clyde Street together.

Honeyman designed Mirrlees and Tait's Scotland Street works in 1861. The west of Scotland supplied about 80 per cent of the world's sugar machinery in the second half of the nineteenth century, and Honeyman was back in 1872 designing an extension. The buildings were all demolished in 1968.

James Buchanan Mirrlees was elected to the town council in 1862 for the area in which his works were located, and became one of the city's eight bailies in 1865. Some of his duties in council life were unremarkable, like the selection of Glasgow's first Medical Officer of Health in 1863, but others were less so, such as officiating at the execution of Dr Edward Pritchard on 28 July 1865, the last public hanging in Glasgow.

He was active in the Free Church, his father having been prominent in the Disruption. Within six days of the new church being set up, the foundation stone of St Matthew's Church was laid in Kent Road opposite the Mitchell Library. He and his brother William became deacons. However, for some reason he severed his connection with the church in 1863. In 1871 he moved to Redlands on Great Western Road in Kelvinside, and supported the campaign to locate a Free Church in the area. This was Honeyman's Westbourne Church, whose memorial stone was laid by Mirrlees in April 1881.

To the surprise of the congregation and his friends, he used the event to criticise the lack of freedom of expression in the Free Church, and to support churchman Robertson Smith who had been accused of heresy for his views on biblical criticism. He warned that such an inflexible attitude was driving people to the Catholic Church, a contention that his cousin William Kidson would have abhorred, being vice-president of the West of Scotland Protestant Association and a campaigner against Catholic nurses at the Royal Infirmary in case they attempted to convert poor Protestants, weakened by illness or disease. Many locals thought that divine retribution had come to James Buchanan Mirrlees on 10 May 1882 when Redlands was badly damaged by fire.

James Buchanan Mirrlees died on 16 November 1903, but the dynasty continued, again through marriage. One of his daughters married Ivor Philipps, who rose to the rank of Major General in the First World War, was knighted in 1917, was Liberal MP for Southampton, and had been chairman of several companies, including Ilford and Schweppes. When James's widow moved out of Redlands it was rented by the Glasgow Provincial Committee for the Training of Teachers as a hostel, until 1921 when the new hostel was built at Jordanhill, part of the project being Honeyman and Keppie's Jordanhill Demonstration School.

The Tennents of Wellpark

The growing city of Glasgow had a great thirst. The Tennents had been farmers in Cumbernauld since the fifteenth century, but in 1556 Robert Tennent moved to Glasgow to become a maltman and brewer in Drygate, rising to the position of a burgess of the city. Eleven family members and several generations later, in 1793, the Wellpark area was purchased for a brewery, with Scotch ale, Glasgow porter and stout being exported to the West Indies and Virginia. By the nineteenth century the Tennents were the largest exporters of bottled beer in the world.

In 1862 the company purchased the Errol Estate, on the north bank of the River Tay, a few miles downstream from Perth, at a cost of £105,955 from Lady Henrietta Duncan or Allen, widow of Royal Naval Captain John James Allen. John Honeyman designed various farm buildings and houses there from 1866 to 1871. The first was the large Daleally Farm, and this was followed by alterations and additions to Port

Daleally Farm, sitting in the fertile Carse of Gowrie between Perth and Dundee, was purchased by the Tennent family in 1862.

Today the horse-mill building at Port Allen Farm has most of its windows bricked up, but the circular steading is open, and despite having been exposed to the elements for around 130 years its roof timbers still appear to be in good condition.

ESTABLISHED 1745

TRADE MARK

Telephone No.
BELL 1900 (3 lines)

Telegraphic Address:
"WELLPARK, GLASGOW"

J. & R. TENNENT, Ltd.

—— *Brewers and Bottlers* of ——

Pale Ale, XXX Stout, and Lager Beer (light and dark)

— FOR ALL EXPORT MARKETS —

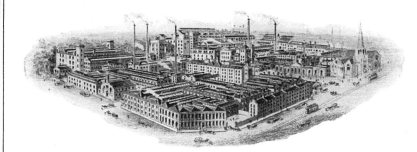

The Oldest Exporters of Beer and Stout in the World

Correspondence in French, German and Spanish

Wellpark Brewery, GLASGOW

And at BIRMINGHAM, LONDON, LIVERPOOL and MANCHESTER

Tennent's Wellpark Brewery comprised an entire community with houses, a school and Wellpark Free Church (the spire of which is visible on the right of the illustration). Honeyman added a hall to the church.

Allen, Balcalk and Northbank Farms. Errol Park House was also altered in 1867 prior to it being burned down in 1874. (It is possible that some elements of the Honeyman fabric were salvaged for incorporation in the replacement building which exists today.) In 1875 he added a hall to the Hay brothers' Wellpark Free Church in Glasgow, the site being gifted by the brewing family. Daleally Farm remains much as it was almost 140 years ago.

At the time Honeyman added a steading to Port Allen Farm, it also doubled as a public house with George Thomson as tenant. He had the lease of the farm, the mill and the pier, Port Allen being the only convenient harbour between Perth and Dundee. From the Carse of Gowrie it exported agricultural products as far as London, and imported wine, porter (bitter beer), sugar and wood. Thomson's nickname was 'Old Snodam', because if anyone annoyed him he would say, 'I'll snod you'. The next tenant, David Miller, employed Honeyman to alter his other farm at Balcalk, although he remained the local publican for only a year as he died in an accident.

Buying a country estate was not unusual for a wealthy family, but, apart from Errol Park House, the buildings commissioned by the Tennents were not grand manors. They were practical farms and houses, suggesting that the purpose of the acquisition was the production of crops for brewing production. It was also unlikely that the lord of the manor of the time would have wanted a country estate for leisure purposes, since he was only an infant. Hugh Tennent was born on 31 October 1863, and his father, Charles Stewart Parker Tennent, died the following year, at which point the first Tennent Trust was set up.

It is highly likely that Honeyman obtained the work at Errol for the Tennents through his accountant brother Michael, who was a witness of a sale of some of the Errol land to a brewer called James Blair in 1869.

On 6 November 1884 it was announced at Hugh Tennent's coming of age party in Glasgow City Hall that he was to become sole proprietor of Wellpark. It is not clear why Hugh's elder brother Archibald did not wish to run the brewery, but he was no doubt happy with the £600,000 his brother paid him from the trust set up by their father. One of the first things Hugh did was to create Tennent's Lager, having visited Bavaria in 1882 and heard how the Germans had been exporting lagers to the Americas since 1875. However, it was not until the 1938 Empire Exhibition that draught Tennent's Lager was introduced to the home market.

At the end of his toast to Hugh at his 21st birthday party, William Robertson, the manager at Wellpark, wished him 'health, long life and prosperity'. The last he managed, but he died aged 27 of acute fever and a fatty heart before he got a chance to marry. The second Tennent Trust was formed, but Hugh and Archibald, who also died without children in 1946, were the last Tennents of Wellpark. Hugh and his father lie in the Necropolis overlooking the brewery that is still one of the largest in Scotland. Curiously, they occupy lair 50 of the Upsilon Section of the cemetery, while in lair 49 lie John Honeyman and his family. One assumes that this is coincidence, since Charles Tennent's funeral was on 24 February 1864, and Honeyman's wife Ann's on 24 March 1864, and they were the first of each family to be buried there.

Industrial projects, 1890 to 1913

Most of Honeyman's work in the 1870s and 80s was comprised of residential, school and church projects, with just a few commercial and industrial commissions. This could have been due to poor economic conditions related to incidents such as the City of Glasgow Bank collapse, or perhaps Honeyman had just lost touch with many of the clients who were commissioning such projects. This changed after 1888 when John Keppie joined the practice.

The Whitevale Foundry in Bridgeton was altered in 1895 and 1900 for David Auld and Sons. The business had been founded in 1832 on the back of steam valve inventions. It was still in business in the 1930s, boasting that various Blue Riband-winning ships (awarded for the fastest Atlantic crossings) had been fitted with Auld's valves – the *Queen Mary*, *Normandie*, *Rex* and *Mauretania*. The John Honeyman and Keppie job books refer to alterations to the Whitevale Mission and Foundry, so it could be that they were linked, either physically or financially.

In 1890 a Hide and Skin Market was built at 34–43 Greendyke Street, Glasgow. Robert Ramsay and Company held a wool auction in it. It replaced a smaller building of 1885 that was destroyed by fire. Industrial use ended in the mid-1970s, after which it fell into disrepair until the category 'B' listed building was converted into flats in the late 1990s by Applejack Design, with the aid of a £500,000 grant from Scottish Homes. It sits beside the Homes for the Future project associated with the Glasgow City of Architecture and Design year of 1999.

Other industrial projects of this period included the Sugar Exchange in Cathcart Street, Greenock (1890), a warehouse at 61 Bishop Street, Anderston (1891), and a store in Cheapside, Glasgow (1892). Later projects were the Saracen Tool Works

The Hide and Skin Market, Greendyke Street, Glasgow.

While it is good to see an old building converted to a new use, in this case flats, many interior details of the Hide and Skin Market, Greendyke Street, Glasgow have been lost, including this magnificent fireplace.

The interior of the Hide and Skin Market, with a few skins left lying on the floor after an auction.

at 272 Bell Street and 13 East Campbell Street (1891–98), founded on the site by Alexander Mathieson and Sons, edge-tool makers, the St Helen's Engineering Works, 150 Helen Street/Harmony Row (1895–98), and the British and Foreign Aerated Water Company (1898, location untraced). Two brick stables were converted for the use of the Apex Motor Engineering Company at 58 Cromwell Street in 1910, which became a driving school for women during the First World War to make up for the shortage of male chauffeurs who had gone off to war. In 1911 alterations took place at the Carntyne Dyewood Mills at 567 Shettleston Road. The British Dyewood and Chemical Company was formed in 1898 and made extracts from dyewoods for colouring and tanning. It made large profits during the First World War from the manufacture of khaki for military uniforms. The company finally ceased trading in 1980.

Until the second half of the nineteenth century, furniture was a craft industry relying on the skill of the cabinetmaker. When it became mechanised, a concentration of manufacturers developed in the Beith and Lochwinnoch area. One of these was Robert Balfour's West of Scotland Cabinet and Chair Works in Beith, which John Honeyman and Keppie altered in 1900. Like most local companies, it suffered in the recession of the early 1960s, becoming Beithcraft before owners McIntosh of Kirkcaldy closed it down in 1983. It was the last furniture company in the area.

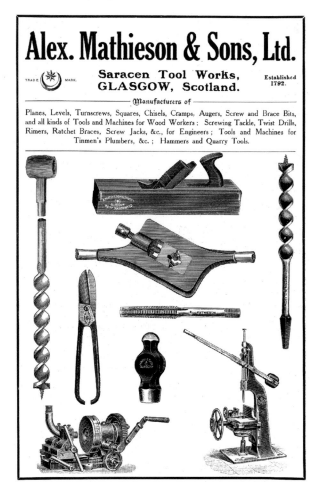

The practice carried out various alterations to Alex Mathieson's Saracen Tool Works, and the lettering on one surviving drawing suggests the hand of Charles Rennie Mackintosh.

Achamore House, Gigha, as it was originally designed,
before a fire required parts of the upper floors to be removed (see page 73).

CHAPTER 6

Victorian businessmen and their country houses

Ardpatrick House, 1864

On the south side of West Loch Tarbert there is a good A-class road on which one can speed down to Campbeltown. On the north side is a narrow, single-track road which winds its way along the Knapdale Peninsula. The remoteness of the area around Ardpatrick House is witnessed by the remains of primary oak forest, which was widespread on the west coast of Scotland in the sixteenth century before it was cut down to create charcoal for the smelting of cannon and cannonballs. In those days, the Dukes of Argyll, and the various branches of the Campbell family that were related to them, cared little about renewable sources of timber.

Ardpatrick House was thought to have been built by a Duke of Argyll in the seventeenth century and enlarged by factor Angus MacAlister from 1769 to 1776. Walter Campbell of Shawfield and Islay purchased it from the creditors of the then owner in 1798. It was also a Campbell who commissioned John Honeyman to extend it in 1864, by adding to the rear of the north wing and rebuilding the south wing.

The Campbell family continued to own the building until it was purchased by Greenock rope-maker John Birkmyre in the 1920s. Walter and Esther (nickname 'Pete') Kenneil acquired it in 1946. Pete's family owned the Edinburgh publishing house Thomas Nelson, and the estate still belonged to their three children and their families at the beginning of the twenty-first century.

Helenslee, Dumbarton, 1866 and 1882

One of the projects inherited from J.T. Rochead in 1866 was a house for Peter Denny, the shipbuilding baron, although Honeyman already knew Denny from a small domestic commission he had carried out for him in 1862. The house in Dumbarton was named after his wife, Helen Leslie. Honeyman changed the design of

In 1864 Honeyman added an extension to Ardpatrick House, an ancestral home of the Duke of Argyll.

the east elevation to locate the main entrance there. He also added a three-storey block, an attic, tower, stable block, lodge and main gate piers. Work carried out in 1882 is thought to have related to alterations to the gate lodge.

In 1924 Colonel John Denny died and the building lay unoccupied for a year. On 7 December 1924, the Kintyre Technical School at Keil House, Southend, at the southern tip of the Mull of Kintyre, burned to the ground. Helenslee was a better location for a private boarding school, being closer to Glasgow, and 51 boys moved there in 1925. Keil School's prestige rose and it survived until 2000 when financial pressures forced it to close. The building went on the market, although a buyer was hard to find.

Helenslee, Dumbarton, was originally built for local shipbuilder Peter Denny and his wife Helen, and was used as Keil School from 1925 to 2000.

Skipness, 1878

Angus Graham's *Memories of a Highland Estate* provide a sketch of life at Skipness at the end of the nineteenth and in the early twentieth centuries. In 1878 his father, Robert Chellas Graham, had commissioned John Honeyman to build a house to replace the eighteenth-century mansion of the Campbells of Skipness, who had owned the estate from 1511 to 1843. The Macdonalds had owned the land in the fifteenth century, but King James IV had been keen to build up the Campbell domain in Argyll.

The Graham family travelled extensively in Europe, and they owned property in Portugal. Robert had met his wife Emily Eliza Hardcastle on a fashionable artistic tour of Rome in 1875. On its completion in 1881, their Highland home was therefore a mixture of Scots baronial tower house with Italianate decorations. The grey schist stone walls matched the walls of the nearby castle, but there were red sandstone dressings and features. The interiors were the usual Victorian clutter of displays of weapons on walls, a Highland cow's head with enormous horns, Italian paintings, family portraits, high-backed Spanish chairs, and a fireplace lined with Dutch tiles.

Although the family sought a 'fairytale castle', there was logic to the planning. The servants' quarters were arranged around a courtyard on one side, and the guest rooms were in a tower on the other. Emily enjoyed hosting large house parties, and asked for bedrooms to be numerous rather than large. The

Skipness House was badly damaged by fire in 1969 and has lost much of its grandeur.

Skipness House.   C.S.66

A less well-known view of Skipness House from the garden side.

main hall could be entered from the front of the building or the garden, and gave access to all the main public rooms on two levels. The schoolroom and nurseries were at the junction between the main part of the house and the servants' wing.

There were also various 'mod cons'. One of the reasons the old house was replaced was the lack of plumbing, the Dukes of Argyll being content with outside toilets. While most rooms in the new house had coal fires, the drawing room and surrounding passages had hot water central heating. Gas lighting required the production of gas from an oily liquid known as 'gasoline' in an outhouse a safe 70 metres away from the main house. A generator powered the machinery that produced the gas. Later, acetylene gas was made from carbide of calcium, although it was less dense than the previous oil-gas and constantly leaked from joints in the gas pipes. The acetylene gas gave a bright light but deposited fine ash which required regular cleaning from the burners.

It may have been very romantic living in a Highland home, but the remote location led to problems with maintenance of the building. The estate workmen could deal with roofing, masonry and woodwork, but Honeyman had designed a large, round, panoramic window in a turret with curved plate glass. This would have been very expensive to make, and glass-manufacturing technology at the time did not allow fine tolerances to fit the stone surrounds, so the windows regularly leaked in heavy, west coast, wind-driven rain. Other tasks involving drains, water and gas were dealt with by a plumber from Tarbert called John MacSporan, whose services ended after he fell off the church tower in Tarbert and died. The various bells that called the servants were maintained weekly by Crawford the butcher when he called.

As Angus wrote:

> The pattern of life for which the House was designed now seems as odd as the fantasies that inspired its architect, and a survivor's memories of that pattern may possess a certain interest. The household servants made the building function. At the top were the lady's maid and cook, slightly lower than these three 'uppers' – table maid, housemaid and laundry maid – and down at the bottom their three 'under' counterparts, along with the unhappy kitchen maid, who devilled for the cook. There was a nurse when the children were young and a dairymaid who sometimes slept in the dairy. Reinforcements were obtained from the village when guests were present.
>
> The head housemaid was Christina MacEwan, a great and irrepressible character, and she, with her subaltern, performed prodigies with baths, fires and linen. The tower bedrooms, for example, were far away from any bathroom, and consequently had to be supplied with cans of hot water for hip baths, and that not only in the morning but at dressing time too, if necessary, after a day's shooting. There were also fires to be laid, lighted, and cleared out the following morning, and although a man from outside brought coal into

the house, its further distribution, including the ascent to the tower, rested with the housemaids.

Flora MacTavish, in the laundry, was out of the public eye, but her standards may be judged by the fact that she would spend a full hour making up a single dress shirt. The chief heroine, however, was the kitchen maid. She had to be up at six to light the kitchen fire to heat the morning bathwater, as well, no doubt, as to prepare early tea for her seniors, and her work would probably never have been finished at all if my mother had not ruled that young people needed adequate sleep, and that she must be free to go to bed by ten o'clock.

It was, in fact, on this account that we had dinner at half past seven, even in the long light evenings of the northern summer, in order to allow washing-up to be achieved at a reasonable hour.

After the family and guests were roused by a bell at 8.30 a.m., a second bell announced prayers at 9.15 and breakfast of porridge and poached eggs soon after. The days could be spent walking in the hills where in August and early September grouse were shot. At Christmas there was pheasant and woodcock shooting. Local streams afforded trout fishing. As Angus reported: 'The flowers for the house were picked and arranged by daughters, though the table maids had the job of clearing up the pantry afterwards'.

In bad weather the older men congregated in the library, and the younger ones in the billiard room. The women settled in Mrs Graham's morning room. On Sundays at 11.00 a.m., Robert Graham led a service for the family, household servants and gardeners in the hall. According to Angus:

We sang two hymns, for which my mother played a harmonium with treadle bellows, and nobody attempted a sermon . . . . By my time, the traditional Sabbath had lost many of its sharpest teeth; hardly anyone in the village now sat behind drawn blinds on Sunday afternoons, and many people went out for sedate walks or visited their family graves. Nonetheless, local feelings about Sunday observance still had to be reckoned with. Shooting or fishing was, of course, unthinkable. Bicycles were a borderline case. The women of the family sometimes registered embarrassment about knitting and sewing, at least in front of the servants, and we used to put the cards and card table away at bedtime on Saturday nights to save the housemaids from contact with them when they tidied things up the next morning.

Other pastimes included calibrating the clocks in the house by using a sun sextant to measure its zenith at noon, an event that took place at Skipness 21 minutes and 21 seconds later than Greenwich. Before radio was available, much time was spent reading newspapers, two dailies, *The Times* and the *Glasgow Herald*, and two weeklies, the *Campbeltown Courier and Argyllshire Advertiser* and the *Lochfyneside Echo*.

Angus thrived in his early years at Skipness, for, despite having been born asthmatic, he survived military campaigns in the Highland Light Infantry at Gallipoli and Palestine to live to 88 years of age, this despite carrying lead shot close to his spine from being wounded at Gallipoli. Being the second son of the family, he had to earn a living, and a botany course at Oxford, combined with brief service with the Forestry Commission in Argyll allowed him to apply for the post of scientific adviser for a forestry company in Quebec. He did not fully lose touch with civilisation as his London tailor visited him annually, to supply him with suits. During the recession of the 1930s he returned home to take up the post of secretary of the Royal Commission on the Ancient and Historical Monuments of Scotland, having been active in Scottish archaeological and historical matters from a young age.

Honeyman's job book has an entry for Skipness from 1867, a year after the estate had been sold to the trustees of Robert Graham, then only eighteen years of age. His mother, Susan, daughter of Dutchman Captain Adoniah Schuyler, was the chief trustee, so in effect she bought it for her son. The design of the new house seems to have started in 1878 with completion in 1881. It was badly damaged by fire in 1969, and the reconstruction work did not recreate the original design.

Achamore House, 1884

In 1882 Honeyman was invited to rebuild a late eighteenth century house for Captain William Scarlett, the third Lord Abinger, on the most southerly island of the Inner Hebrides, Gigha. Like Skipness this was a country house for a well-to-do family, containing all the comforts for a country gentleman and his guests to enjoy. By 1884 the new house was complete. One of the towers was left open and was said to be the post of a small piper boy who was pushed through a hatch from the staff quarters to summon the household to dinner from the various parts of the grounds.

Achamore House, Gigha.

The Honeyman and Keppie job book indicates that fire hydrants were being installed in 1896. Whether they failed to stop a conflagration that year or were a belated response to it, much of the original Honeyman building was destroyed by fire. Only the billiard room survived unharmed.

The island was purchased by Sir James Horlick (who produced the bedtime drink) in 1944, and he set about recreating the gardens. When he died in 1972, he left them to the National Trust for Scotland. The rest of the island was sold to the Longdale family who occupied Achamore House until 1992 when Derek and June Holt moved there from Stobo Castle. The island was up for sale again in October 2001 when the bid from the 110 islanders was accepted, despite being the lowest at around £4 million. The Isle of Gigha Heritage Trust received help from the lottery-supported Scottish Land Fund and Highlands and Islands Enterprise's community land unit, but had £1 million of its own to find. The sale of Achamore House, this time as a private house rather than the laird's residence, contributed to this.

William Miller and Glasgow Cross

There may have been some doubt as to whether Honeyman or Alexander 'Greek' Thomson carried out the first designs for Knockderry Castle in 1856 (see chapter 2).

For his new house, Roundelwood, William Miller seems to have requested a modern version of Knockderry Castle.

However, the next major extension in 1869 was definitely by Honeyman and for a new owner, Bailie William Miller. In 1883 there is another reference to an extension in Honeyman's job book, although at the same time he was designing Roundelwood in Drummond Terrace, Crieff, for William Miller JP. This was possibly a retirement home for the Glasgow businessman. Honeyman also seems to have designed a house in Woodside Terrace, Glasgow, for him in 1876.

In 1874 he carried out alterations to Miller's shop at the John McIntyre Corner at the north-east corner of Glasgow Cross. William and his brother Gavin were described as retailers and commercial warehouse wholesalers in general goods. The building was one of the first cast-iron framed warehouses in Glasgow, having originally been designed around 1850 by William Spence. Ironically, John Keppie and Henderson's plans for the redevelopment of Glasgow Cross in the 1920s eventually led to its demolition, although initial reluctance by the site owner to be part of the development led to only the north-west corner being rebuilt. The original John McIntyre Corner still remains an empty site today, although planning approval was obtained in April 2004 for a new building. Another shop appears to have been designed by Honeyman for the Miller business in Sauchiehall Street in 1883.

The *Bailie* magazine of 18 June 1873 is not particularly complimentary about William Miller, who by this time had retired as a bailie of the city:

> Decent man, he looks it only, for in reality he is – well it might be sinful, if not libellous, to call the ex-Bailie stupid; but there can be no harm in saying that there are one or two cleverer men in the Council . . . .
> This valuable quality of being dull, pre-eminently respectable, and pliable – and yet clever at one and the same time – is so highly

Glasgow Cross with William Miller's shop on the corner in the foreground.

This caricature of William Miller from the Bailie *matches the satirical savaging of the accompanying text. His shop, on the right, has been turned into a hustings stage.*

appreciated by the gentlemen who manage us all, that ex-Bailie Miller enjoys quite a plurality of offices.

Of the Finance, Law, Property, etc. Committee, he is Convenor; High School Committee, Sub-Convenor; Parliamentary Bills Committee, Member; Gas Supply Committee, Sub-Convenor; Gas Works Committee, Member; Gas Finance Committee, Convenor; Tramways Accounts Committee, Sub-Convenor; Stirling's Library Committee, Member; Police Finance Committee, Convenor; Statute Labour Committee, Member; Health Committee, Member; Police Parliamentary Committee, Sub-Convenor; Purchase of Property, Convenor; Disposal of Assessment Objections Committee, Convenor.

This is a goodly list of offices. Even a man of consummate ability might hesitate to undertake the discharge of duties so multifarious; but ex-Bailie Miller has the courage. Whether he does the work or no, he looks as if he did; and that is what is wanted of him by the gentlemen who place him in office. Ex-Bailie Miller is eminently moral – in fact he is nothing if not moral. To raise the morality of the citizens to an approximation to the high standard of his own, he shut up the back doors of the public houses; he caused panes of glass to be placed in the doors of public house boxes to serve the same purpose for which spy holes are placed in the cell doors of criminals; and, in short, he showed and continues to show, every disposition to whip with scorpions those of the public who cannot afford to be immoral in private.

Honeyman would not be particularly interested in what the gossip columns of the day said about Miller. From 1869 to 1885 he received six commissions totalling £18,230 worth of building works, and would also have had access to this influential man for other business contacts. The caricature of Miller in the *Bailie* magazine has him standing at Glasgow Cross with the Tolbooth Building on his left and instead of the John McIntyre Building on the right is a politician's hustings stage. He has in his hands papers relating to his various offices, including one where the 's' is written backwards as if by a child.

John Keppie and Henderson returned to Roundelwood in 1931/32 to carry out a refurbishment of the house for the occupation of David MacBrayne. One of the modern features installed was parquet flooring.

Craigie Hall, 1872, 1892 and 1898

Today it is strange to talk about Craigie Hall, Bellahouston, as a country house, but when John Honeyman designed it for merchant Joseph McLean the suburbs of Glasgow had not yet reached it. It is of particular interest in the history of the Keppie practice as it was originally a creation of Honeyman, completed in 1872, was altered and extended by John Keppie, assisted by Charles Rennie Mackintosh, in 1892, and the music room and organ case were designed by Mackintosh in 1898. The different styles of the three architects are apparent in the different parts of the house.

In 1869, Honeyman had carried out alterations to Haughead House in Govan Road for Joseph McLean. However, it is believed that he had to move to make way for railway works. The original Honeyman house from 1872 is very classical, with the rich detailing and stained glass of the period.

Detail from the seat in the library of Craigie Hall. The female face might be that of Jessie Keppie, and hers the heart that the crack has broken through.

Craigie Hall, Bellahouston, was originally designed by Honeyman, but contains later internal alterations by John Keppie and Charles Rennie Mackintosh.

When builder Thomas Mason, of Morrison and Mason, purchased Craigie Hall in the early 1890s, he called the practice back to design stables, a conservatory, a library and a bedroom wing. Mason's company built the City Chambers between 1883 and 1890, and certain interior details of Craigie Hall suggest that John Keppie was being influenced by what his client had seen in this building.

The library of 1892 has sinuous, carved woodwork, and on the side of a chair is the face of a woman with a heart below. If Mackintosh had someone in mind when he was sketching this, it must have been his girlfriend of the time, Jessie Keppie. What is thought to have been the original sketch for this was found among Jessie's personal effects in a collection at the School of Art. The side of the chair now has a crack in it, down through Jessie's face and heart, symbolic of the break-up between her and Mackintosh a few years later, when he transferred his affections to Margaret Macdonald.

Thomas Mason sold the house to the Green family from Preston. They were travelling show people, and in one of their tents they had a bioscope. When cinemas became popular in the 1920s they cashed in, opening Green's Playhouse in the centre of Glasgow, catering for audiences of up to 3,000. It became a concert venue for pop groups in the 1970s and was renamed the Apollo. The building was demolished in the 1980s, and in its place today is a modern multi-level, multi-screen cinema.

Craigie Hall was almost demolished in 1980. A Manchester-based building company had purchased the ground and applied to have the building knocked down in order to develop the whole five-acre estate for new housing. John Gerrard of the Civic Trust visited the building to assess its worth, but since it only had category 'C' status at the time it had little statutory protection. The exterior of the building was relatively plain, but he was amazed by what he saw inside – not just the elaborate Honeyman detailing, but features that showed possible Mackintosh influences. Roger Billcliffe, then Keeper of Fine Art at Kelvingrove Art Gallery and Museum, and his colleague Brian Blench, confirmed as much.

The race began to upgrade the house to a category 'A' listing that would ensure its protection. The builder on site sent a telex to his Manchester head office to tell

The organ casing in Craigie Hall, designed by Charles Rennie Mackintosh.

them of the manoeuvrings of the authorities. They replied, instructing him to demolish the building over the weekend. Fortunately, he left early on the Friday for a weekend break before he received the message, and by Monday the 'A' listing had been confirmed.

In August 1980, local engineer and Mackintosh enthusiast Graham Roxburgh purchased the house and set about restoring it. For many years it was used as office suites, with Graham based there, until in 2004 it was sold to a hotel company as its head office. Graham went on to carry out an even more ambitious project, having Mackintosh's House for an Art Lover built in Bellahouston Park, just across the road from Craigie Hall.

Lynhurst, 1878/79

If most of Honeyman's commissions were for Glasgow or Greenock businessmen, Lynhurst is an exception. In 1878 he enlarged and altered the home of Galashiels mill-owner Walter Cochrane. Stables and offices were added in 1879. The building had originally been called Langhaugh, and been built in the 1850s for an Admiral William Clark. It is not known how Honeyman obtained this commission, since there are no other buildings in the area designed by him. A possible connection was through the volunteers, one

In the 1870s many wealthy Galashiels mill owners could afford to build mansions like Lynhurst in Abbotsford Road.

Lynhurst was taken over by the Scottish Co-operative Society as a convalescent home, renamed Abbotsview and extended.

of the Cochrane family, Adam, being in charge of the 1st Selkirk Rifle Volunteers from 1866, otherwise known as the Gala Forest Rifles. Honeyman helped found the Dumbartonshire Volunteers.

Walter was a third generation miller, with grandfather Adam Cochrane founding water-powered Mid Mill in 1792. This then passed to his sons John and Walter, with the third brother Archibald selling his share to them in 1833. This Walter was the father of the Lynhurst Walter, his mother being Janet Lees, daughter of the owner of Galabank Mill.

Until 1845 the family of eleven had lived in the middle of Galashiels in what is now Paton Street:

Walter had built the house but had no money to finish it properly by the time the family moved in, and the interiors had no doors. The Mother stood on bath night at the door to keep the older children away while the young ones were in the bath. Life was spartan with no carpets, but tweed cloth was laid out on the floors. Horsehair covered the sofa and chairs. They ate porridge night and morning and Scotch kale with barley. Water was pumped from a cellar well and carried upstairs. Waste water was run into the garden by a hose through an open window. These houses were very well built but in those days there was no plumbing system and the outside sanitation was very primitive.

Local mill-owners, including Walter Cochrane, were proud of Scotland's great nineteenth century author, Sir Walter Scott, and grateful to him for raising the profile of the area, his romantic novels helping to make tweed cloth popular. At a meeting of the Manufacturers' Corporation in 1820 (motto: 'We Dye to Live, and Live to Die'), one of the clothiers sang his own composition, albeit in a style more reminiscent of McGonagall than Scott:

> The Thames, long of Britain the glory and pride,
> Must now yield to Scotland and lovely Tweedside;
> For the harp lies unstrung in fair Twickenham's bowers,
> And the roses of Windsor have shed their last flowers.
>
> Ah! love you to charm and enlighten our isle,
> To share both the people and sovereign's smile;
> We rejoice in the favour that altered your lot
> And raised up plain Walter to Sir Walter Scott.
>
> While Tweed shall roll on in her sylvan career,
> Thy name shall be honoured, and hallowed thy bier;
> While the peasant shall point to thy turrets so fair,
> And say, the great minstrel, Sir Walter, dwelt there.

The Cochrane family moved out of town to a grander house in Abbotsford Road in 1845. Walter junior went into partnership with his brothers Archibald and Adam to build the steam-powered Netherdale Mill in 1857 for £10,400, with the first self-acting mules in the town. By 1878 he could afford to buy Lynhurst, another house in Abbotsford Road, and commission Honeyman to spend £4,769 on it. The annual turnover of woollen goods in Galashiels in the 1870s was around £500,000 with the wage bill amounting to £100,000. From the proceeds of spinning local and Australian wool, the mill-owners had plenty of money to build a string of mansions along Abbotsford Road.

The entrance hall at Lynhurst displays the typical clutter of a large Victorian house.

The Cochrane family also managed to survive as shareholders of the City of Glasgow Bank, being among the few who fully satisfied the claims of the liquidators.

Walter died in Gaza, Palestine, fighting with the British Army in the First World War. His brother Archibald died in Ceylon in 1915 from heat stroke. Before he died he wrote to his sister, 'We all have to do our bit for the war effort, so we only have one horse now for the carriage instead of two'.

The Cochranes must have moved out of Lynhurst by 1906, as by then it had been much enlarged and renamed Abbotsview, and was in use as a Co-operative Convalescent Home. In April 1984 it was demolished to make way for a housing estate.

Uncovering something new or of particular relevance is one of the joys of historical research. The census of 1881 finds Walter Cochrane with his wife Agnes, children Walter (five), William Elliot (three), Adam (eleven), mother-in-law Elizabeth Armstrong, cook Jane Pirie, housemaid Helen Cruise and nurse Agnes Smyth. Also staying on that night is a visitor called John Honeyman, an architect and a widower.

Cowden Castle, 1875 and 1894; Murdostoun Castle, 1881

The link between these two buildings is sisters Alice and Ella Christie, daughters of John Christie, a Glasgow steel baron. He commissioned the Honeyman practice to carry out alterations to Cowden Castle, near Dollar, in 1875 and 1894. The design of the latter alterations took place in late 1892 and 1893 and included an octagonal tower topped by a weather vane with art nouveau overtones. It is possible that Mackintosh had a hand in this, and it precedes his design for the *Glasgow Herald* water tower.

Today only the base of the octagonal tower of Cowden Castle survives (left, above the greenhouse). This may have been a forerunner by Mackintosh of the Glasgow Herald tower.

Ella Christie (rear left), Robert King Stewart (rear right), John Christie and Alice King Stewart – as fine a group of clients as any architect could wish for.

The garden at Cowden also contained a steel and wrought iron suspension bridge over the River Devon with a Glasgow Style motif.

Mrs Christie died in 1894 and John in 1902, leaving the estate to Ella, who created a famous Japanese garden in 1907. Cowden Castle gradually fell into disrepair and was demolished in 1952.

Alice married Robert King Stewart whose father Robert had purchased Murdostoun Castle at Bonkle, Newmains, near Wishaw, in 1856 when he retired. Honeyman designed an extension in 1881. Robert senior had been Lord Provost of Glasgow, and his main achievement was the introduction of a water supply from Loch Katrine. This was not an easy task, given the £1,200,000 estimated cost. Ella Christie tells the story:

One bailie saw nothing but bankruptcy staring in the face of the Corporation if they undertook the task of supplying the city with water; but another more sensibly supported the scheme remarking, 'Look at Glasgow at the present moment – at the mercy, humanly speaking, of every epidemic with which the country is visited'. . . . After a lengthy debate, the Council voted 30 for and fourteen against the motion. Objections were then raised on the plea that Loch Katrine water was deficient in lime and this deficiency would give the children rickets. The discussions dragged on for years, until 1854, but at long last the cause of common sense triumphed and Glasgow was provided with a plentiful and clean supply of water. Queen Victoria performed the ceremony of turning on the supply in 1856.

Robert King Stewart had the same progressive ideas and public spirit as his father. 25 years after the Water Scheme had been carried through, another 'illuminating' idea suggested to him in 1881: Why not install at Murdostoun the new electric light which was being used elsewhere?

Alice and her husband had seen it in use for the first time in Paris. Her diary for March 1880 notes: 'Went for a walk along the Avenue de l'Opera which looks very well lighted by the new Electric Light'. This was the Edison system, well adapted for outside purposes or public buildings, but much too bright for private houses. The new system was regarded with suspicion. Lord Salisbury, it is true, started to wire Hatfield about this period, but a fatal accident to a workman brought the scheme to a standstill for a time: it was too dangerous.

The architect, Mr John Honeyman, was greatly interested in the wonderful new light, and with the courage one much admires he launched with full confidence into the project. Messrs Anderson and Munro of Glasgow made and laid the wires. These were enclosed in rubber tubes, and a testimony to their excellent quality is their duration, as they have only recently been renewed (1936). Every bracket had to be specially designed, as much less clumsy fittings than gas ones were suitable. Mr Honeyman drew the designs for the billiard table lighting, and also a most artistic central pendant light for the central hall.

In the days of faint gaslight, men played billiards, which has two white balls and one red, scoring taking place by a variety of pots, in-offs and cannons. Only when electric power was available could snooker become popular, the brighter light making the different colours easily distinguishable.

Then the question of generating power arose. For this a small steam engine was used, looked after by a young lad, and fed by a coal stove. If late hours were kept, an electric bell was rung to rouse the sleeper. Every bulb cost seven-and-sixpence, and at first these were broken constantly, as the boy ran the engine too hard. The light was turned on for the first time in September 1882. We had a party of friends staying with us at the time, and we all, with the head electrician from Glasgow, waited at the engine house to see the current turned on; then came a wild rush to the house and every room was seen ablaze with light! Far too much ablaze, as at least a dozen bulbs fused that first night!

We never regretted this pioneer work. During the first year or two many curious visitors arrived to see the successful installation, and by 1886 a certain number of private mansions had adopted the new invention. In time, accumulators were invented, and water power, with a dam on the Calder, replaced the sleepy boy and his engine.

Lord Kelvin came to see the installation, the practical use of the idea which his brilliant scientific brain had conceived. He took the keenest interest in the new experiment and constantly reiterated that electricity would be the light of the future. He also, one day, remarked during his visit that he was happy to think that he had been the first individual to generate light on the planet.

A correspondence went on in *The Times* last year about the earliest installation, but I think this account settles the matter definitely. Possibly small houses may have had wires run by an inventive owner, but not a fully finished installation such as I have described.

Ella would not have made these claims lightly, being a fellow of the Royal Geographical Society of Scotland and a fellow of the Royal Scottish Academy. Alice King Stewart received the OBE. Murdostoun Castle is now a nursing home and brain injury rehabilitation unit.

The lower section on the left formed the 1881 extension to Murdostoun Castle.

Paisley Library and Museum.

CHAPTER 7

Paisley and the Coats family

Paisley Library and Museum, 1870, 1882, 1904 and 1934; Coats Observatory, 1883

John Honeyman received commissions from the Coats family of Paisley, who were not only entrepreneurs in the thread industry but also benefactors both in their local area and in other parts of Scotland.

James and Peter Coats formed the company J. and P. Coats when their father James retired in 1830. They were joined soon after by their brother Thomas. James died in 1845 at the age of 42, and it was Peter and Thomas who were the clients of Honeyman, the former for the Free Library and Museum, and the latter for the Coats Observatory. James junior, their nephew, was also a philanthropist who contributed to developments in both buildings as well as a wide range of charitable ventures. They

Peter Coats, entrepreneur, philanthropist and client for Paisley Library and Museum.

were typical of many other successful industrialists who spent a lot of their wealth on their community. As Andrew Carnegie said: 'The man who thus dies rich, dies disgraced'.

In the middle of the nineteenth century, books were almost exclusively the preserve of the well-off, although there was a Paisley library from 1802, funded by wealthy citizens. At Carlile's Mill in New Sneddon a library was opened by one of the daughters of the Carlile family in the 1830s. Some churches had libraries and there were Encyclopaedia Clubs. The Paisley Philosophical Institution, founded in 1808, purchased books but lacked suitable premises to store them where they would not perish in winter. By 1864 they had raised £3,000 towards the construction of a museum and library.

The Free Libraries Acts of 1864 and 1866 allowed councils to raise rates to run libraries for the free use of the community. Local mill-owner Peter Coats offered to buy a site for the new building and to pay for its construction. The Philosophical Institution then used its funds to purchase 5,000 books to add to the 7,743 volumes from the existing Paisley library and another 1,481 from other sources.

At a meeting on 22 January 1867 the Philosophical Institution set out its requirements:

The interior of Paisley Library.

First, a large hall, in which all may meet to read books, and to enjoy the best literature of the day; in the second place, side rooms filled with standard works, which may be consulted, and from which extracts may be made; and thirdly a lending department so that families in the town may obtain books of the highest character to study at home. The Museum, as not by any means a mere jumble of curiosities to amuse, but a series of assorted objects to instruct – a many-leaved volume delineative of the most beneficial forms in nature, and expressive at the same time, of scientific thought and conclusions.

Honeyman was appointed in June 1868. The building was to be designed in Grecian Ionic style, as befitting a civic house of learning. The site cost £3,000 and the building in excess of £15,000. Peter Coats, who received a knighthood for his benevolence, must have been an ideal client. The original budget was £3,000, but money seemed to be no object in the task of producing a library that Paisley could be proud of. The whole building had hot water central heating with the correct amount of ventilation to ensure that the books were kept in the best condition. A librarian's house was built alongside the museum. 'The most critical eye is unable to detect a single want in all the arrangements of the building', a report of the time said.

On 23 September 1870 the buildings were formally handed over by Sir Peter Coats to the magistrates and town council. It was believed to be the first building of its kind in Scotland, a source of great civic pride. 'The designer has not been lavish of ornament, but good effect is gained without elaboration, and the whole character of the building is that of chasteness and repose'.

By 1880 the library had proved such a success that it required an extension. Honeyman was called back and again Sir Peter provided the funds. Accommodation was provided to make the library function better, to provide an extra room for the reference department and to add a sculpture room and picture gallery. These were completed in 1882. In 1902 the Coats family was again sponsoring an extension and appointed John Honeyman, Keppie and Mackintosh. Mackintosh himself appears to have designed the very respectful classical extension, and his drawings remain in the building. The library also included space for a display of Paisley shawls. The extended building opened on 1 December 1904, and further galleries were added in 1915.

At their AGM on 5 October 1880, the Paisley Philosophical Institution proposed that the society 'should purchase a telescope, with a view to having it placed on some part of the new building in connection with the Free Library and Museum, subject to the approval of Sir Peter Coats and the Town Council'. Thomas Coats stepped forward to fund its purchase. Peter Coats had already acquired ground around the museum for possible extensions, and the site extended from High Street back to Oakshaw

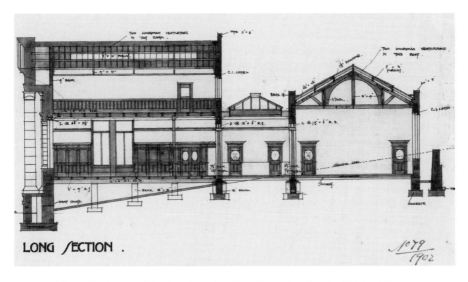

LONG /ECTION .

The lettering on this drawing showing the extension to Paisley Library suggests that it was designed by Mackintosh.

Coats Observatory.

Street. This was where the observatory was built. Honeyman was advised on technical matters by Professor Grant of the University of Glasgow, having already effected alterations to the Royal Observatory at the University of Glasgow in 1862. The foundation stone was laid on 8 March 1882, the ceremony including the building into the base of the walls a time capsule containing journals, coins and portraits of Thomas Coats and his wife.

Once again Honeyman was working for a philanthropist who developed the commission as he thought proper, unconstrained by money. There was advantage in having an astronomical clock alongside the telescope, and a photographic room. It would also be useful to accommodate various meteorological instruments. The official opening on 1 October 1883 was a low-key affair due to Thomas Coats being on his deathbed. He passed away two weeks later, having only been in the building once since the telescope had been installed. It was believed that the internal ramps were designed to accommodate his wheelchair.

James junior took over as benefactor, purchasing new equipment and carrying out various improvements including an extension in 1898. He also had electricity installed and a connection between the mean time clock at the observatory and the town hall clock to ensure that the latter was always accurate. The clock at the observatory was calibrated by observation of the positions of various stars, the practice used by navigators before reliable ships' clocks were invented. James Coats also maintained his family's support of the library with a section devoted to books for the blind.

James Coats junior was perhaps the most generous philanthropist of all his family, although he was modest and became a recluse after he retired in 1903. He was brought up to believe that philanthropy was a duty and an obligation, donating money to Paisley Infirmary and other local institutions, sending the elderly on seaside holidays, and providing shoes for the children of Paisley's poor each winter. When he died in 1912 around 20,000 Paisley people lined the route of his funeral, and the town's shops and public houses were closed in respect for the man.

His generosity was also felt beyond Paisley. In 1901, while sailing his yacht *Gleniffer* (with the help of a crew of almost 40), he landed on Ailsa Craig. Dismayed by the fact that the two lighthouse keepers had no reading material, he gave them the books aboard *Gleniffer*, and assuming that other lighthouse keepers were in a similar situation, he sent packages to all lighthouses in Scotland. Each contained books, two pounds of tobacco and two pipes.

His yachting trips took him all round Scotland as far as Harris where he bought tweed from the local weavers. His next philanthropic venture was to set up rural libraries in the Highlands and islands. Between 1903 and 1912, approximately 4,000 Coats libraries were established, chiefly in western and northern Scotland, each with around 300 books. Coats had some books translated into Gaelic for native speakers. While the books were intended for adults, the libraries were usually housed in schools with the local schoolmaster acting as the librarian. This was propitious, since with the school leaving age rising in 1901 from twelve to fourteen, more adult reading materials were required. All schools were candidates for a donation whether they were state-run, Roman Catholic or Episcopalian.

To encourage rural people to read, James employed two lecturers over a four year period to travel to Coats libraries and give talks on literary subjects. One of these, D.T. Holmes, a former head of English at Paisley Grammar School, gained such celebrity status from these tours that he was invited to be the Liberal candidate for Govan, a seat he held as MP from 1911 to 1918. His grandson, Tony Benn, was also keen on politics.

Although another extension was added to the museum in 1934, the next major commission for the Coats family was city-centre headquarters offices at 159–175 St Vincent Street, Glasgow, in the 1980s, completed by Scott Brownrigg and Turner just before they merged with Keppie Henderson. The company was called Coats Patons by this time, and used the new building to effect corporate cultural changes that were long overdue. The prevailing hierarchical system had four different grades of lavatories and dining facilities. All of this vanished the day they moved into the new premises.

David Collin, a director of the practice at this time, remembers in the first few days watching Sir William Coats, in the new self-service canteen, carrying his tray to the only available seat, which was next to a somewhat sad looking commissionaire. However, they were soon locked in amiable conversation with much waving of a well-laden knife by the commissionaire. Their ability to enjoy further lunchtime liaisons was curtailed by the recession of the early 1990s, which enforced changes and cuts in the organisation. Eventually Coats Viyella, as it became after further restructuring, succumbed and another city centre office block lay empty.

Other Paisley buildings

In 1870, while designing the museum and art gallery in Paisley, Honeyman was appointed to design a building to replace the former Tolbooth on a prominent site on High Street at the corner of Moss Street for the City of Glasgow Bank. The Tolbooth tower had been leaning dramatically and was demolished before it threatened public safety and fell down. The new bank opened on 22 October 1872.

This was the only project Honeyman carried out for the bank, and, given later events, it was just as well. Today one thinks of the main banks as completely sound and immune from failure, but they are subject to normal market trading, and in the nineteenth century there was less public accountability for private companies. In 1857 business failures by companies the Western Bank had lent large sums to caused it to collapse, and the City of Glasgow Bank was affected by this. By the mid-1870s it had 133 branches in Scotland, but it invested unwisely on projects like the Racine and Mississippi Railroad and the New Zealand and Australia Land Company, the latter failing in 1866. It could not afford to call in debts from its major borrowers lest it made them bankrupt, and thus it was locked in a vicious circle. The managers started to falsify the balance sheets (audits were unheard of when the City of Glasgow Bank was founded), but the problems mounted until, as share values fell, the bank bought up its own shares in an attempt to stabilise them. On 1 October 1878 the bank stopped trading. With unlimited liability in an unincorporated bank, the shareholders were responsible for the debts, and of 1,819 of them, only 254 remained solvent. Many of these shareholders were Honeyman's friends and clients. They were not consoled by the fact that the manager, Robert Stronach, was sent to prison for only eighteen months for falsifying accounts.

Before all this happened, Honeyman carried out two commercial projects in Paisley town centre in 1876, at 9 Moss Street and for McInnes and MacFarlane in Gilmour Street. Such commercial projects were lucrative, the latter costing £5,034.

Honeyman's High Street/Moss Street corner building in Paisley (background).

The last meeting of the board of the City of Glasgow Bank.

Glasgow Magdalene Institution.

INCORPORATED BY ROYAL CHARTER.

Sir John Neilson Cuthbertson, *President.*
J. D. Bryce, Esq.; Sir John Burns, Bart.; Jas. A. Campbell, Esq., M.P.;
Rev. Dr. Douglas; James S. Napier, Esq., *Vice-Presidents.*
Alexander Sloan, Esq., C.A., *Hon. Treasurer.*
R. W. Sinclair, *Secretary,* 15 Stirling Road.
And a General Board of 42 Directors.

The cover of a Magdalene Institution report.

CHAPTER 8

The Victorian social safety net

Poorhouses

In 1859 Honeyman designed poorhouses in Govan and Campbeltown. He also carried out alterations to the asylum at the Lochgilphead Poorhouse in 1886. It is not a building type the practice has obtained many enquiries for since.

With the gravitation of people to the cities in the nineteenth century, the problems of dealing with the migrating poor mushroomed. Scottish legislation on the issue dated from 1579, and the Poor Law Act of 1649 confirmed poor relief as the responsibility of the local parish, with the obligation on the landed classes to help in times of need.

In Scotland the parish of one's birth was responsible for giving relief unless one could prove at least three years' residence elsewhere. The church raised money mainly from voluntary donations, although sometimes fines from civil courts could be directed towards poor relief. For 200 years, while the country consisted of relatively stable rural parishes, this system worked. However, a Royal Commission was set up in 1843 to respond to changing circumstances at a time when a recession in the industrial areas – which lasted from 1841 to 1844 – was adding to the problem.

One could imagine the room for abusing the system. Immigrants might falsify residency length to obtain poor relief, or claim that they had been born in the parish. A common ploy was to claim to have been born at sea and have no other parish to apply to.

The 1845 Act, which resulted from the Royal Commission, set up boards of supervision in each parish. Glasgow's board consisted of 33 local businessmen, most of whom were elected, although some were chosen by magistrates or the church. An inspector of the poor was appointed and parishes with over 5,000 people were expected to build a poorhouse. The inspector or the board would adjudicate cases.

The first Govan Poorhouse, and the one on which Honeyman worked, was in old cavalry barracks on Eglinton Street. This was at the eastern edge of the combined Govan and Gorbals Parish, which at the time also crossed the River Clyde to include Partick and Hyndland. Maps and plans of the buildings before and after they became a poorhouse suggest that Honeyman's work involved converting the two stable blocks into male and female dormitories, as well as adding a chapel for 400 people and two small hospital wards.

The records of Govan Poorhouse only go back to 1876, as opposed to in Glasgow where registers of poor are in existence from 1851 onwards. Fortunate family history researchers will find details of where their antecedents came from and reports about

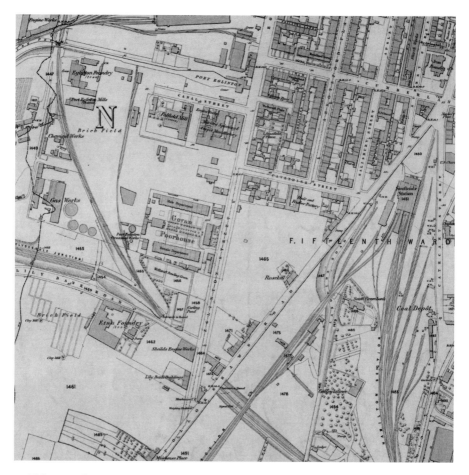

This map shows Govan Poorhouse at its original location to the west of Eglinton Street before it had to move (in 1872) to make way for the Cathcart Circle railway line. Falfield Cotton Mills, altered by Honeyman in 1856, are just to the north, served by the canal at Port Eglinton.

how they came to be in their predicament – or at least their versions of them to the inspector.

The site on the west side of Eglinton Street was acquired to construct the railway line which serves the Glasgow south suburban network, and the poorhouse moved to a new site at Merryflats in 1872. The buildings, which are currently part of the Southern General Hospital, consisted of a poorhouse with associated 240-bed hospital and 180-place lunatic asylum. Honeyman was not involved in their design, but Keppie Design's options study of the site in 2001/02, as part of the Greater Glasgow Health Strategy Review, heralds the likely end of their use as acute hospital buildings.

The association of a hospital and lunatic asylum with the poorhouse reflected the nature of the latter's intake. Able-bodied people who were capable of working were not admitted. Conditions within the poorhouse were intentionally spartan and the social stigma of entry such as to ensure that only those in desperation entered.

The largest group of entrants, around two thirds, were the sick, either from disease, accident at work or malnutrition. The next largest groups were married women with children and women with illegitimate children. The former had to persuade the authorities that their husbands had deserted them, and were usually required to provide details of their men so that the parish inspector could pursue them. This could involve legal action being taken to the countries of the Empire or to America.

Honeyman designed the poorhouse in Campbeltown. He was recommended to Campbeltown Parish by the inspector of the poor in Govan, although one of the seven sites considered for the new buildings was part-owned by 'John Honeyman of Glasgow'. In the minutes of one meeting of the poorhouse committee the architect is referred to as John Honeyman junior, suggesting that Honeyman's father was known locally.

The minutes of the Campbeltown Parochial Board and its poorhouse committee reveal features of local political decision-making and its relationships with central government, in this case the Board of Supervision in Edinburgh, which both Honeyman and later generations of architects in the practice would see repeated again and again. Among these features are the following:

The wall around Campbeltown Poorhouse kept scroungers and the undeserving out, and those with infectious diseases inside.

Politicians take a long time to make up their minds and agree. The first enquiry to determine whether to build a poorhouse took place in 1841, and a committee was appointed in 1846. It was reinstated in 1851; a motion was carried on 18 May 1852; in June 1855 the project was off; and in August 1855 it was back on again.

Central government does not trust local organisations to make prudent decisions, sometimes with good cause. The Campbeltown Parochial Board had agreed to pay £650 to the United Presbyterian Church for a site for the poorhouse; the Board of Supervision made them think again and they got another one, albeit subject to flooding, for £24.

Politicians are over-optimistic about the cost of a project when they are trying to get it launched. On the basis of another poorhouse whose cost equated to £20 per inmate, a budget of £1,200 to £1,500 was set. After architect Robert Matheson of Her Majesty's Board of Works in Edinburgh prepared plans, the first estimate was £4,089. 42s. (£58 per inmate).

Robert Matheson resigned in January 1859 and was paid off for £21. 11s. – Honeyman's total fee was £119. 7s. John Honeyman had drawn up plans for a poorhouse in Govan for 100 inmates at £25 per bed, although a smaller building in a rural area, where labour and building materials were less easy to source, should cost proportionately more. Honeyman's brief at Campbeltown in February 1859 allowed for 42 inmates, with less ancillary accommodation than Matheson had been asked to include.

> *To save money, a reduced specification is requested.* The boundary wall was reduced in height, and plaster was coated directly onto the inside of the stone wall instead of applying it on timber laths (battens) to help prevent moisture from the outside reaching it; both of these were rejected by Sir John McNeil of the Board of Supervision in September 1860.
>
> *It is assumed that the cheapest tender price received will be the final cost.* The tender price in 1859 was £1,564. 15s. (£37 per inmate) and the final cost after it opened on 25 November 1861 was £3,015. 9s. 9d.
>
> *To save money, site supervision is reduced.* It was only found that the builder had reduced the amount of field drainage around the building when it flooded.
>
> *The client's brief changes during construction when it is difficult to hold the contractor to competitive rates.* A typhus outbreak in February 1859 showed the need for a small hospital attached to the poorhouse, but the extension was not instructed until July 1860.
>
> *The public sector organisation inherits a long-term debt.* At the time the poorhouse and hospital were completed in October 1871, three outstanding loans totalling £2,882. 3s. 11d. were consolidated, to be paid back over nineteen years at 5 per cent interest; the original intention was for £1,500 maximum to be paid off over ten years.

The main difference between then and now is that the six members of the parochial board of 1871 had to provide personal security for the loans. One cannot imagine too many local authority councillors or hospital trust board members who would be willing or able to do the same today.

The system of poorhouses was affected by the 1908 Old Age Pensions Act, the 1911 Unemployed Act and by the change in local government in 1930 when parish councils became town or county councils. Nevertheless, the 1845 Poor Law Act was not repealed until 1948 when the whole system was taken out of the hands of local government, and the modern Welfare State was born.

The Glasgow Magdalene Institution

Many of John Honeyman's clients subscribed to this institution which looked after 'fallen women'. His elder brother Michael was a director, as were such notable figures as John Blackie junior (from the publishing family), George Burns (a founder of the Cunard Line), James Campbell MP (cousin of Sir Henry Campbell-Bannerman, future Liberal prime minister) and Richard Kidson (benefactor of Park Free Church in Helensburgh). Its constitution began:

> *First* – That a Society be now formed, under the name of THE GLASGOW MAGDALENE INSTITUTION, for the repression of Vice, and the Reformation of Penitent Females.
>
> *Second* – That it shall be the object of the Society to seek, by all competent

means, the suppression of the resorts of profligacy, and the abatement of the various agencies which contribute to the prevalence of prostitution in the City, or among the community: and, at the same time, to provide temporary Homes for Females who have strayed from the paths of virtue, and who are willing to return to them, and similar refuge or other protection to females who may be in imminent danger of being led astray.

The Magdalene Institution at Lochburn, Maryhill, with the Honeyman building on the right.

In 1863, the City of Glasgow United Working Men's Abstinence Society reported that within 'little more than 800 lineal yards of frontage, there are resident 1,034 families; while there are no less than 43 public houses and 42 brothels in that small compass'.

That year, the Magdalene Institution wrote to the Lord Provost of Glasgow, John Blackie junior, urging him to abolish the Glasgow Fair:

At the Fair time it is plain that the number of prostitutes is frightfully large, probably augmented by the flocking of loose women from other places, and by the appearance on the streets of some who ply their horrible traffic only at certain times. Houses of accommodation are greatly multiplied; and yet they are unable to accomplish all that heated passions demand of them.

The members of the Magdalene Institution were not complete killjoys, and urged another holiday with more 'pure' amusements, also noting that 'the Fair falls at a proverbially wet season'. It seems that some things never change.

A survey carried out in 1849 estimated that there were 211 brothels in Glasgow with around 500 prostitutes, and another 500 walking the streets. An example was given of a brothel owner who bought a property for £590 and made £416 a year from prostitution. Another leased a building for £46 per annum and made £200 each year from the trade.

The temptations of the Glasgow Fair and the demon drink were not the cause of the problem. The main reason for girls becoming involved in prostitution was the lack of any welfare facilities for the large number of people flocking to Glasgow for work. Half of the girls coming to the Magdalene Institution for help were orphans, and two thirds 'had not had the benefit of a mother's care'. More than a quarter of those taken in were under sixteen years of age.

In addition to the personal effects on the girls and women involved, there were social consequences with sexually transmitted diseases leading to increased infant mortality rates and adult insanity. Illegitimacy rates were estimated to be 6.8 per cent of all births in Glasgow and 7.6 per cent in Edinburgh, although one might speculate as to how accurate these figures were. As if to show how uncivilised the nasty French were, the corresponding rate for Paris of 32.9 per cent was quoted in a Magdalene Institution annual report.

93

Legislation attempted to deal with the problems of alcohol abuse and prostitution. The Police Act of 1846 allowed police to enter 'refreshment houses', or public houses as they were increasingly known, to deal with disorderly conduct or if they suspected that prostitutes were operating there. Harbouring prostitutes or admitting to pubs boys and girls under fourteen years of age could lead to a penalty of £10 or 60 days imprisonment. Given the profits that could be made from prostitution, the latter sentence was more effective.

The Police Act of 1862 actually made prostitution illegal, with streetwalking an offence, no proof of annoyance to passers-by or local inhabitants being necessary for conviction. The police could also inspect lodging houses, their powers of entry to such premises being possible merely to inspect sanitary conditions, for which the legislation set minimum standards.

The Magdalene Institution commented on the new Police Act in its annual report, feeling that it treated women as the culprits rather than the victims:

> Vice ought to be reprobated in man as firmly as in woman . . . the inexperience of victims is taken advantage of to a frightful extent by those who, to gratify their own evil passions, remorselessly consign poor female lives to perdition.

In law, evidence has always been easier to attach to the woman. Early poor law, which saw illegitimacy as a root cause of poverty, sought to place responsibility for the upkeep of the child on the man rather than the woman. The progressive legislation was soon repealed due to numerous citings of wealthy men in paternity cases. Too bad that DNA testing was not available then.

The Criminal Law Amendment Act of 1885 raised the age of protection of girls from thirteen years to sixteen. The Magdalene Institution reckoned that this should rise to eighteen, and again called for the law to be amended so that it was equally applicable to men and women 'in the matter of street solicitation and other immoral practices'.

Half of the inmates at the Magdalene refuges came from service, and the newsletter reported:

> a want of proper superintendence and of that watchful endeavour to inculcate and approve those religious and moral sentiments which are the best guardians of virtue in any class of life. The practice of allowing servants to be out on the Sabbath evenings is another occasion of evil. It were better to have them home at the close of the afternoon's service, allowing them a week evening occasionally to visit their friends.

Another moral danger was highlighted:

> Your Directors take the opportunity of advertising to an occasion of evil, perhaps too little thought of, and all the more dangerous on that account, resulting from the practice, now so common, of separating households in summer, and leaving servants in town without superintendence. The consequences are serious. Scenes of profligacy occur in houses of which the respectable occupants may never hear, and at which they would be dismayed – male visitors being admitted in their absence. In this way, it is to be feared, that many young servants are first corrupted; nor do the young men of the

family left in town during the week always escape uninjured. The subject is one eminently deserving attention on the part of heads of families.

This hints that, while the rich businessmen and their families escaped smoggy Glasgow in the summer for the coastal retreats which Honeyman had designed for them, the servants left in town were having a ball, and the sons of the family were obtaining licentious experiences at the expense of the female servants involved, in true 'Upstairs Downstairs' fashion. It is likely that many girl servants who became pregnant or whose sexual liaisons were infringing respectable upper middle class values, were defined as 'females who have strayed from the paths of virtue' and were consigned to the Magdalene Institution.

The institution had a probationary home at 17 Stirling Road, Riddrie, Glasgow, that could accommodate 62 young women. In 1864 a site was found in the pleasant suburb of Maryhill at Lochburn for a larger refuge to supplement the existing one. It was designed by Honeyman and opened in October 1867. It contained workrooms, dormitories and a chapel, and was intended 'to combine a pleasing simplicity of exterior with the best internal arrangements, and at the most moderate cost'. This could hold 130 'inmates', as they were called. Here they could be employed in laundry and needle-work, earning two-thirds of their keep, the rest coming from charitable subscriptions. In addition to the directors of the institution mentioned above, many of Honeyman's other clients subscribed to the charity, the minimum annual amount being £1.

In 1878, £700 was raised to build a new laundry at Stirling Road. Correspondence to subscribers advertised the laundry services to them and their friends. 'No powders, nor any deleterious substances are used in the process of washing, all goods are hand washed and grass bleached'. Washing without detergents must have been soul destroying.

The Maryhill refuge had twelve matrons and female superintendents. In 1878, 96 of the 294 inmates were released to their family or found places in service, usually after two years of 'industrial and educational training'. Literacy was taught, 16 per cent of admittees being unable to read and 32 per cent unable to write. Religious teaching was also at the heart of instruction, with only the truly penitent being accepted for redemption:

> The matrons have no power, nor do they ever attempt to detain girls against their will . . . unless the stage of true sorrow for sin and a settled desire to amend has been reached, no real reformation can be expected. The grace of God alone can change the heart.

There was a Ladies' Committee, no doubt made up of wives of subscribers, who visited women after they had been sent into service to enquire after them.

In 1878, 32 women were sent to hospital. The reasons for this were not given, nor is there any indication of what happened to the babies which inevitably would have been part of the predicament of many girls and women. Perhaps it was a condition of entry to the institution that babies be adopted. There were no nurseries in Honeyman's accommodation brief.

The annual reports do indicate that many young women were helped to find a happier life. Letters published from past residents of the institution, many from Canada and Australia, tell of a fondness for their time there, and an appreciation that the wardens cared about what happened to them after they left.

Monday, April 1, 1878

Dear Mrs Nott,

You will be glad to hear that my father was down seeing me on the Fast-day. When they came and told me, I was quite surprised to see him. He told me the way that he did not write while he was out of town working, and he was wishing he could come and see me. I am glad to say that he is not drinking any more now. He was glad to see me looking so well. He had not much time to wait, as he had to go to see friends. My little brother is in a shop working. The master and them all was quite surprised to hear that he had come to see me. I thought I would just write and let you know that I had seen him. My kind love to all the girls, and also all the ladies. No more at present, but remains yours most truly,

S. A.

November 24th, 1884

My Dear Miss Weir,

You will be thinking me very unkind in never answering your kind letter, but you must excuse me as I have been so busy getting ready for my situation and now I have got settled in it, and I like it very much. There is just one Lady, so I have not much to do, and I get out every Sabbath forenoon to go to church, so I have a great deal to be thankful for. Give my kind love to Miss A, Miss M, Miss B and all the rest of the Superintendents. Hoping all the girls are behaving themselves. I always remember Mr Sinclair's bible class. I hope he may have souls for his labour. I can bless the day I came to Lochburn house. It was there I saw the light, and the burden of my heart rolled away. With my best love, I remain your humble servant,

J. McN.

John Honeyman and Keppie designed new baths and made other alterations at Lochburn, Maryhill, in 1896.

Other houses of refuge

After the Magdalene Institution in Maryhill, Honeyman was asked to design the Glasgow Protestant Institute for Orphan and Destitute Girls at 7 South York Street by its secretary Robert Muncie in 1869. It continued in this use until the 1890s when it became a 'sanitary reception house'. The building survived until the 1970s, changing its address to 339 Moffat Street and then Cumberland Street, both in the Gorbals.

While a small alteration was carried out at 4 Hill Street, Garnethill, for a house of shelter for females in 1871, the next major commission was after the Glasgow Juvenile Delinquency Prevention and Repression Act of 1878, which set up commissioners to provide houses of refuge and reformatory and industrial schools. Michael Honeyman was their treasurer, and in 1881 John Honeyman received the commission for a house of refuge at East Chapelton, Milngavie Road, Bearsden. The Italian-style, two-storey building cost £9,570 including the site, and had accommodation for 60 girls. John Honeyman and Keppie carried out alterations in 1896. The building has long since disappeared. The 1901 census lists a superintendent, a teacher, four other staff and 33 inmates. At an adjacent lodge lived the janitor and his wife, Robert and Janet

Fulton, with their grown-up son.

Another organisation looking after the welfare of young women, this time in Glasgow's East End, was called the Glasgow House of Shelter for Females. Set up in 1878, its president Alexander Ferguson appointed Honeyman to design a new building in 1883, which included an extension of an older building dating from around 1828. Called the Prison Gate Mission, it was intended to rehabilitate ex-offenders. Their report stated that: 'Our Bible Woman meets the female prisoners at the prison gate on their liberation'. Two homes were run by the charity, once more running a large washhouse and laundry to keep the inmates busy for their stay of up to a year. They then tried to find them occupation in the outside world.

Honeyman and Keppie carried out further work in 1895 and 1900, after which it was called the Whitevale Mission Laundry. In the 1920s it was a working boys' home which it remained until the 1950s when it became an annex of Stow College. Today it is still occupied, as offices and a community information centre at 15 Whitevale Street, just off Duke Street, and is possibly the oldest building in the area.

The Canal Boatmen's Friend Society of Scotland, 1892 and 1931

It was not only young women who needed to be protected from vice in the city. The Canal Boatmen's Society was originally called the Scottish Mission of the Seamen and Boatmen's Friend Society, with James S. Napier as one of the honorary vice-presidents. Its mission was:

> To promote the social, moral, and religious welfare of seamen and canal boatmen. The means employed are – preaching the gospel in their Bethels and in the open air; the promotion of day, evening and Sabbath schools; the establishment of mothers' meetings; penny banks and temperance societies; the circulation of books, tracts, copies of the scriptures, and general visitation. This society employs thirteen missionaries, three day school teachers, and occupies eight stations.

Since the Canal Boatmen's Institute was intended to improve the moral welfare of men working on the Forth and Clyde and Monkland Canals, it is not clear if Mackintosh's design of naked women draped around the clock face was a joke or not. Photographs suggest that the clock was not completed in this way.

Its place of worship was the Seamen's Hall, over the collector's office on North Speir's Wharf, Port Dundas. This was insufficient for its needs, and in 1892 John Keppie was responsible for a new building, seating 274, at 162 Port Dundas Road. Charles Rennie Mackintosh assisted him, and the open timber roof of the hall is believed to be to

Bargemen's Institute
Port Dundas
Honeyman and Keppie
Architects Glasgow

The Canal Boatmen's Institute, Port Dundas, was lost to make way for the M8 inner ring road,
which followed part of the route of the redundant Monkland Canal.

his design. He also designed a clock face on the tower at the corner of the building, illustrated in the *British Architect* of July 1895. It is not clear if this was ever installed or if it was a joke by Mackintosh, for it consisted of four nude young women draped around the clock face. One cannot imagine the directors of the institute being happy about Mackintosh corrupting the young canal boatmen. A major extension was made to the building by John Keppie and Henderson between 1929 and 1931, but it was demolished to make way for the northern section of the M8 inner ring road in 1967.

Genoa Scots Church, 1877

In 1877 Honeyman received a commission from the Scottish Presbyterian Mission to build a church in Genoa, Italy. By the second half of the nineteenth century there were about 400 British and 50 American ships visiting the port each year. Three large societies catered for the welfare and souls of sailors abroad, the Roman Catholic 'Apostleship of the Sea', the Church of England 'Missions to Seamen', and the Free Churches of Britain 'British Sailors' Society'. My research has not been able to show how the Scottish Presbyterian Mission fitted into this. In 1969 the Church of Scotland Overseas Council produced a pamphlet explaining why the Established Church in Scotland unusually had its own mission in Genoa, and states that the date of its inauguration was 17 January 1892. The only other mission noted at this time was run by the Mediterranean Missions to Seamen associated with the Anglican Diocese of Gibraltar, a building that was destroyed during the Second World War. Honeyman researchers indicate that his building of 1877 was also destroyed in the war, so the two might have been the same. Alternatively, Honeyman's church may have subsequently been transferred to the Church of Scotland's control.

The pamphlet traces the Church of Scotland's beginnings in Genoa to a young Scotsman called Donald Miller, who in the middle of the nineteenth century went to work in Italy. His uncles ran the shipping line P. Henderson and Co., popularly known as the Paddy Henderson Line (later owned by Honeyman client James Galbraith – see chapter 12). He returned home to train for the ministry in the Free Church of Scotland, and on ordination was appointed chaplain to the Scottish community in Genoa. His work involved visiting ships as they lay in the harbour, but in September 1869 he formed the Genoa Harbour Mission to raise funds which were used to purchase a boat called the *Bethel*. This was soon too small for the number of sailors coming for evening service, and the mission hired rooms ashore until a larger boat called *Caledonia* was purchased and put into use on Christmas Eve 1881. In July 1885 a steam launch called *Iona* was purchased to ferry the sailors to the mission from their boats. *Caledonia* later moved to Naples and the property at Via Bruno Buozzi was acquired and inaugurated on Sunday 17 January 1892. A land base was now essential anyway, since steamships could berth in the dock instead of out in the harbour, and sailors could walk straight off.

The missions were not merely set up to preach to the men. 'We have to provide counter attractions to temptation. No doubt many will feel that the pendulum has swung too far the other way and that there is too little of the Gospel in our Missions and too much entertainment'. Food was the first requirement of a sailor, taste buds dulled by months of ship's cooking. Before the First World War there was a large British community in Genoa and the neighbouring Italian Riviera, and amateur societies organised concerts. Later, English-language films were shown, and young ladies were brought into the mission to teach sailors how to dance.

In 1969, when the Church of Scotland published a pamphlet on its history, the mission was still thriving, its activities becoming more ambitious and including visits to the opera in Verona, sightseeing tours of Pisa and Florence and ski trips into the Alps.

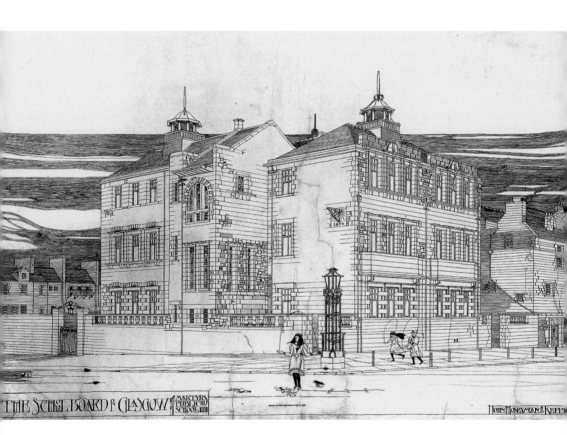

Martyrs' School, Townhead, Glasgow.

CHAPTER 9

Victorian schools

The 1872 Education Act formed the basis of Scottish education as we know it today. From the beginning of the nineteenth century, with the movement of people from the country to the towns, various voluntary bodies and churches had taken responsibility for addressing the necessary changes in education. However, about 90,000 children slipped through the net and received no education at all, and half of those who did were in schools with no government inspection. The 1872 Act sought to rationalise school provision and plug gaps in the system.

Scotland had a proud tradition of universal education. The Scottish Education Act of 1696 was probably the first of its kind in Europe, and spawned the Scottish Enlightenment. The parochial school, while concentrating on providing an elementary education for all, was proud of the fact that schoolmasters would tutor talented boys for university entrance. About half of those attending university came from parish schools, the rest from fee-paying grammar schools for the better-off. The opportunity of a good education was appreciated as the royal commissioners noted in 1865:

> The poor Irish immigrant, the Highland Crofter in Ross and Sutherland, the weaver of Maybole, or the fisherman of Cellardyke, are all educated by an appreciation of the benefits of education, and would gladly see their children better able to read and write than themselves.

As well as parish and grammar schools, there were a number of other establishments relying on philanthropy. Schools like George Heriot's, George Watson's, Donaldson's and Fettes in Edinburgh, and Hutchesons' in Glasgow, were originally intended for the poor and orphans. Ragged and industrial schools were seen as an alternative to begging, and an Act of Parliament in 1855 required courts to send children under eleven to such schools rather than prison.

After the Disruption in 1843, all church denominations tried to provide their own schools. John Honeyman was responsible for a small school for Kirkintilloch Kirk Session; its foundation stone was laid on 27 April 1854 and it was completed on 14 November that year. In 1857 Lennoxtown Oswald School was built, now Oswald House in Crosshill Road. Finnieston Free Church commissioned schools in 1861 where the Scottish Exhibition and Conference Centre is now situated.

Two charitable schools were designed by Honeyman. The foundation stone for Gorbals Youth School at 14 Elgin Street was laid on 11 June 1868, and the building was opened in the spring of 1869. It went bankrupt after the 'headmaster was found running a private school on his own account, with no sign of the two assistants the Gorbals Youth management thought it was paying for'. This became an opportunity for Hutchesons' Hospital (the word 'hospital' in such a charitable foundation merely indicated that it was a residential establishment for the needy). It had been looking for accommodation for girls, having provided schooling for boys since 1650. Since there were no charity commissioners in Scotland, the application for a new school required the Hutchesons' Hospital Act of 1872. The separate girls school was finally opened in the former Gorbals Youth School on 4 August 1876. Honeyman carried out

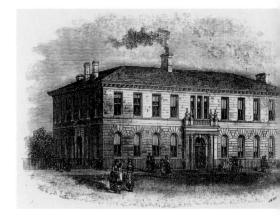

Gorbals Youth School became Hutchesons' Girls' School and was used as the Jewish Talmud Torah School in the years prior to its demolition.

alterations to Hutchesons' Girls' School in 1887, and Honeyman, Keppie and Mackintosh made further changes in 1904. It subsequently became a Hebrew College, the Talmud Torah School, before being demolished, the Jewish population moving out to the suburbs as their circumstances improved.

The other charitable school of this era was for the Glasgow Protestant Institute for Orphan and Destitute Girls at 7 South York Street, Little Govan. The Dean of Guild approval application was made by Honeyman to the council on 27 May 1869 on behalf of the secretary of the institute, Robert Munsie.

The oldest parish school by Honeyman, still in use as a school, is in Aberfoyle, next to the church designed at the same time. Honeyman owed the opportunity to architect J.T. Rochead, whose main claim to fame is the spectacular Wallace Monument in Stirling, designed in 1859. Rochead retired in 1869 due to ill health and Honeyman acquired three unfinished projects – Helenslee, Dumbarton (which became Keil School), North Park House, Queen Margaret Drive, Glasgow (which became the headquarters of BBC Scotland) and the Aberfoyle church and school. He added an extension to the school in 1890. The benefactors of the original 1870 parish school were a Mr and Mrs R. Hampson. Mrs Hampson's brother, E.G. Joynson, had Honeyman and Keppie carry out alterations to The Glassert, Aberfoyle, in 1891, and J. Walter Joynson to his house Altskeith, Kinlochard, Aberfoyle, in 1898 (now the Altskeith Hotel).

The 1872 Education Act required school boards to be elected in each parish and burgh throughout Scotland. These were empowered to acquire land, raise money and provide adequate accommodation for seven to thirteen-year-old children. In addition they were encouraged to provide instruction for the

Aberfoyle School.

under-sevens (they did so for five and six year olds), and evening schools for children thirteen and over. 'Any sum required to meet a deficiency in the school fund, whether for satisfying present or future liabilities, shall be provided by means of a local rate within the parish or burgh in the school of which the deficiency exists'. This started off as a few pennies in the pound, rising to almost a shilling in the pound by the end of the century. School boards were overseen by the Scotch Education Department (as it was called until 1914).

Some of the 50 or so secondary or grammar schools in Scotland became independent. Eleven others including Glasgow High School, Paisley Grammar, Perth Academy and Stirling High School chose to come under the school board structure, although they were not supported by the school rate. The universities saw the lack of funding for a secondary school in each town as a weakness of the Act, as the mandatory elementary education of a thirteen year old did not adequately prepare boys for university attendance.

Although overseen by the school boards, for some time the Roman Catholic and some Episcopalian churches continued to run their own schools, concerned about the possible secularisation of education under the standard curriculum required to obtain grants from the Scotch Education Department. Honeyman received a commission from St Joseph's Mission in Gourock for a school which opened on 4 August 1877.

However, his main school clients were the school boards of Govan, Glasgow and Gourock – Fairfield, Govan (1874/75); Burnbank, Henderson Street, Woodside (1874–76); Tureen Street, Calton (1874–77); Rockvilla, Maryhill (1874–76); Gourock Eastern (1875–77); and Gourock Middle, Binnie Street (1876). Tureen Street later became a specialist school for the deaf, and was associated with the Deaf and Dumb Institute in West Regent Street, in whose vacated premises Keppie Design is now located.

The initial School Board of Glasgow had fifteen members, eight of them clergymen, the others being local businessmen, some of whom, such as Michael Connal, James Campbell and William Kidson were well-known to John Honeyman. He designed Ferniegair House for Kidson in Helensburgh in 1867, and Parkhall at Killearn for Connal in 1879.

The school boards were elected in each area every three years until education became the responsibility of local authorities in 1918. Glasgow was the UK's biggest constituency since London was split into districts. One of the main factors in the selection of board members was religion. Of the fifteen places on the Glasgow School Board, at least three were guaranteed for Roman Catholics. At the first election in 1873, there was a group of candidates who referred to themselves as 'Christian Secularists', who felt that religion should not be taught in non-denominational schools, an argument being that most teachers were neither qualified nor motivated to teach religion. There were at least four ministers in this group, as well as a prominent trade unionist, George Jackson. A second group standing for election also contained Protestant ministers and lay people, among

Fairfield School, Govan.

Henderson Street School, Glasgow.

Tureen Street School, Glasgow, is one of the few Honeyman schools to have survived.
It is now a community centre.

them some of Honeyman's clients. One of these was Harry Alfred Long who made clear his condemnation of Roman Catholicism and his belief that the Pope was the Antichrist. Between 1873, when he topped the poll with 108,264 votes (twice as many as the second-placed member) and 1900, he totalled 535,069 votes, which he claimed was the highest ever in any UK democratic process.

Neither Protestant group wished the Catholic representation to rise from the minimum three to gain a majority on the board, as it had done in Liverpool. In the election of 1873 there was a concern that the competition between the two Protestant groups would let the Catholics in. In the event, Harry Alfred Long's group was most successful, and a compromise was reached dictating that religious instruction should be largely confined to morning assembly, with individual attendance subject to parental approval. Trade unionist George Jackson did not obtain sufficient votes to gain a place on the board, despite predictions that he might top the poll. Harry Alfred Long summed up the election result:

When the good news passed into the open some men wept for joy, others threw up caubeens [Irish berets], and yet other some danced, jumping for joy. The overwhelming majority over the priesthood sent a thrill over all Scottish bluedom. The covenant blue banner was justified. Thousands bowed in grateful adoration to God. The Bible and Catechism were safe. One of our best leaders, himself returned, said, 'The greatest Protestant triumph of the nineteenth century'.

Of the district's population of 513,664, there were 87,294 children between five and thirteen, with 228 schools providing schooling for 52,644 of them. The average attendance was 42,655. From 1873 to 1882 the board erected 27 schools to accommodate 25,267 pupils. John Honeyman received three commissions from Glasgow: Henderson Street (985 pupils, opened August 1876), Rockvilla (926 pupils, opened November 1876) and Tureen Street (785 pupils, opened August 1876). James Salmon obtained four schools, H.H. Mackie five, D. Thomson and Turnbull four, James Thomson two, with others such as John Burnet and Campbell Douglas and Sellars (where John Keppie trained) receiving one each.

The Scotch Education Department gave loans for new schools at a rate of 3.5 per cent over a 50-year period (it rose to 4.25 per cent in 1879), on condition that the cost per scholar did not exceed £10 and that the minimum area per scholar was ten square feet. The SED tried to impose standard classroom sizes and room proportions on the board, but relented in response to opposition from various schools. I seem to remember the same debate between central and local authorities about standard classrooms in the late 1990s.

The Glasgow board made a policy that boys and girls should be taught in the same classroom, but be separated from each other in sections and have separate entrances, exits and playgrounds. The ventilation of schoolrooms was considered very important at a time when children usually came from homes with poor sanitation and washing facilities. The standard specification was 'the admission of fresh air from the lower sashes of the windows – the vitiated air being extracted by apertures in the ceiling of the rooms by Munn's Patent Ventilator'.

The 1872 Act made it the responsibility of every parent to ensure that their children from ages five to thirteen received education in reading, writing and arithmetic. Up until 1890, parents had to pay fees for their children's education unless they succeeded in pleading poverty to the parochial board, whereupon it would pay. The school board ensured that there was at least one school with low fees in every district of the city, the scale beginning at 1½d. per pupil per week. The third child in a family attending school allowed the eldest to be admitted at half fee, and the fourth led to the eldest receiving free schooling. The minimum fee resulted in about eight shillings per year. Barony, City and Govan areas charged a uniform fee of £1 per year.

The High School of Glasgow was thought important enough to have its own board committee. If an average 1,000-pupil city school obtained £1,000 per year in fees, the £5,204 income to the High School for 770 pupils allowed the classics, mathematics, science and music to be taught. When the board inspected it in 1873 it

> found a very considerable attendance of scholars, yet there was no regular curriculum of study or any Rector or other recognised head of the institution. The premises were considered far from suitable for the Grammar School of so great a city.

The members of the board may well have had civic pride to the fore in their considerations, but they could also afford to send their children there, so self-interest could well have been a motivation. They purchased premises in Elmbank Street in 1877, previously known as the Glasgow Academy, and commissioned the most famous local sculptor of the time, John Mossman, to erect statues of Homer, Cicero, Galileo and James Watt outside. The building remained in use as the High School until the 1970s when Glasgow Corporation withdrew grant support for fee-paying schools. Keppie Henderson designed new premises for the independent High School of Glasgow (1975–78) at Anniesland.

By 1885, elementary drawing was becoming widely available in schools, and the board thought that commercial design and art was important enough to the city for it to apply to the UK Department of Science and Art in Kensington for a grant to build an art school. It was turned down, and Glasgow had to wait until 1899 for Mackintosh's building to be realised, or at least the first phase of it. In the meantime the board established schools of art in the High School and Thomson Street School for evening students. Other evening classes were held in mathematics, magnetism and electricity, physiology, chemistry, solid geometry, machine construction, building construction, botany, physiography (physical geography), applied mechanics, theoretical mechanics and steam. Allan Glen's School, which Mackintosh had attended, was allied to Anderson's College, to become part of the Glasgow Technical College in 1887.

Apart from a few alterations to existing buildings, Honeyman was not called on to design more schools after 1877. John Keppie and Charles Rennie Mackintosh designed the next ones. Little Dovehill School required an additional 365 places for drawing, science and cookery classes. It was opened in February 1895 and illustrated in the *Builder* on 11 May of that year. The appointment of the practice to replace the Martyrs' School at Townhead on 8 January 1895 gave Mackintosh his first opportunity to design a new building, only a short distance from where he was brought up. The previous Martyrs' School had accommodation for 472 pupils, and the new school opened in August 1897 with a roll 920 pupils (the design was featured in the *Builder* of 31 July 1896).

Honeyman and Keppie entered a design competition for Paisley Technical School in 1895. They submitted two designs, which were placed second and third, and were illustrated in *Academy Architecture* and the *British Architect* on 27 February and 29

May 1896. They were more successful with the Glasgow School of Art competition the following year.

By 1904, when the commission was given for Scotland Street School, Mackintosh was a partner in the practice. The board had to pay a lot of money for the site, which was in a high-value industrial area. It cost £13,500 in 1904, compared to £2,100 for the additional land required for Martyrs' in 1895, and £2,247 to £4,358 for the Henderson Street, Rockvilla and Tureen Street schools in 1874. This probably meant that the board was particularly conscious of costs when it came to the construction of Scotland Street, although Mackintosh did not help matters by having one set of drawings approved by the board (January 1904) and giving another to the builder (August and September 1904). Alison Brown at Glasgow Museums reckons that Mackintosh was found out when someone else in the office sent tiling layout drawings to the board for approval in November 1905, and they noticed changes in various features. Why was it necessary to have stained glass in school windows? Meetings were called and the board was not happy with Mackintosh's attitude. He did however manage to keep the tiling layout he wanted and the voids in the stair towers, but the stair railings had to revert to the original plain metal design. The final cost was £34,219, exceeding the £32,700 loan obtained from the Scotch Education Department.

When it opened in 1906, Scotland Street School had a roll of 205 boys and 172 girls. The perspective drawing of the building was set up by one of Mackintosh's assistants, William Moyes, who emigrated to Australia around the time the building was completed. However, Mackintosh clearly wished there to be no doubt that he had designed the building by having his own name written above the practice name of Honeyman, Keppie and Mackintosh.

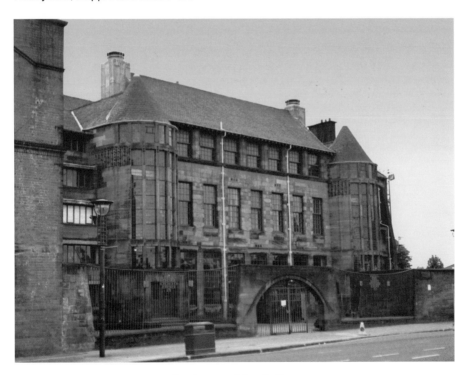

Scotland Street School, Glasgow.

The original artist's impression of how The Cliff, Wemyss Bay, would look.

CHAPTER 10

The Skelmorlie years

Nine years after setting up in practice as an architect, John Honeyman, aged 32, married Rothesia Chalmers Ann Hutchison, daughter of merchant Charles Hutchison, on 3 June 1863. Honeyman's joy was short-lived as Ann (as she was known) died at 2.00 p.m. on 20 March 1864, aged 34, exactly one week after she had given birth to John Rothes Charles Honeyman. John's elder brother Michael registered both the birth and death at Cathcart on 21 March 1864, presumably because John was too distraught. Under the section of the certificate marked 'Cause of Death' it was noted 'not certified'.

Although the most likely cause of Ann's death was a birth complication, there was a typhus and cholera outbreak in Glasgow that year. The rich and poor were both susceptible to the effects of the dreadful sanitary conditions of mass housing arising from the influx of people to the city. Ann's death may explain Honeyman's later keen interest in societies involved in public health and poverty. He also experimented with inventions for drainage traps and ventilation systems. From 1884 to 1895 he applied for eleven patents, five of which were accepted.

The Police Act of 1862 had set standards for new houses. Honeyman became president of the Sanitary and Social Economy section of the Royal Glasgow Philosophical Society, and was appointed as a consultant to Glasgow's City Improvement Trust when it was formed in 1866. He was joined by John Burnet, Alexander 'Greek' Thomson, David Thomson, Clarke and Bell and J.T. Rochead. These architects were each paid 50 guineas for their advice. In 1900 Honeyman was appointed president of the Architecture and Engineering Section at the Public Health Congress in Aberdeen.

In other fields he helped found the Glasgow Archaeological Society in 1856, and was among the first members of the Architectural Institute of Scotland, joining in 1853. He became president of the Glasgow Architectural Association in 1866, later called the Glasgow Institute of Architects. In 1883 Honeyman was still campaigning for legal reform, leading a Glasgow Institute of Architects delegation to the House of Commons on 29 June, along with James Thomson and Campbell Douglas. They handed in proposals to the Lord Advocate that building regulations be set up, separate from the Burgh Police and Health (Scotland) Bill. The Police Acts covered a wide range of social issues from sanitary provision to building use, but the police were more interested in uncovering illegal drinking dens and whorehouses than enforcing sanitary standards, and the GIA proposals envisaged the type of building regulations we have today.

Honeyman married for a second time in 1867, at St Saviour's Church, Paddington,

London to Falconer Margaret Kemp, daughter of a wealthy retired Greenock merchant and ship owner. A year later on 27 April 1868, at their home at 13 Somerset Place, Glasgow, William Frederick Colquhoun Honeyman was born. (Just over a month later, in the poorer east side of the city at 70 Parson Street, Charles Rennie McIntosh, as his name was spelled at the time, was born.)

The rich did have one big advantage over the poor in trying to avoid nineteenth century urban pestilence. They could purchase rural and coastal retreats to enjoy the fresh air and tranquility. John Honeyman was rich and he had married into money. With dozens of churches and houses in his portfolio, he obtained his first high profile public building in June 1868, Paisley Library and Museum. The pressure of work and the time he was spending on committees led to Honeyman's principal assistant, John Bennie Wilson (1850–1923), who started working for the practice in 1867, being given more and more duties. So in 1869, Honeyman, Falconer, John junior and baby William moved down the Clyde Coast to Skelmorlie. The twelve years from 1869 were Honeyman's happiest and most prosperous.

The Rev. John Lamond summed up the lifestyle Skelmorlie and neighbouring Wemyss Bay afforded:

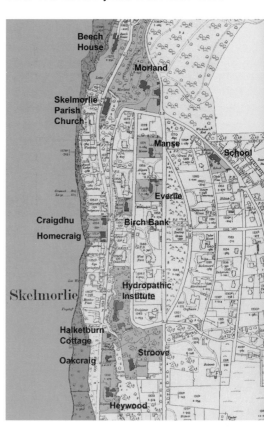

> There were days in Skelmorlie when the glory of heaven was well nigh outrivalled, so marvellous were the sunsets. These days were called 'pet days' by the local people. The estuary was never empty. Day and night some steamer or sailing ship was on the waters, and in the summer season the yachts with fairy-looking wings went gliding to and fro, giving life and animation to the scene. To live on the Clyde is to be drenched with Beauty.

Most people had a house in Glasgow or Greenock but lived in Skelmorlie in the summer, where life centred around the yacht and house parties. There was also bathing and tennis in summer, and for those who returned for Christmas, curling and skating when the old reservoir froze over. Guests were invited to stay. Among John Burns's visitors at Castle Wemyss were General Sherman, commander-in-chief of the US army, and explorer H.M. Stanley. David Livingstone was a visitor to the Kelly

Honeyman's house, Stroove, was situated next to the hydropathic institute in Skelmorlie, while the MacNair family lived four houses beyond at Birch Bank. Herbert MacNair was the same age as Honeyman's son John junior, and they probably went to school together. The buildings highlighted were designed or altered by Honeyman, along with several others beyond the area of the map.

Estate in Wemyss Bay, and he probably exchanged memories of the area with Stanley in the six months they spent together in Ujiji in 1871/72. Livingstone's host at Kelly was James Young, the Glasgow scientist who developed paraffin. After Livingstone died, Young invited the two African servants, Susi and Chuna, who had carried his embalmed body over a thousand miles to Zanzibar, back to stay with him. They built a replica of their master's hut in the garden, and local people could still remember it hidden in the undergrowth in the 1960s.

Plans had been in existence from 1834 for the creation of a holiday resort at Wemyss Bay, which it was claimed was two hours from Glasgow by road or sea. At the time there were four houses on the bay, let out to wealthy Glasgow merchants. On the site of one of these now sits Dunloe, designed by John Honeyman and Keppie in 1890. In the 1850s and 1860s more than 30 homes were built. Development of adjoining Skelmorlie took place later. The local minister, the Rev. John Dow, did not promote the coastline as enthusiastically as his later colleague quoted above: 'From the keenness of the easterly winds in winter and spring, it may be doubted whether the climate is well adapted for patients liable to spitting blood, or inflammatory infections of the linings of the lungs. In such cases, Rothesay is better.'

The opening of the railway to Wemyss Bay on 15 May 1865 certainly gave quicker access to the steamer to Rothesay. However, it also brought Skelmorlie into commuting distance of the Glasgow area and allowed it to be developed as a dormitory and holiday village. Originally, the Greenock and Wemyss Bay Railway Company intended to build the station on the site of Captain T.O. Swinburne's house, Villa Clutha (named after the local term for a small boat), but altered its plans and moved it a few hundred metres south to its present position. This was fortunate for Honeyman, as he received the commission to redevelop Clutha in 1866, the first of over 20 houses he designed or altered in Wemyss Bay and Skelmorlie. A second commission followed in 1866 for alterations to Skelmorlie Bank, a large house altered by Honeyman again in 1897, which later became the Strathclyde Hotel, a convalescent home and a holiday home for deprived children, before being demolished.

While carrying out these two projects, he picked a site for a house for himself which he called Stroove. His old home is still there today. He could not have chosen a better spot on the hill overlooking the Firth of Clyde, and as a keen sailor, he could view new ships going through their paces on what became known as the 'measured mile' opposite Skelmorlie. The Halket Burn runs through the extensive gardens of Stroove on its way from the reservoir serving the village to the sea, past Halketburn Cottage on the Shore Road below Stroove. *Who's Who in Glasgow in 1909* stated that:

he had the pleasure of possessing his own yacht . . . in which he and his wife and sons had many a pleasant and eventful cruise along the beautiful west coast. Like many another lover of white sails and blue water, he found that at busy periods of his life, an occasional cruise of

The view from the side of Honeyman's house, Stroove, with Rothesay on the Isle of Bute in the distance.

ten days or so was the best possible means of regaining vigour and enjoying mental rest.

Stroove was built with fifteen rooms, necessary for entertaining guests and for accommodating live-in servants. At the 1871 census, merchant Charles McLean and his wife Agnes were staying. Honeyman had just finished extending McLean's home, Glenearn House in Bridge of Earn. Three servants were looking after them: Barbara Mackenzie, a nurse from Inverness; Maria Clark, a housemaid from Ireland; and Marion McClymont, a cook from Elgin. By the time of the 1881 census, Honeyman's elder sisters, Christina and Agnes, had come to stay. John junior was by this time seventeen years old and an architecture student at the Glasgow School of Art, which he attended from 1881–84.

Next door to Stroove was the hydropathic institute, erected in 1868. With the introduction of pumped saltwater up the cliff in 1875, Turkish and salt water baths were added. Dr Ronald Currie was responsible for the health facility. He had been one of Professor Joseph Lister's students in Glasgow in 1860 at the time he was introducing antisepsis into surgery. Currie lived in Skelmorlie until he died in 1923, part of the time at Oakcraig, the house Honeyman extended for him in 1874.

Four plots beyond the hydropathic institute was a house called Birch Bank. Mr Brown of Brown and Poulson had originally commissioned it, along with three adjacent houses so that he could control who his neighbours were. George Best MacNair and his wife moved to Birch Bank in 1872 with their three daughters and the four-year-old baby of the family, Herbert. When Herbert grew up he was to become Charles Rennie Mackintosh's friend at the Glasgow School of Art and later his brother-in-law. The family was well-off and George was able to retire early from the directorship of a shipping company. Census information has him living on his own means, and when he died at Birch Bank in 1910 his wife described his profession as 'gentleman' on the death certificate.

To adapt the house for its new occupants in 1872, Honeyman carried out a number of alterations, including adding a new laundry. Birch Bank today is split into three twenty-first-century sized family homes. Its folklore, passed on by its current occupants, suggests that Mackintosh built cupboards in a bedroom. He is reported to have visited the MacNair family at Skelmorlie in the 1890s, and may well have built the modest cupboards, but using standard sections of wood and hinges from the local joiner, since there are no stylistic clues in their design to set them apart from other features in the room. Herbert MacNair later recounted how he, Frances and Margaret Macdonald decorated the main staircase with a mermaid motif, the mermaid being the Clan MacNair crest, but no traces remain today. (I have used the spelling 'MacNair' throughout this book, although the family sometimes used 'McNair').

Honeyman doubled the size of The Cliff with the addition of the part of the building seen on the left in this picture. The practice returned in the early 1890s, and the stained glass in a window added to the old part of the house to light a stair landing looks suspiciously Glasgow Style.

At the same time as this, Honeyman designed The Cliff in Wemyss Bay for Henry Martini, a merchant whose office was in Hope Street in Glasgow and whose town house was Lynholm in Hamilton. He was also vice-consul for Denmark. The £4,386 house was extended for the next occupant, Stewart Clark MP, in 1881 and 1884. The building has since been converted into flats with the loss of the main staircase and some other internal features.

Honeyman came to Skelmorlie just after the end of the American Civil War, and would have heard about it at first hand from local people who were involved. Henry Watson was a landscape gardener who had laid out the grounds of some of the first houses in the village, including Halketburn Cottage (altered by Honeyman for a Miss Boyle in 1872), and Ashcraig for West Indian sugar planter, A.D. Campbell (the second occupant of this house was a Miss Isabella Stewart who had Honeyman carry out alterations in 1873). Henry Watson had two sons, Richard who ran the local wine merchant's, a highly valued social facility, and William, an engineer who travelled extensively and settled in Louisiana, just in time for the Civil War. As a Confederate he ran the blockade, first in sailing craft and then in Clyde-bought steamers which had shallow drafts to allow them to penetrate the River Clyde up to Glasgow at low tide. William Watson survived the war, returned to set up business in Greenock, and built three houses in Skelmorlie named after the battles he took part in: Oakhill, Pea Ridge and Beechgrove. The last of these was one plot to the south of Stroove. From his home in Skelmorlie he wrote two books on his experiences, *Life in the Confederate Army* and *The Adventures of a Blockade Runner*.

A number of other notable people lived in Skelmorlie around the time Honeyman was there. George Burns, who founded the Cunard Line with Robert Napier, lived in Wemyss House. Both were Honeyman clients, the former's Glasgow offices in Jamaica Street being completed in 1864.

From 1852 to 1890, Skelmorlie Castle was let to John Graham. The job books suggest that Honeyman may have carried out work to Graham's offices at the Life Association of Scotland at 123 St Vincent Street, Glasgow in 1864, and he designed £3,280 worth of alterations at Skelmorlie Castle in 1877. Graham opened the galleries of the castle to the public to display his paintings by Gainsborough, Turner and Landseer. The job books also suggest that Graham sponsored a boarding school in 1878/79, but it has not been traced. When Graham vacated the castle in 1890, it was let to one of the Coats of Paisley, clients of Honeyman for the Paisley Library and Observatory.

Sir William Pearce built Cardell in 1860,

Skelmorlie Castle.

Cardell, Skelmorlie, was the home of Sir William Pearce of Fairfield's Shipyard.

and Honeyman carried out alterations to the house for tenant Daniel Macfarlane. Pearce took over Fairfield's Shipyard in Govan in 1868 after John Elder died, and appointed Honeyman to design its offices. Unfortunately, before they were completed in 1891, Sir William died, and Honeyman designed a memorial to him in Govan at a cost of £1,212.

Two houses were designed in Skelmorlie for Greenock sugar merchants. Having already completed the town house Woodburn for Hugh Walker in 1865 at 2 Newark Street, Greenock, Honeyman designed Chaseley in Skelmorlie for him. It still exists as the Beechwood Nursery on Shore Road,

Chaseley, Skelmorlie, was originally the home of a rich Greenock sugar merchant, and its most recent incarnation has been as the Beechwood Nursery.

although it had been converted to a hotel before the Second World War. Along with the adjacent Skelmorlie Bank, altered by Honeyman in 1866, it had been purchased by the Lanarkshire Coalmasters Association as a convalescent home for women of mining families.

The other Greenock sugar merchant was Laurence Robertson who in 1876–77 had £5,793 worth of alterations and extensions carried out to the 1862 villa Moreland. It had previously been the home of William Thomson before he moved to Largs. Later better known as Lord Kelvin, this mathematician and physicist helped to develop the law of the conservation of energy, and the absolute temperature scale is now measured in degrees Kelvin. While living in Skelmorlie in the mid-1850s, his theories on electrical telegraphy made possible the underwater telegraph wire between Ireland and Canada, a distance of transmission not previously thought practical. Laurence Robertson invited Honeyman back in 1893 to spend £2,600 more on Moreland. It ceased to be a single residence in 1982, the main staircase being lost in the alterations. The music room was left in its original condition, including the inglenook seating and stained glass panels depicting Industry and Effort by Stephen Adam.

The Kyles of Bute Hydropathic, 1878–80

A short ferry journey from Wemyss Bay is the Isle of Bute, from where Port Bannatyne was a short horse-and-cart ride from the pier at Rothesay. From 1878 to 1880 Honeyman designed a hydropathic institute here, an establishment that tells us much about Victorian society.

Honeyman lived next door to a hydropathic institute at Skelmorlie, and later, when he moved to Bridge of Allan, he also found a house next to one. Perhaps Dr Currie in Skelmorlie recommended Honeyman as the designer of the Swanstonhill Sanatorium at Port Bannatyne, which became known as the Kyles of Bute Hydropathic. It was converted from an old residence.

Hydropathy came to prominence in Victorian Britain from Austria, where Vincenz Preissnitz had developed techniques of using wet compresses to treat injuries. Two

Scottish physicians, Dr East and Dr Paterson, introduced them to Scotland at their hydropathic institutes at Dunoon and Glenburn. Turkish baths were introduced by the 1850s. Henry Parrat's 1889 *Guidebook to all the Hydropathic Institutes in Great Britain* stated:

> Scotland can boast some of the finest hydropathic establishments in the world; and it would be no exaggeration to say that there are few noblemen's residencies that can compare with some of these. These palatial establishments are generally constructed with a view to external beauty of design as well as to the completeness of the accessories.

The Kyles of Bute Hydropathic at Port Bannatyne.

With reference to Honeyman's building he continues:

> The climate on the Isle of Bute is generally mild, and yet bracing; it is also very free from fogs or mists. The house in winter is well heated throughout, and all the comforts and enjoyments of the visitors most thoroughly attended to. The grounds of the establishment extend to fifteen acres, beautifully wooded, and laid out in shaded walks, and in the summer season are rendered most attractive by the variety of the foliage and luxuriance of the plants. The house arrangements are admirably conducted; the public rooms comprise handsome drawing room, billiard and reading room, etc. The baths comprise Turkish and the ordinary baths, besides salt water baths, hot and cold. Also superior lawn tennis, boating and fishing. Summer terms, inclusive, £2. 12s. 6d. to £3. 3s. 0d. per week.

(Honeyman paid Isabella, his secretary, £1 per month in the early 1890s, so hydropathy was a rich man's pastime.)

Most hydropathics would admit day visitors, and Honeyman would partake of treatments at Skelmorlie and Bridge of Allan on this basis, much as we would today at a health club. A Turkish bath would cost two shillings, a plunge bath one shilling, with vapour, electric and other special baths at various rates. A huge amount of water was used, from fresh water storage or pumped up from the sea, and architects would have to call on the services of civil and heating engineers in the design of buildings.

Medical treatments were claimed for indigestion, constipation, pains in the bowels, enlargement of the liver, eruptive fevers, diphtheria, abscesses, boils and many other complaints. As well as different types of baths and compresses, mineral water could be drunk, injected or, 'a small tea-cupful of tepid water, thrown up into the lower bowel by means of a small tin syringe, or other convenient instrument. No difficulty, suffering, or danger, attends this process. Any nurse may employ it.' I wonder how much the Victorians believed the sales pitch:

> Every cure is wrought by the inherent powers of the living organism itself, all

that treatment can do is to place the patient in the circumstances in which nature can work to most advantage; and we maintain that, of all known modes of cure, hydropathy is that which fulfils this condition most fully, and with the least approach of doing harm.

So said the Rev. Alex Munro MD in 1864.

The link between pure thoughts and pure, cleansed bodies was evident in church thinking. Honeyman's sponsor at Park Free Church, Helensburgh, William Kidson, gave a lecture at the church to the Young Men's Society in 1881, extolling the virtues of hydropathy, and its importance among the best in society. He painted a picture of a visit to one establishment:

An ex-Bailie of Glasgow, a genial old gentleman, who was there with a number of his family, spoke to every one, and was a general favourite. Two little stout gentlemen, twins, who were inseparable, and who wore the same dress, and the same little fancy caps, excited some interest. Provost Swan of Kirkcaldy, who was there part of the time, took a hearty interest in all that was going on. Everyone seemed desirous to add to the general enjoyment. There was a profusion of good milk, served up in glass decanters, and the tea in particular was the delight of the ladies.

In the morning the inmates flock with alacrity into the drawing room, and gather round a table as eagerly as flies buzzing round a plate of treacle, but the sweets on this occasion are not saccharine, but sweet letters, newspapers, postcards, and packets. After reading papers and writing letters, when we look from our parlour windows, we are sure to see ladies in fashionable 'Pinafore' dresses, and gentlemen in Highland costume, having a lively game at lawn tennis.

Honeyman's conversion of the Kyles of Bute building at £9,414 was modest compared to the £45,000 spent at Craiglockhart in Edinburgh or the £70,000 spent building the Peebles Hydro. However, the crash of the City of Glasgow Bank in 1878, with a final call on shareholders in 1881, had a profound effect on many clients of hydropathic institutes, and in 1884 Craiglockhart, Dunblane and Peebles hydros went into liquidation. Edinburgh architects Peddie and Kinnear had previously taken their fees in shares in the first two of these as their clients ran out of cash, and they lost the lot.

The more modest Kyles of Bute Hydro stayed in business right up to the Second World War when it was requisitioned by Graham Henderson (the Keppie practice's fourth principal) for use as the headquarters for the 12th Submarine Flotilla, and renamed HMS *Varbel*. It was the base for men who manned midget submarines and 'human torpedoes' from 1942 to 1945. It made a comeback as a hotel after 1945, when its sales brochure stated that 'Although the term "Hydropathic" has lost much of its original meaning, salt and fresh water plunge baths, Sitz baths, douches, spine and shower baths within the building itself are at your service free of charge.' By the 1970s and 80s the hotel business in Clyde Coast resorts was suffering from the competition of cheap flights to the Mediterranean. The building became derelict and was demolished in 1990.

Throughout his life, Honeyman was clearly interested in maintaining a healthy lifestyle, but good health could not be guaranteed. His golden age at Skelmorlie ended in 1881 when, on 7 January, his wife Falconer died of tuberculosis. Both his sons

William and George also contracted it. William died of consumption in 1885 on board the steamship *Wellington* while travelling to Italy in the hope of recuperating. George is believed to have been committed to a sanatorium. In his grief, Honeyman sold Stroove to Donald Macdonald, a Greenock sugar merchant, and moved to 24 Newton Place, Glasgow. In 1888 Honeyman gave a job to William's lifelong friend and neighbour Herbert MacNair.

Stroove continued to be used as a private house until the Second World War, Keppie Henderson adding a chauffeur's cottage for Captain C.S. Scott in 1920–22. It was subsequently purchased by Mr and Mrs Hally Brown who intended to convert it into a cottage hospital in memory of their two sons who died in the Second World War. However, when the National Health Service was formed the building was not required, and various uses followed, including as a community centre and a holiday home for the Skelmorlie Foundation. In 1997 it was purchased by the YMCA, and it is now back in private hands.

The relationship of the practice with the area did not finish with Honeyman's departure. Apart from alterations to Skelmorlie School in 1894, he returned to undertake two major projects, Dunloe House in Wemyss Bay in 1890 with John Keppie, and Skelmorlie Church between 1893 and 1895 with Charles Rennie Mackintosh.

Dunloe House, 1890

Dunloe was designed in 1890 for Ninian Bannatyne Stewart of Keil. Honeyman had designed a fernery, an entrance gate (now the entrance to neighbouring Blair Lodge), a stable block and other alterations at Ascog Hall,Bute, in 1862 for Alexander Bannatyne Stewart, Ninian's father and son of the founder of the drapery warehouse Stewart and

McDonald. Honeyman would probably have known A.B. Stewart in his position as chairman of the council of the Glasgow Institute of Fine Arts, although he was also commodore of the Bute Aquatic Club and flag officer of the Royal Northern Yacht Club. He had a passion for growing orchids, and the fernery allowed him to pursue this.

Ninian could afford to build such a grand house thanks to an inheritance. Unfortunately, a live-in mother-in-law came with it. Actually she was also his aunt, Ninian having married his cousin, Maria Amelia Stewart, in 1888. Perhaps this was an attempt to keep the drapers' business in the family. Ninian was first noticed in the research for this book taking out a bond of £15,000 in 1865 with Robertson Buchanan Stewart and

This sketch of Dunloe House, Wemyss Bay, was by Alexander McGibbon, one of a number of talented draftsmen who were in the practice during the time Mackintosh was there.

Alexander Bannatyne Stewart from another of Honeyman's clients, the Tennent family of the Wellpark Brewery

117

in Glasgow. He also secured property on the east side of Mitchell Street in Glasgow, where Fraser's is now located. In the 1950s Fraser's combined the Stewart and McDonald and Wylie and Lochhead premises which extended from Buchanan Street to Mitchell Street. Ninian gave his place of abode in 1865 as Torquay.

This was the second house Stewart had commissioned in Wemyss Bay, Honeyman having designed Ardvar for him in 1880. His grandson, Commander Ninian L. Stewart OBE RN, told me that Ardvar was left unoccupied after Ninian senior's death in the 1920s. It was eventually demolished in the 1950s.

The practice used Dunloe to promote the new partnership of John Honeyman and Keppie. It appeared in the *Builder* in August 1891 and in the September/October 1891 issue of *British Architect*. The fireplace in the main reception room is today close to the original perspective, although Keppie's favourite decorated frieze device has gone. Some of the original drawings are framed in the hallway of the house, which is full of interesting features and details. Above the internal doorways there are brass panels with human faces, some with open mouths, others with closed mouths. Apparently this was a sign to Gaelic-speaking servants that if they entered a private, restricted area of the house, denoted by a face with an open mouth, they would be shouted at.

When the house was being marketed in 2001, the selling agent FPD Savills included a number of interesting historical details:

During the Second World War Dunloe House was used as a Catalina flying boat station where naval commanders could keep an active watch for German U-boats arriving on the western approach to the Clyde. After the war, Dunloe was returned to a fine private house and is thought to have been host to a number of notable visitors including Haile Selassie, and also to Princess Margaret who regularly stayed in the turreted bedroom whilst visiting the nearby Ardgowan Estate.

Unfortunately, none of this is true. The U-boat indicator loop detection installation was elsewhere in Wemyss Bay and the Catalina flying boats were based at Largs. Maria

The original proposal for the dining room at Dunloe, and the same room seen in 2001.

Amelia Stewart lived alone in this huge house during the Second World War. Also, it was Lord Inverclyde at Castle Wemyss who put up Emperor Haile Selassie during his exile from Abyssinia (now Ethiopia) after Mussolini occupied the country from 1936 to 1941. Lord Inverclyde also met Princess Margaret and the rest of the royal family during the Clyde Fleet Review in 1947, when King George VI and Queen Elizabeth were celebrating their silver wedding. Princess Elizabeth and Prince Philip had just become engaged. Lord Inverclyde merely escorted them along Wemyss Bay Pier to the station where the royal train was waiting.

The house's occupants did experience drama in 1907. The measured mile, along which new boats underwent speed trials, stretched from Skelmorlie Castle in the south to a point opposite the hydropathic institute. Occasionally, boats under trial collided with other shipping on the Clyde. The worst such occurrence took place on 18 September 1907 when a ship called the *Maori* was completing its northward run and was turning in Wemyss Bay. Another craft, the *Kintyre*, was struck on its starboard side and sank within five minutes. Captain John McKechnie stayed on the bridge with chief engineer William Lennox until everyone else was safely off. Luckily there were no passengers, only crew. The two men went down with the boat, but only Captain McKechnie managed to swim to shore. Lennox was never seen again. Commander Stewart's father, also called Ninian, was playing in the garden of Dunloe with his sister when the collision occurred. They launched a dinghy but only managed to recover the ship's log. They later presented it to Captain McKechnie in the Wemyss Bay Hotel, where Dr Currie had been summoned from the hydropathic institute to attend to the survivors.

In 2001 the owner of Dunloe tried to sell the house for single occupation, but without success. There are large servant areas to the rear that could be separated from the main house, and Keppie Design's Edinburgh office was approached in 2002 by a developer who wished to split the building into sections more appropriate for twenty-first century family units. Surprisingly, Dunloe had not previously been listed by Historic Scotland, but the prospect of alterations to it very quickly led to it being spot-listed.

Skelmorlie Church, 1895

By 1890 the congregation of the parish church in Skelmorlie had outgrown the original 1856 building, famous locally because of the organ installed in it by the Rev. Walter Boyd. He made this change prior to receiving authority for such a daring innovation from the Presbytery in Edinburgh, and many believed it was the first organ played in the Church of Scotland. Conservative parishioners were shocked at the thought of musical entertainment in the house of God, and nicknamed the church 'Boyd's Theatre'.

Despite design ideas having been

The enlarged Skelmorlie Church, with the original building to the left of the tower.

Skelmorlie Church includes details, like this lamp standard, which suggest that Mackintosh assisted Honeyman in the design.

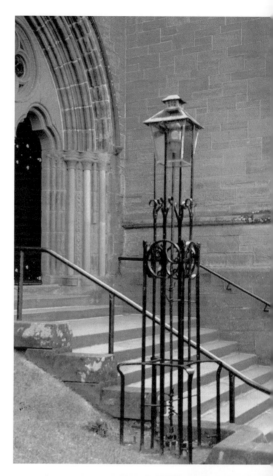

presented by the previous minister, R.H. Fisher, and Laurence Robertson, for whom Honeyman had previously designed a house, it was perhaps inevitable that Honeyman was invited back to design the new church. Not only was he still well-known to many of the congregation, he had designed Skelmorlie Manse for the Rev. Robert Stewart in 1874. The old church building became the church hall, seating 250 people, with the new church able to accommodate 550 worshipers. An entrance tower links the two sections. The cost was £5,813. 19s. 6d.

By the time design work started in 1893, Mackintosh was beginning to contribute more to projects. He was collaborating with John Keppie on the *Glasgow Herald* Building, the Glasgow Art Club and the Conservative Club in Helensburgh, but he also had an interest in Honeyman's passion, ecclesiastical buildings. In 1893, Honeyman was 62 years old, and it must have been obvious to Mackintosh, and indeed his two bosses, that this was an important part of the business on which Mackintosh could specialise. It is not clear at what point in 1889 Mackintosh joined the practice, although it is assumed that his art school project for a country church was carried out just before he started with John Honeyman and Keppie. It would have done his prospects with the practice no harm.

The church projects in the early 1890s had almost all been alterations to existing buildings, requiring a respectful approach to the design –

These stained glass windows in Skelmorlie Church commemorated Honeyman's second wife and two sons, who died of tuberculosis.

Gargunnock Parish Church, East Kilbride Parish Church communion table and chair, North Berwick Free Church, Glasgow Cathedral, Loretto School Chapel, Iona Cathedral, Rhu Parish Church and Bellahouston Church (now Ibrox Parish Church). There would have been no opportunity for Mackintosh to develop his own artistic ideas on these projects, so there is little evidence of his involvement. Mackintosh and MacNair are known to have visited Iona Cathedral to survey it with Honeyman, and it is likely that Mackintosh helped Honeyman with restoration work at Glasgow Cathedral, which was close to his home, and was of interest to him at various times. Skelmorlie Church shows a simplicity of detailing which suggests that Honeyman was helped by a younger man. Mackintosh's signature is certainly on the lamp at the front door and certain internal details on the stair. The lamp was given a category 'A' listing in 1980 by Historic Scotland.

Local builder W.W. Oswald used red stone from nearby quarries, and Honeyman brought in Glasgow stained glass designer William Guthrie and one of the leading wood carvers of the time, John Crawford. A number of donations were made to furnish and fit out the church. John Honeyman's contribution was three stained glass windows in memory of his wife and two sons. The subjects were St Columba of Iona, St Mungo of Glasgow and St Ninian of Whithorn. The first two were particularly pertinent due to Honeyman's work at Iona and Glasgow Cathedrals. They remain today a commemoration of Honeyman's Skelmorlie years.

Skelmorlie Church.

*Being close to the beach at Portobello, the sandy soil caused problems
in the design of the foundations of St Philip's Free Church.*

CHAPTER 11

Edinburgh churches and Bridge of Allan

Historically, the Keppie practice was based in Glasgow, and obtaining work in Edinburgh was often seen as bridging a cultural divide. In Glasgow, if one was asked what school one came from, it was to elicit one's religious background. In Edinburgh, the same question invoked allegiance to an old school tie fraternity. Religion aside – and I have rarely, if ever, found this a barrier to commercial collaboration – a Glaswegian might say that in Glasgow one was judged on what one could do, as opposed to Edinburgh, where who one was might have had a bearing. The opening of an SBT Keppie office in Edinburgh in 1994 was an attempt to bridge the divide, but it took a long time to establish and be successful.

John Honeyman was a west coast man who had been educated at Merchiston Castle School in Edinburgh, and he sent two sons to Loretto. He must have failed to cultivate professional contacts in the east since the bulk of his commissions were in the west, although his skills as a church designer did spread to the capital city, and there are three churches there that he designed – St Philip's Portobello, St Michael's on Slateford Road, and Loretto School Chapel.

The completion of St Michael's heralded a new chapter in John Honeyman's life because he married his third wife there. With her, he left his central Glasgow house and sought peace in the spa town of Bridge of Allan, where he spent the rest of his life. The church he joined there had work carried out to it by himself and his assistant, Charles Rennie Mackintosh.

St Philip's Free Church, 1877

St Philip's Free Church in Portobello did not have much luck when it came to experiencing fires. The first conflagration occurred on the Sabbath, 8 November 1874, when the Free Church congregation was based in Regent Street. Mr Baird, the session clerk, was alerted to a fire in the gallery, which by the time the fire brigade arrived had spread to the roof. This collapsed within an hour. It did not help that a man sent down the street to a stopcock, which would have increased the water pressure, turned it the wrong way. The hoses stopped. 'The bell, when it was reached by the fire came down with a great crash, ringing its own death knell as it fell, and was broken in a hundred pieces on the pavement of the vestibule.' Later, some of the congregation remarked how the atmosphere in the church during the service that day had been 'close and stifling', and the smell of burning wood had been noticed. No one bothered investigating since the furnace had frequently overheated before.

The Established and United Presbyterian Churches both offered to share accommodation until a new church could be built, but the Free Church congregation had a mission hall in Pipe Street, and on occasion held services in Portobello Town Hall. By early 1875 they had decided to temporarily re-roof the old church and purchased cane-bottomed chairs from the Agricultural Hall in London to replace the burnt pews.

Funds were sought for a new church. The insurance money came to £2,000 and £2,651 was raised from members of the congregation in sums from 2s. 6d. to £200. The minister, Robert Ireland, was the most generous contributor.

The congregation obtained plans from various Edinburgh and Glasgow architects. This was probably not a design competition, since, 'the style of

St Philip's Free Church, Portobello.

Mr John Honeyman being generally preferred,' he was appointed in January 1875. By March he had prepared plans and estimated a cost between £6,000 and £6,500. The church had already paid £535 for the site, and requested that he restrict the budget to £6,000. However, when construction work started in July, excavations exposed a deep layer of sand that had to be penetrated to find a good base for the concrete foundations. For good measure they were made broader and deeper under the tower and steeple. Masons' wages also rose heavily during the construction period, and the builder almost went bust. The final cost of the building was £8,920. 8s. 1d. A bazaar in the summer of 1878 and one at Christmas 1888 raised the deficit.

On 19 July 1877 the building was sufficiently complete to hold a service and lay a memorial stone. The time capsule below it contained coins, almanacs, newspapers, an account of the building, and a narrative of the fire, all sealed in a glass jar. It was said that the former Regent Street church, 'could not boast of any extraordinary architectural beauty. The new building on the contrary, is a model of architectural beauty, and reflects the greatest credit on Mr John Honeyman, its architect'.

In those days, each family secured the same seat at Sunday service, and it was decided that their places would match as closely as possible the corresponding position in the old church. The seat-letting committee (it must have been a really important task for a committee to be appointed for it) thought it had solved the problem, but on the evening set aside for the formal apportioning of seats there was a three hour clamour before everyone finally agreed to a position.

Rather than merely being called the Free Church of Portobello, it was named St Philip's. This was a reference to the evangelist in the Bible, but it was also pertinent in celebrating the ministry of the Rev. Alexander Philip from 1849 to 1861. From 1929 until about 1962 it was called Portobello St Philip's (Joppa).

In January 1881 the Rev. Robert Ireland was directing operations to clear a heavy snowfall from the approaches to the church. He caught a chill and died from complications three weeks later, having been the minister for 20 years. He was buried in Portobello Cemetery and a large runic cross of red granite, designed by John Honeyman, was erected in his memory. Honeyman, or at least the practice, returned to the church twice more. In 1885 it advised on the pulpit installation, recommending the placing of a large tapestry screen behind it to improve acoustics, and in 1906 plans were submitted for an organ chamber costing £1,900. The Deacon's Court chose a cheaper option at £1,300. It is no longer there, but photographs suggest that a design by Mackintosh may have been adapted for use.

The second major fire in the church's history took place on Thursday 3 December 1998. The junior choir were due to gather for Christmas concert rehearsals at 6.30 p.m., but on arrival were met by fire engines. These attended to the fire more efficiently than their counterparts 124 years before and it was extinguished by 8.00 p.m. Nevertheless, the roof was lost, and restoration was not completed until four years later.

St Michael's, 1883

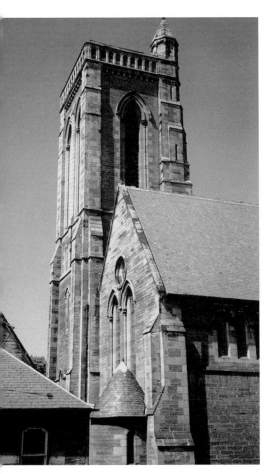

St Michael's Church on Slateford Road started life as a mission church for the districts of Dalry, Tynecastle and North Merchiston. The original building seated 500 people and was referred to as the 'Iron Church'. As a temporary building, its walls would probably have been made of corrugated iron. This could not have been a comfortable place in which to worship. It must have been cold in winter, warm in summer, and heavy rain or hailstorms would be very noisy.

While the congregation at St Philip's had £6,000 to spend on their new church (although the final cost was nearly £9,000), the £15,000 estimated for the new St Michael's Established Church promised a much grander edifice. Church histories do not indicate why John Honeyman was chosen as the architect, but by this time his reputation would have gone before him.

The triangular site was purchased for £1,176 in 1879. The following year, John

St Michael's on Slateford Road in Edinburgh was one of Honeyman's largest churches and the venue for his third marriage.

Campbell joined the congregation and was immediately made responsible for the project's finances. The building was intended to seat 1,000 people with the specification that the average pew width allowance was to be 20 inches (50 centimetres). St Michael's considered a slim spire, but the tower, which is a landmark on Slateford Road, was erected instead. The difficulties facing those who look after our architectural heritage are exemplified by this building, for which the present congregation of the church (which had an average monthly income of £3,582 in 2003) has a report suggesting that up to £1.7 million worth of restoration work is required, primarily to the tower. £500,000 was promised in August 2002 from Historic Scotland and an application for £800,000 was made for Lottery funding.

Construction commenced in January 1881 and the building was officially opened at 3.00 p.m. on Wednesday 28 November 1883. It attracted much attention in the industry press, appearing in the *British Architect* of 4 November 1881 and 28 December 1883, the *Building News* of 7 December 1883 and 18 July 1890, and the *Builder* of 29 December 1883. John Keppie added an organ case in 1894/95, purchased from Messrs Brindey and Foster at a cost of £964.

The Rev. James MacGregor of St Cuthbert's, who conducted the official opening service, was asked to recommend the new minister. His reply was: 'There is only ae minister in the Church of Scotland fit to fill the charge, and that is George Wilson o' Cramond'. Wilson was from humble beginnings, having become a millwright after leaving school. When he moved to Edinburgh he became involved in the Temperance and Anti-Popery Crusade and decided to join the ministry. It is not clear why these two issues were linked.

Bridge of Allan and Holy Trinity Church, 1895 and 1904

In 1884, soon after it was opened, St Michael's was the venue for the wedding of John Honeyman and Sarah Anne Horne (known as Anne). George Wilson conducted the ceremony. The period when Honeyman was designing wonderful churches like St Michael's and Westbourne was one of personal trauma. His second wife Falconer died of tuberculosis in 1881 after the couple had spent twelve very happy years together in Skelmorlie. Their two sons also contracted the disease and died.

Minewood, Bridge of Allan, was Honeyman's retirement home. Robert Louis Stevenson had been a previous occupant.

The address on the marriage certificate of 1884 is 7 Blythswood Square, Glasgow. Both John and Anne were noted at this abode, suggesting that they had been living together before the wedding. John was 52 and Anne was a 39-year-old spinster, born into a more humble farming background at Soulbury, Buckinghamshire. One might imagine the social repercussions that Honeyman would have put up with for personal solace and happiness. Family certainly stood by him, brothers Michael and Patrick being the witnesses at the wedding.

After they were married, the Honeymans moved from Glasgow to rent a house called Melburn at Bridge of Allan. They then moved to Mine Cottage later that year, before settling at Minewood in 1886. Bridge of Allan was a Victorian spa town, and as at Skelmorlie, Honeyman lived beside a hydropathic institute.

The *Stirlingshire Directory* for 1886 states:

It is chiefly to its mineral wells that Bridge of Allan owes its principal claims to attention. These are situated on the Airthrey Estate, the property of Lord Abercromby, and within a few minutes' walk of the village. They are highly celebrated for their medicinal virtues, externally and internally, and have proved of great benefit to numerous invalids. There are convenient baths, and the hotels are admirably suited for the reception of families and other visitors; while the walks around are beneficial auxiliaries in improving the health of the invalids. Among the business establishments, besides the inns, are large bleaching and dye works.

The works referred to were Keirfield beside the Allan Water, run by the Pullar family. Laurence Pullar lived in Bridge of Allan. Honeyman must have become acquainted with him, for he was asked to design workers' houses at the Tulloch Works, Perth, a few years later. The Pullars' son Frederick came to a tragic end on Airthrey Loch in February 1901, trying to rescue a fellow skater, Miss Kate Rutherford, who fell through the ice. Fred was a talented inventor who had been developing electric motors at the time of his death. He had also invented the Pullar sounding machine for measuring the depths of freshwater lochs. With Sir John Murray, he had been surveying the depths, temperatures, volumes of water, pondweed, and the nature of the soils of Loch Katrine, Loch Achray, Loch Ard and Loch Leven for the benefit of fishermen. Had he lived, the family's involvement in the dyeing and dry cleaning business which still retains their name, might have extended beyond the First World War.

Minewood's location close to the hydropathic institute meant that it had previously been rented by other visitors to the town. One of the regulars was the family of Robert Louis Stevenson. One wonders if Honeyman realised that the initials 'MIS' on a window were those of Robert's mother, Margaret Isobella Stevenson, scratched onto the glass with her diamond ring by her nine-year-old son in 1860. The pane of glass is still retained within the modern window today. The woods, rivers and caves (Minewood got its name because old copper mines were in the hill behind the house) around Bridge of Allan in which he played on holiday were believed to have been an inspiration to Stevenson in his later life as an author.

John and Anne's only son, Herbert Lewis, was born in Bridge of Allan on 12 November 1885, just months after the death of John's second son, William. (By contrast Herbert's obituary in *Archaeologia Aeliana* said he was born at 24 Newton Place in Glasgow, and if so this indicates that his father still had a residence there in 1885.) He may have been named after Herbert MacNair, William's lifelong friend from the age of four at Skelmorlie. In a gable of Minewood Cottage, Honeyman had a stone plaque inserted with the initials J.H. and A.H., and below this the Latin inscription *horas non numero nisi serenas*, which roughly translates as, 'Let there not be many hours without tranquillity'.

The family joined Holy Trinity Church in Keir Street, Bridge of Allan, Honeyman and Charles Rennie Mackintosh carrying out additions and alterations to it in 1895 and 1904. The first involved the church hall and church officer's house extension, and these were formally opened on 27 April 1895 by the Very Rev. Dr J. Marshall Lang of the Barony Parish in Glasgow, ex-moderator of the General Assembly of the Church of Scotland. That day an article on the building appeared in the *Bridge of Allan Reporter* describing 'plans prepared by the eminent architects, Messrs Honeyman and Keppie, whose names are sufficient guarantee of the excellence and good taste of all of the arrangements and details of the building, and of the workmanship'. The drawings submitted to the Dean of Guild for approval noted that 'Honeyman Patent Ventilators' were to be used in the roof. The congregation noted that these, 'afforded plenty of fresh air, with a total immunity of draught'.

By 1901, John Honeyman was chairman of the trustees of the church, and probably felt that he could not personally profit from the donation of £800 from two ladies of the

Although interesting in themselves, these Mackintosh chancel furnishings at Holy Trinity Church, Bridge of Allan, are a slightly incongruous insertion within the otherwise traditional church.

congregation in 1903 'towards improving and modernising the church organ'. He therefore brought in Charles Rennie Mackintosh to design the new chancel furnishings. (Honeyman might have gained indirectly since Mackintosh could have used the £20 fee to help buy out Honeyman's share of the business in the years from 1902 to 1904.) Mackintosh designed the pulpit, communion table, organ screen and chancel rail. A photograph from 1923 shows that choir pews had also been supplied, but they have since gone. The organ screen may also have included three chairs for the three canopies.

A Bridge of Allan history credits the design of the United Presbyterian Church (later Trinity UF Church) at the corner of Well Road and Henderson Street to Honeyman and Mackintosh. It was, however, designed by the architects Malcolm Stark and Rowntree, Glasgow, in 1895. It was demolished in 1948, although doors and some glass were used in a refurbishment of the Western Arms Hotel, and a coloured glass window commemorating the Rev. James Muir's ministry was relocated to Holy Trinity Church, where it still remains today. The mistake about Honeyman's involvement could have arisen because a George Honeyman had been involved in the building of the new church.

Although Honeyman later rented a house at 6 Ailsa Drive, Langside, Glasgow, the move to Bridge of Allan probably weakened his links with Glasgow society. It perhaps explains why he did not attend the inauguration of Elder Park in Govan on 27 June 1885. He had designed this for Isabella Elder in memory of her husband John, founder of Fairfield's Shipyard. Various pillars of society were present, and perhaps Honeyman did not feel comfortable attending the event with his younger, farmer's daughter wife, who was at that time pregnant.

Loretto Chapel, 1893

The memory of the death of his two sons was still fairly recent when Honeyman was invited to design a chapel at their old school, Loretto. A committee had been formed in February 1891 to raise funds 'to build a really working chapel at an estimated cost of about £3,000', to replace the iron chapel of 1876. The whip-round of old boys was so successful that construction work started in June of that year. The inaugural service in the 300-seat chapel was held on 31 March 1893.

It was constructed of Hailes stone with oak panelling up to window level, and plain white wood above. An account of 1911 stated that: 'The design is not elaborate – some people think it too severe – but the chapel has a simple dignity, and is not without beauty.' Various internal embellishments were later carried out, including the installation by R.S. Lorimer (later Sir Robert) in 1902 of oak seating to commemorate former pupils killed in the Boer War. Only four bays of the original chapel remain following Sir Robert Matthew Johnston-Marshall's enlargement of the building in 1962.

Apart from choir practice, the chapel was only used on Sundays. The headmaster felt that he could not combine the spiritual and secular matters of a morning school assembly in the setting of the chapel. In the school hall, 'he could so happily bring the most trivial and mundane matters into the realm of the gospel'. Perhaps he just did not wish to drag himself and the boys outside on cold, wet winter days to and from the far end of the grounds, past the stables, where the chapel was located.

Loretto School Chapel (2)

Honeyman's two sons by his second marriage studied at Loretto School,
and their father later returned to design the chapel.

Rockingham, Kilcreggan.

CHAPTER 12

Helensburgh
and the Rosneath Peninsula

After Skelmorlie and Wemyss Bay, Helensburgh contains the largest cluster of projects by Honeyman. Like many Glasgow people, John Honeyman senior purchased a house in the area to which he could retire.

Helensburgh was a new town, lying in the Parish of Rhu (spelled Row until 1927). In 1776 Sir James Colquhoun set out to create a community of bonnet makers, linen and woollen weavers, and placed an advert in the *Glasgow Journal* offering land for this purpose. He called the town after his wife Helen. Unlike the new towns of the twentieth century, it took some time to develop. The grid pattern layout of 1777, by Charles Ross, was extended by Peter Fleming in 1803, the year after Helensburgh attained burgh status. Henry Bell started the first seagoing steamship service in the world from Helensburgh in 1812. A gas supply was introduced in 1846, the railway reached it in 1858, and a proper water supply was obtained in 1868 with the opening of the Mains Hill Reservoir.

The Rosneath Peninsula, stretching out to the west of Helensburgh between the Gare Loch and Loch Long could be reached by boat from Helensburgh, Greenock or the Cowal Peninsula. Today villages like Cove seem somewhat remote and are bypassed by those heading by car from Glasgow to Inveraray or Oban, but the fleet of small craft in the nineteenth century allowed easy access to the many villages that grew up here and along the Firth of Clyde. There is something invigorating about the short, relaxing, and often bracing sail from lowland Renfrewshire to highland Argyll to escape the cares of urban life.

Knockderry Castle, 1856, 1869 and c.1883

The commanding position that this castle enjoys, overlooking the entry to Loch Long, lends credence to the legend that the dungeons of an ancient Viking fort lie below the Victorian building. The castle which stood on the site at the beginning of the nineteenth century was reputed to have been the Knockdunder Castle in Sir Walter Scott's novel *Heart of Midlothian*, and was commemorated in the stained glass windows in the dining room of the current building. Another window by Sir James Guthrie from 1887 depicts the Battle of Largs where the Scots defeated the Vikings.

It is difficult to believe that this grand mansion was one of Honeyman's first designs, and there has been debate as to whether Alexander 'Greek' Thomson had a part in it. Honeyman's job books are clear that in 1855/56 he was working for John Campbell, and the records of the time have the latter living at Knockderry Castle. The Campbells were the feudal landlords of the area, but after this time Honeyman's clients for grand houses were the 'nouveau riche' industrialists rather than the landed gentry.

Knockderry Castle, Cove.

The original Scots baronial building constructed for John Campbell now forms the west wing. Honeyman extended Knockderry for Glasgow merchant William Miller (see chapter 6) in 1869/70, with further alterations being made around 1883. The carpet manufacturer John S. Templeton was the next occupant of the house, but he turned to William Leiper in 1896 to double the size of the building and add a grand banqueting hall with minstrels' gallery. Templeton had a hydraulic-powered lift installed in the east tower, which was still in operation when the house was put up for sale in September 1964, as was the original boiler in the basement dungeon. Above the new main entrance was carved the inscription 'As built on rock so be our lives'.

Andrew Carnegie visited on 15 May 1901, when he wrote from Knockderry to the Lord Provost of Glasgow offering financial support to the libraries in the city. In 1905 John Keppie, as president of the Glasgow Institute of Architects, judged the design competition for the new Mitchell Library (see chapter 17), built with the help of £26,000 received from Carnegie, the total project cost being £52,850.

When I visited Knockderry in 2000 it was closed, with a sign at the gate warning potential trespassers to keep out.

Little houses and big houses

With his father and at least one of his sisters living there, the Helensburgh area was a 'home from home' for Honeyman. As a young architect he would be asked for favours and would have been happy to gather experience and cash from small domestic projects. In the 1850s and early 1860s he designed the Free Church manse in Cardross (now a house called Bowmore), a house for Patrick Stead in Helensburgh (thought to be Lansdowne in Victoria Road, latterly a boarding house for pupils of Lomond School), a house in Cove for Henry Young (untraced), Letrault, Rhu, for Hugh Baird (possibly the brewer), Lochside, Garelochhead, for a Mrs McPherson, Rockingham, Rosneath Road, Cove, for a Dr Gossling, and lodges at numbers 5 and 15 King's

A Honeyman-designed house at King's Crescent, Helensburgh.

Crescent, Helensburgh. Although all of these commissions were small, involving houses which cost as little as £250, they led to bigger prizes. One of the lodges was for Robert Henderson of P. Henderson and Co., merchant ship and insurance brokers. His business partner, James Galbraith, commissioned Towerville, a larger villa.

Honeyman also started working for local benefactor Richard Kidson, designing Helensburgh Free Church Manse in 1859 (now a nursery school). A few years later the same source gave him his first major ecclesiastical project in the area, Park Free Church. His client's relatives, William and Charles Kidson, commissioned new houses in 1867 and 1869. Ferniegair House, Rhu Road Lower, Helensburgh, cost £7,500 and a conservatory and stables at Glenoran, Rhu, cost £6,314. Both buildings have been lost.

In 1866, £1,767 worth of alterations were carried out to Laggary House, Pier Road, Rhu, which is the second-oldest remaining house in the village, dating from around 1830. Alterations were also made to Kilarden, Rosneath, in 1870 for writer W.C. Maughan, author of *The Annals of Garelochside* and *Rosneath Past and Present*. His family still lived in the house at the end of the twentieth century. In 1869, Honeyman designed an extension to his father's house, Park Cottage at 1 King Street, at a cost of £1,642. It was demolished in the early 1970s and two modern bungalows have taken its place.

Park Free Church, 1863

Honeyman secured the commission for this church in Helensburgh from the town's East Free Church congregation in 1862. When in Helensburgh, he regarded this as his 'home' church as his sister Christina was a member. Richard Kidson, a church elder, purchased the site and offered to match pound for pound any money raised by the rest of the congregation and their supporters. Sir John Colquhoun reduced the feu duty from £14 to £1, a gesture that was equivalent to a donation of £300.

The foundation stone was laid on 16 July 1862 and the church was opened on 14 June 1863, the collection that day raising £598 towards the cost. It is believed Honeyman thought that this was one of his best-designed churches. He described it as in the style of the Gothic architecture that prevailed during the first half of the thirteenth century. Internally, it is split into three aisles carried on columns of polished Peterhead granite. It accommodated 830 people on the basis that 20 inches (50 centimetres) of space be allowed for each person, and cost £5,600.

In 1888, William Leiper, then the Helensburgh architect in residence and much in demand, remodelled the interior, partitioning the chancel off from the main part of the church and forming a vestry and session room with halls above. The church was only closed for six weeks for the work to take place. Following the union of the United Presbyterian and the United Free churches in 1900, the church became known as Park Free Church.

Park Free Church, Helensburgh.

Helensburgh Town Buildings, 1878

Richard Kidson was Provost of Helensburgh on two occasions, and it is possible that Honeyman received this commission through him. Situated at the corner of East Princes Street and Sinclair Street, Honeyman's building replaced a theatre that had been converted for use as the civic building. Scots baronial was the style thought appropriate, and the foundation stone was laid on 15 August 1878. The sculpted head of Henry Bell was used as the keystone on the arched entrance. As well as building the *Comet*,

The Town Buildings, Helensburgh.

Bell had been elected the first provost of the town, serving from 1807 to 1811. A later addition is a plaque to commemorate local man John Logie Baird, who invented a system of transmission of pictures by radio waves, later known as television.

A 1906 extension along Sinclair Street by local architect A.N. Paterson was built to accommodate the fire station and police office. Engraved on the wall beside the latter are two sets of handcuffs, and there is a stone effigy of a cat, which is said to have caught Paterson's attention and affection when it frequented the building site during construction.

Shandon House, 1883

Honeyman added a billiard hall to this 1849 house for A.C. Henderson JP who lived in the building from 1883 until around 1899. It must have been a grand billiard hall, or more likely a number of alterations took place to suit Henderson when he moved in, since the cost was £1,350.

The building became a boys' preparatory school before being purchased in the

Having added a billiard hall to Shandon House in the 1880s, the Keppie practice returned in 1990 to assess the feasibility of converting it for MOD use for the adjacent Faslane submarine base.

1920s by Nelson Mitchell, who went on to live in the house for 40 years. From 1965 to 1986 it was St Andrew's List D School, with the Archdiocese of Glasgow selling it to Barratt the builder in 1989, who in turn sold it to the MOD in 1990. Shandon House escaped the same fate as West Shandon, an 1852 J.T. Rochead building and home to Robert Napier, which was demolished in the 1950s to make way for the Faslane submarine base. However, in 1990 SBT Keppie carried out a feasibility study for Shandon House to be converted as the base of the Commachio Company, a select group charged with the security of Britain's nuclear submarines. If I tell you more I will be infringing the Official Secrets Act.

Princes Street Church, 1884

This Congregational Church in West Princes Street occupies the site of the town's first place of worship, the Tabernacle. Honeyman extended what had originally been called the Independent Church (built in 1850), which then became the church hall. Richard Kidson's daughter was a member, and she channelled family money into church affairs. The new church was necessarily bigger than its replacement and perhaps lacks its charm. Internally, Honeyman used Peterhead granite columns between the nave and the aisles.

The Dean of Guild approval drawings were signed on behalf of the Honeyman practice by architect D. McNaughtan (this is probably Duncan McNaughtan, 1845–1912). With the ongoing workload, Honeyman must have had two assistants working for him, since Peter McGregor Chalmers was also in the 140 Bath Street studio at the time. However, while Chalmers arrived as an apprentice, McNaughtan was a very capable architect, having designed the French Renaissance Maryhill Burgh Hall in his own right from 1876 to 1878. He later had a successful practice with his son Alan from the mid-1890s to around 1908. By coincidence, he extended Dumbarton Sheriff Courthouse from 1895 to 1900, on which Keppie Design started a programme of redevelopment works in 2002.

Camas Eskan, 1886, 1891 and 1896

This house sits a few miles east of Helensburgh, opposite Craigendoran Pier, which was closed in 1972. The original building dated from 1648 but was remodelled by David Hamilton in 1840. Honeyman carried out alterations for William Middleton Campbell in 1886, and the practice was back to make more changes during the 1890s. Honeyman and Keppie's assistant at the time, Donald Stoddart, left to join A.N. Paterson (see the Town Buildings extension above) in 1900, and in 1915 he made further alterations. After brief spells as a sanatorium and a geriatric hospital, it was converted to luxury flats in the 1970s.

Craigrownie Church, 1889; Rhu Parish Church, 1892

The original 1852 Craigrownie Church at Cove, halfway up the hill overlooking the Clyde estuary, was extended to provide more accommodation. A lithograph of the original building, which hangs in the church vestry, illustrates how much was added. In 1893 the practice was invited back to prepare a colour scheme for the interior, but it did not meet with approval: 'the scheme of painting appears more suited to a place of amusement than for a church'. The committee rejected it and asked the local painter to put the decor back to the way it was in 1887 before the works began. It is possible that an assistant in the office had gone over the top with his ideas and upset the rather conservative congregation. Honeyman would not have been happy, and might have stormed back to the office to enquire: 'Who's to blame – was that you MacNair? Mackintosh? McGibbon? Mitchell?'

In Rhu, Honeyman was once again extending a church, lengthening it without disturbing William Spence's magnificent 1851 octagonal tower at the front. The Gothic windows in the transepts and the nave are probably by Honeyman, who definitely designed the carved, timber pulpit. The church had to close for several months while the works were carried out, and it reopened in June 1892. There is a black marble memorial in the church to one of Honeyman's earliest clients, Robert Napier, who had erected a tomb to Henry Bell in the graveyard and donated the church's bell in 1851.

Helensburgh Conservative Club, 1894

Described at the time as 'one of the most artistic in Scotland', the Helensburgh and Gareloch Conservative Club at 40 Sinclair Street had two shops at ground level to generate revenue, with a public hall, reading and smoking rooms, caretaker's flat, and

Access to the upper level clubrooms of the Conservative Club, Helensburgh, was to the left of the Paterson and Christie shopfronts.

top-lit billiard hall and committee rooms above. The street elevation is interesting because it presents a mixture of features, partly a result of John Keppie trying to keep his client happy with Prince of Wales feather patterns in leaded-glass windows along with a statue of St Andrew (the crest of the club), and Charles Rennie Mackintosh having fun with stylised trees, foliage and other sensual shapes carved in the red sandstone. It was officially opened in December 1895, and because of the Mackintosh contribution was category 'A' listed in March 1992.

Hill House, Helensburgh, 1904

John Honeyman was still an active member of the Glasgow Archaeological Society when Walter Blackie joined it on 19 December 1901. The two may even have shared the compartment of a train together after an evening at a society meeting in Glasgow, Honeyman living in Bridge of Allan and Blackie in Dunblane, the next stop. A partner in Honeyman's brother's law firm, William George Black, had married into the Blackie family in 1899. However, it was Talwin Morris who recommended Mackintosh to Blackie in 1902 for the design of his new house in Helensburgh. Morris had been appointed art director at the Blackie publishing company in 1890, and was in Mackintosh's artistic circle. He and his wife Alice leased Dunglass Castle at Bowling. When Morris moved out in 1899, Dunglass was occupied by the Macdonald family, whose two daughters, Margaret and Frances, married Charles Rennie Mackintosh and Herbert MacNair respectively. A number of paintings and pieces of furniture and furnishings were designed at or for Dunglass. In 1979, two Mackintosh enthusiasts found five Mackintosh-decorated panels reused as roofing materials on the turreted dovecote.

It transpired that Walter Blackie had been a Mackintosh fan without realising it. He later wrote:

> The new school of art was nearing completion. I had watched with interest its growth into the imposing structure that emerged, vaguely wondering who was architect, when Morris named Mackintosh and recommended him as architect for my projected villa house. I was at first taken aback, thinking so distinguished a performer would be too big a man for me. Morris, however, persisted in his recommendation and undertook to get Mackintosh to call upon me. He called the next day. When he entered my room I was astonished at the youthfulness of the distinguished architect.

They formed a productive client-architect relationship, leading to completion of the villa in March 1904.

Walter Blackie and his family lived in the house for fifty years, and Campbell Lawson and his wife for twenty years thereafter, until the Royal Incorporation of Architects in Scotland took it over in 1972. Ten years later it was transferred to the National Trust for Scotland, which now manages it so that visitors can enjoy today the rich mixture of interiors, furniture, furnishings and exteriors. Mackintosh even made his only major attempt at garden design there, which is surprising, given his father's passion for horticulture and his own fascination with flowers.

Hill House, Helensburgh, before the garden had matured.

The hall of Windyhill, Kilmacolm, a Mackintosh building owned by the author's former boss at Scott Brownrigg and Turner, Jim Fisher.

CHAPTER 13

The Mackintosh years to 1907

The year 1889 was one of the most significant in the history of the practice. With John Keppie joining in December 1888, it was the year when it went from being the vehicle of a single practitioner to that of a partnership, and with the introduction of a new assistant, Charles Rennie Mackintosh, there would be three strong influences in the direction of the practice by 1895.

In 1889 John Honeyman was 58 years old and he wanted to ensure the continuation of the practice he had founded. His friends and contacts were still offering him work and he needed the help of younger men to service it. He was bored with the mundane tasks of running an office, having experienced the ups and downs of booms and recessions over the previous 30 years. In 1888 he had taken on 21-year-old Herbert MacNair, son of ex-neighbours of his in Skelmorlie, but young MacNair's real interest was painting, and he was unlikely to be more than an assistant. Besides, Honeyman wanted a partner with some experience and an ability to gain work. An architect friend, Campbell Douglas, came up with the solution. Douglas's partner Sellars had died and he was also choosing a new partner, favouring his assistant Alexander Morrison. This left no room for the career of John Keppie to develop. Keppie had been the favourite of Sellars. In both 1886 and 1887, he had won silver medals in the Royal Institute of British Architects' Tite Prize – for a classical church and a post office. When the Campbell Douglas and Sellars practice was concerned that it was being threatened by others with Paris-trained architects, it sent Keppie to the Atelier Pascal for eighteen months to learn the latest ideas in design.

The young John Keppie doesn't have the flamboyant artist's cravat of Charles Rennie Mackintosh, but sports a jaunty tie and buttonhole.

Sellars had won the design competition for the new Victoria Infirmary in Glasgow in 1882. Keppie helped him develop the project,

John Keppie won a silver medal in the Royal Institute of British Architects' Tite Prize for this design for a post office.

John Keppie assisted James Sellars on the design of the Victoria Infirmary, Glasgow, before he left the practice to join Honeyman.

140

although various delays meant that construction work did not start until 1888. He also worked with Sellars on buildings for Glasgow's first International Exhibition in Kelvingrove Park in 1888. The Moorish theme was probably the result of Keppie's studies in Paris.

John Keppie was born in Glasgow in 1862, the son of a tobacco importer with a home in the prosperous Hillhead area of the city, and one in Prestwick. He studied at Ayr Academy, the University of Glasgow, and the Glasgow School of Art. Keppie retained a keen interest in art throughout his life and enjoyed friendships with many of the 'Glasgow Boys'. A tour of northern Italy in 1886 with an artist friend led to sketches and watercolours of Lucca, Florence and Siena being published and exhibited through the Glasgow Architectural Association and the Glasgow Institute of Fine Arts.

On 29 November 1889, John Keppie attended the highlight of the Glasgow social calendar, the grand costume ball at the Art Club. He went as 'The Squire' with one of his sisters, probably Helen, dressed as 'Lady Betty'. Also there was his sweetheart Helen Law, but his hopes of a future with her were dashed when painter E.A. Walton, several years Keppie's senior, announced his engagement to her. Less than a month later, Keppie's father died, and he took on new responsibilities as he and his brother had to look after their mother and four sisters, especially his younger one, Jessie, to whom he was closest.

Keppie never married, although he continued to be attracted to eligible women. One of these was 'Glasgow Girl' Bessie MacNicol. In 1897, when Keppie was 35 and she 28, she had been painting a portrait of his friend, Edward Atkinson Hornel, at the latter's studio in Kirkcudbright. Writing to him, she told of Keppie's interest:

John Keppie (seated left) was a friend of E.A. Hornel (standing). This photograph was taken at Hornel's studio at Kirkcudbright, which Keppie designed and is today owned by the National Trust for Scotland. Hornel's sister Tizzie is on the right.

John Keppie came up to see me the day after I returned from Kirkcudbright, and was inviting me to go for a cycle run with him. I have got a new kind of cycling skirt, which is divided so far up, but is just like a walking skirt when I am standing. I put the Mater into fits when I was in the shop buying it, by dancing a hornpipe behind the woman's back. I am getting on splendidly and am quite a scorcher. I have not gone more than ten miles yet but can pass machines and people without running them down for certain.

'A Girl of the Sixties'
by Bessie MacNicol

It is easy to understand Keppie's attraction to this vivacious woman. However, that summer she suffered particularly badly from hay fever, and a few months later took ill with a liver complaint. She was treated with mercury, which sent her into fits of depression. If there had been any hint of romance with John Keppie it did not survive the illness. In 1899 she married another suitor, the physician and painter Alexander Frew, but died at the age of 34 while expecting her first child. Her gynaecologist husband could do nothing for her. Four years later Frew committed suicide. Bessie MacNicol's portrait of Hornel remains to this day above the fireplace in the dining room of Broughton House, Kirkcudbright. Keppie designed Hornel's studio and gallery in 1909, and he would have seen the portrait each New Year when he and Jessie Keppie visited Hornel and his unmarried sister, Tizzie. Until his dying days, Keppie treasured Bessie's painting *A Girl of the Sixties*, which reflected her old-fashioned romanticism and reminded him of her youthful talent, cut short. Keppie bequeathed the painting to Glasgow Museums and Art Galleries when he died.

In 1889 Jessie Keppie was completing her first year at the Glasgow School of Art. Ladies were day students at the school while men worked as apprentices during the day and obtained theory in the evenings. That year Jessie received a silver medal in a national competition for her design of a Persian carpet. On the same page of the school's annual report, Charles Rennie Mackintosh is detailed as obtaining a National Queen's Prize for a design for a Presbyterian church.

Mackintosh was one of the best of the crop of young architects to pass through the art school after Francis Newbery took charge of it in 1885. In the same set of tests – advanced local examinations in design ornament – Mackintosh received a first class prize and Jessie Keppie a second. This was the year Mackintosh also won the Alexander Thomson Scholarship.

Charles Rennie McIntosh (this spelling was used until he changed it around 1892; John Keppie also had relations who spelled the family name as 'Keppy') was born in 1868 in the Townhead district of Glasgow, living in a top floor tenement flat. His family were not living in poverty, but their lifestyle was far-removed from the privileged upbringing that John Keppie had received in Hillhead. When Charles was a child, his father, William, obtained promotion in the police force, and the family moved to the suburb of Dennistoun. Here Charles had a garden in which to draw and develop the love of nature that was to be his lifelong inspiration.

At Reid's Public School and Allan Glen's School he did not do well academically, and it has been suggested that he suffered from dyslexia. Allan Glen's was technically oriented, and Mackintosh probably learned perspective, solid geometry, woodwork and metalwork. With drawing his main interest, he decided at the age of sixteen that he would like to become an architect. This did not meet with approval from his father. He was a strict Presbyterian, a keen sportsman (captain of the Glasgow police tug-of-war team), and had risen through the ranks from inspector in 1865 to superintendent in 1889 because of his organisational skills.

Charles was very different – scholastically weak, and with a contracted sinew in his foot, not physically strong. His father probably thought he should learn a craft and start wage-earning work straight away. However, Charles persisted and was apprenticed to John Hutchison, based in St Vincent Street. He received no pay in his first year, but after five years he had the chance to earn £2 a month.

The new practice of John Honeyman and Keppie presented a great opportunity for him. He had long admired Sellars, and working with his chief assistant was the next best thing. The Honeyman practice had become somewhat stale prior to Keppie joining it, and there were more fashionable ones in Glasgow like John James Burnet's. However, at such a practice Mackintosh would have been unlikely to have been given much freedom to develop, design control being kept firmly in the hands of the partners.

The volume of work increased so much at John Honeyman and Keppie that in 1889 an extension had to be built at the rear of the offices at 140 Bath Street. Keppie had brought the Anderson's Medical College building from Sellars (now part of the University of Glasgow), and continued to gain occasional work from previous Campbell Douglas and Sellars' clients for several years. Examples include alterations and the installation of new lifts to the Bank of Scotland building in George Square built by his previous employers in 1874, and a dispensary for the Victoria Infirmary.

Charles Rennie Mackintosh.

Honeyman had started work on the Cardross Drill Hall, and two large industrial projects were underway – the Fairfield shipyard offices in Govan, and a hide, wool and tallow auction market at Greendyke Street, Gallowgate. A complete remodelling and large extension of an 1862 mansion called Dunloe at Wemyss Bay probably gave Keppie a chance to show his mettle to Honeyman.

A busy office that is full of new enthusiasm will, while welcoming a well-paid industrial project for financial security, seek more prestigious projects to demonstrate the talent in its ranks. Honeyman entered the competition for the Sydney Houses of Parliament.

Mackintosh was also keen to enter competitions, obtaining the Alexander Thomson Scholarship, which allowed him to tour Italy from March to July 1891.

To work on deadlines for competitions and possibly other projects, Keppie, Mackintosh and MacNair sometimes went to Keppie's house at Prestwick. At the weekend they were joined by a group of Jessie Keppie's friends from the art school – Agnes Raeburn, Katherine Cameron, Janet Aitken, and the two Macdonald sisters, Margaret and Frances. Keppie rented two bungalows at Dunure, about three miles north of Culzean. They referred to this as 'the Roaring Camp' and to themselves as 'the Immortals', contributing to a literary and artistic magazine edited by Lucy Raeburn, Agnes's sister.

As a group, the Immortals did not last long. Francis Newbery realised that

N°5.

ST VINCENT STREET ELEVATION

*Mackintosh's 1898 competition design for the National Bank
at the corner of Buchanan Street and St Vincent Street was unsuccessful.*

Mackintosh, MacNair and the two Macdonald sisters had compatible ideas, and by about 1895 they had become known as 'The Four'. This also led to the end of the romance that Mackintosh had with Jessie Keppie, a relationship which at one point was regarded as an engagement. 'Toshie' and Jessie were the same age. Margaret Macdonald was three years older, and the maturity and radical nature of her work may have been an attraction. In 1895 or 1896 Mackintosh made a silver jewel box for Jessie, although the motive for this may never be known. Either his romantic attachment to her lasted longer than thought, or it was a token of affection for Jessie after she had accepted the inevitable – that his relationship with her friend was to be a lasting one.

Mackintosh made this jewel casket for Jessie Keppie.

The Immortals at Dunure. Jessie and John Keppie are on the right, Margaret Macdonald to the far left, and Frances Macdonald at the back. MacNair and Mackintosh are at the front.

Harvest Moon was gifted to John Keppie by Mackintosh.

This photograph of the Honeyman and Keppie staff was taken in 1889 or 1890, and the line-up is believed to show (left to right) David Forbes Smith, Alexander McGibbon, Herbert MacNair, Charles Rennie Mackintosh and Henry Mitchell.

A portrait of Alexander McGibbon painted after he became Professor of Architecture at the Glasgow School of Art.

G.A. Paterson's intricate sketch of a door from the Certosa di Pavia illustrates how Honeyman and Keppie seemed to be able to employ the best draftsmen in town.

EXTERIOR PERSPECTIVE.
DESIGN FOR A ROYAL MAUSOLEUM.—BY MR. JAS. B. FULTON.

Tite Prize, R.I.B.A., 1899

Reprinted from "THE BUILDER," FEBRUARY 4, 1899.

This James B. Fulton sketch of a mausoleum won the RIBA Tite Prize in 1899.

The time spent at his house in Prestwick also allowed Keppie to assess the abilities of Mackintosh and MacNair. The latter had limitations and his heart was not in architecture. Being of independent means, he could afford to leave John Honeyman and Keppie in 1895 to set up his own practice, designing furniture and painting. But limited success with this led to a move to Liverpool in 1898, where he became Instructor in Design at the School of Architecture and Applied Art. He made a brief return to Glasgow the following year to marry Frances Macdonald.

While MacNair is well-known today, largely because of his membership of 'The Four', there were other very talented assistants in the Honeyman and Keppie office in the 1890s. When Francis Newbery took up his post in 1885, John Keppie and Alexander McGibbon were receiving instruction in construction under the auspices of the Glasgow Architectural Association. Newbery persuaded the whole class to transfer to the School of Art. From 1882 to about 1886 McGibbon became a draughtsman in John Honeyman's office, and he was there again when the famous group portrait was taken. By this time he had started teaching at the art school. McGibbon was a skilled draughtsman and became a freelance perspective artist, hiring his skills to several practices. He preferred this to designing buildings, a task for which he gained a reputation for being chronically indecisive in not knowing which design option to work up. Like today, architects wanted presentation drawings prepared for a competition at the last minute, and he often followed an evening's tutoring at the art school with perspective drawing from 10.00 p.m. to three or four in the morning. He later became the first Professor of Architecture at the School of Art, retiring at the age limit of 65. A much-loved character, he was described by those who knew him as 'a big chap with short legs so that his coat hems were only just above his toe-caps'.

While the practice was designing the *Glasgow Herald* Building, the paper's editor, Charles Russell, possibly sought a favour from John Keppie by asking him to give an apprenticeship to Donald McKay Stoddart, son of Russell's predecessor as editor, James Hastie Stoddart. This he did, Donald Stoddart training with Honeyman and Keppie from 1893 to 1896 before travelling in France and Italy and returning as an architect on £60 per annum in 1899. In 1900 he left to join John Keppie's old boss Campbell Douglas.

Architectural historian David Walker described James Black Fulton as 'one of the greatest architectural draughtsmen of all time'. Fulton worked at John Honeyman and Keppie in the mid-1890s, before deciding to try his luck in London. Among many awards, he won the Tite Prize in 1899, the Soane Medallion in 1902, and the RIBA silver medal in 1900. A successful career was ended by the First World War, which badly affected his health. He declined the offer of a commission and enlisted as a private soldier, suffering extreme hardships in the trenches. In 1920 he returned to Glasgow to become Professor of Architectural Design at the Glasgow School of Art, but took ill and died on 11 April 1922. He must have had a son, since there is a Dean of Guild application made by the practice in 1920 for the erection of a barrel store for James Fulton junior at Drygate.

Mackintosh stayed with John Honeyman and Keppie to develop his career. John Keppie quickly realised his talents and allowed him more and more participation in projects. During 1892 and 1893 he worked with Keppie on the Canal Boatmen's Institute at Port Dundas, Glasgow, the Glasgow Art Club interiors and the Conservative Club, Helensburgh. By the time work on the *Glasgow Herald* Building started in 1893, Mackintosh was leading sections of the design, and in 1894 he made a contribution to the design of the anatomical department at Queen Margaret College (now part of the BBC Scotland Headquarters).

Mackintosh also worked with Honeyman during this period. The latter was taking advantage of the burden lifted by his new partner to concentrate on his ecclesiastical and conservation interests. MacNair recalled spending happy days with Mackintosh and Honeyman in 1891 as they sketched and surveyed Iona Cathedral, although restoration work did not take place until 1902. Mackintosh may also have helped with refurbishment works in Glasgow Cathedral in 1890 and 1891, and possibly assisted Honeyman later with his contribution to *The Book of Glasgow Cathedral*, published in 1898. Mackintosh had spent the first ten years of his life just around the corner from the Martyrs' School site and a few hundred yards from the cathedral. Honeyman also worked on a new parish church in Skelmorlie from 1893 to 1895, and the lamp standard outside is attributed to Mackintosh, being similar to the one he illustrated in a perspective of the Martyrs' School in 1896.

In 1892, Mackintosh's annual salary rose from £40 to £88, and by 1894 it was £144. From then until the turn of the century, partners' takings for both Honeyman and Keppie were roughly equal. It is likely that they brought in the work, were briefed by clients, and that Mackintosh as principal assistant architect was involved in some way on most projects. A more junior architect and two apprentices were also part of the team.

On some projects Mackintosh had freedom to do most of what he wanted – phase one of the art school, Garscube Road Free Church (now Queen's Cross Church), Windyhill in Kilmacolm, Westbourne Free Church Mission (now Ruchill Church hall), and the *Daily Record* Building. In others he is known to have contributed to the design to some extent – an inn at Lennoxtown (demolished), alterations to St Paul's Church Mission Hall, Shuttle Street/College Lane (demolished 1979), Manchester House, Sauchiehall Street (demolished 1973), Redlands in Bridge of Weir, Biggar Manse, 233 St Vincent Street (the

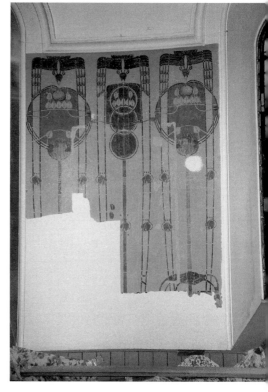

Originally built as the Garscube Road Free Church, Queen's Cross Church is now the home of the Charles Rennie Mackintosh Society.

A Mackintosh mural at St Serf's Church, Dysart that had been painted over and was only rediscovered in 2004.

Mackintosh roof trusses have survived various subsequent alteration works), Alton Dyke in Kilmacolm (much altered since), Westdee in Queen's Place, Glasgow (illustrated in the German magazine *Dekorative Kunst*), St Serf's Church in Dysart (where a Mackintosh mural was rediscovered in 2004), and Auchenbothie Lodge in Kilmacolm.

Other projects he may have assisted on were Cowden Castle, Dollar (demolished 1952), Little Dovehill School extension (demolished), Saracen Tool Works, and the restorations of St Michael's Church, Linlithgow, and Brechin Cathedral (along with a house in Brechin called The Mary Acre in 1902, which displays hints of his influence). Other projects in the office during this period included the Bellahouston Dispensary, a factory for the British and Foreign Aerated Water Company, St David's Church hall in Kirkintilloch (now the Indian Cottage restaurant), an extension to St Helen's Engineering Works (demolished), a house in Barrhead (untraced), alterations to 324 Gallowgate (untraced), alterations to Belhaven United Presbyterian Church (a Sellars' building which since 1954 has been the Greek Orthodox Cathedral of St Luke), alterations to Gourock Parish Church (now Old Gourock Church), alterations to the West of Scotland Cabinet and Chair Works in Beith (untraced), an extension to 244 St Vincent Street, extensions to houses at Moncktonmill and Ayton House in Kelvinside (both untraced), and workmen's cottages in Tulloch, Perth.

Researchers today have a handicap since the late Frank Worsdall borrowed a number of old practice drawings from the City of Glasgow District Council's archives and some were lost when his house went on fire. Whoever was responsible for the design of these buildings – Honeyman, Keppie, Mackintosh, or a combination – the office was very busy.

Having designed the mission hall for Westbourne Free Church in 1899 (Ruchill Church hall), Mackintosh might have expected to receive the commission for the permanent church, but perhaps he was too busy finishing the art school and working on Windyhill to keep the Westbourne client happy. Clients require architects to be in charge of the design and ensure that the cost and programme are not exceeded. If a client feels that the architect is not spending enough time with them – and this meant face to face contact in the days before telephones were widespread – they will lose confidence and choose another practice the next time. Another theory is that Mackintosh was insensitive to the symbolism which his Free Church clients would interpret from some of his architectural detailing. It is surprising that he was allowed to incorporate features in Queen's Cross Church which reflect pre-Reformation or Anglican thought in church design, but which Mackintosh would merely have regarded as artistically appropriate to his composition.

In 1900 Mackintosh married Margaret Macdonald in Dumbarton. The Macdonald family had moved to Dunglass Castle on the north shore of the Clyde in 1890, the previous tenant being Talwin Morris. The newly married couple rented a house in Mains Street in the centre of Glasgow and spent much of the early part of 1900 designing its interiors. Margaret had a private income of £250 to £300 per year to contribute to its costs. Mains Street is now Blythswood Street, and the 1992 office conversion on the corner of Bath Street by SBT Keppie is called Mackintosh House. It contains reproductions of many Mackintosh and Macdonald features.

With Honeyman starting to reduce his workload in 1901, Mackintosh began to assume the role of a partner, the practice being renamed John Honeyman, Keppie and Mackintosh in 1902. Having to gradually buy his share of the business from Honeyman, Mackintosh continued to earn a salary of £240 until 1903. In 1904 he drew £435 as a partner, Honeyman £615 and Keppie £648. Honeyman's final payment from outstanding projects was £94 in 1905.

Offices for J. Pullar and Sons at 202 Bath Street in 1902 may have been under the control of Mackintosh, and his first major projects as a partner were the Hill House in Helensburgh, the Willow Tea Rooms and Scotland Street School. The Annan family had taken photographs for Honeyman, Keppie and Mackintosh over the years, and in 1903 the practice was appointed to design the Annan showroom at 513 Sauchiehall Street (now the Royal Highland Fusiliers' Museum). While various sections of the building are attributed to Mackintosh (although the likes of the lift metalwork are executed somewhat crudely, perhaps due to budgetary constraints), the style of much of the rest suggests Keppie's hand. If this is so, it disproves the contention that they had lost the ability to collaborate by this time.

In 1903 Mackintosh designed a corner shop in the small village of Comrie for a friend. Perhaps such a modest building did not attract the Mackintosh scholars interested in the development of his architectural style, as the first reference to it is in an article by David Walker in 1968. There is no attention drawn to it today, which is surprising given the tourist potential of Mackintosh. The category 'A' listed building is not marked in any way, not even by a small plaque on the wall.

The years 1905 and 1906 were difficult ones for Mackintosh artistically, although they were financially rewarding as his £1,541 partnership share exceeded Keppie's £1,234. Keppie continued to be a pillar of society, being president of the Glasgow Institute of Architects in 1905/06 (he also held this position in 1919/20), and elected deacon of the Incorporation of Wrights in 1906. Mackintosh's remuneration probably reflected his role as prime working principal in the office. However, the practice saw a general downturn in work of the sort that would have interested him. The largest projects in the office in 1905 were two commercial developments on Sauchiehall Street for cabinetmaker James Simpson and for a Dr Walker. Mackintosh laid out the Wellesley Tea Rooms in the latter, but the fittings were designed by someone else. His extension to Paisley Library was in progress, but it was a very

This shop in the centre of Comrie is a simple but attractive example of Mackintosh design.

This building at 309–313 Sauchiehall Street was designed for cabinetmaker James Simpson.

EXPLOSIVES

NOBEL'S EXPLOSIVES
COMPANY, LIMITED,
GLASGOW

BLASTING EXPLOSIVES,
PERMITTED EXPLOSIVES
FOR COAL-GETTING

THE WORLD'S

TRADE MARK

Alfred *Nobel*

GLASGOW.

STANDARD

DETONATORS
ELECTRIC DETONATORS
SAFETY FUSE

CORDITE
MILITARY & SPORTING
AMMUNITION

NOBEL~GLASGOW

*Mackintosh's client for Auchenibert,
Killearn, was assistant general manager of
Nobel's Explosives Company in Glasgow.*

respectful classical addition to Honeyman's 1868 building. By that time he was also having difficulty realising his aspirations for Scotland Street School within public sector budgetary constraints. John Keppie proposed Mackintosh as a fellow of the Royal Institute of British Architects in 1906, paying him a glowing tribute for his work on the school. Keppie himself was busy on the design of McConnell's Building in Hope Street (today the Theatre Royal is opposite it), having just completed Barony Parish Church, Auchterarder.

Mackintosh's client at Auchenibert, Killearn, was Francis James Shand. He had joined Nobel's Explosives Company under its manager, Thomas Johnston, being assistant general manager from 1884 to 1909, when Johnston died and he took over. The company had originally been set up by Sir Charles Tennent (a friend of Isabella Elder) as an opportunity to develop Alfred Nobel's ideas about dynamite when he could not obtain backers in the City of London. A bleak spot was found for a factory at Ardeer, near Irvine, and it commenced production in 1873. It was founded as a limited liability company, unusual at this period, and with no ownership by a family, managers could develop their careers on their own merit. Francis Shand was a member of a rare species of the day, a professional manager. In deals done with other major companies, the world market for explosives was carved up with Europe for the Europeans, the British Empire for the British, the USA for Du Pont, and other areas by arrangement. At one point, the British government thought it was receiving competitive tenders from suppliers of cordite when, in fact, all of the companies were subsidiaries of Nobel's Explosives Company. The Anglo–German company had to split in two so that it could supply both sides in the First World War.

Mackintosh found it difficult to work with Shand, and it has been assumed that this led to him giving up the commission for another architect to complete it. However, Mackintosh had previously worked for a number of clients with whom he did not share a common design philosophy. All architects resign themselves to the fact that they will only encounter a small number of sympathetic clients in their working lives (like Newbery, Cranston and Blackie), and that much of their output will be the result of compromise. One can imagine, in the late 1890s, John Keppie pressing Mackintosh to confirm that he was mature enough to take on the responsibilities of partnership, balancing the good of the practice and its employees with his own personal artistic aspirations, ever mindful also that he would soon be married and perhaps have children to bring up. Mackintosh the pragmatist wrote to Shand in September 1905: 'If you

153

want a house in the Tudor or any other phase of English architecture, I can promise you my best services.'

Perhaps Mackintosh, when he was contemplating his appointment outside the pub at Killearn, realised that he was working for an explosives manufacturer, and that the countries where he had received artistic recognition were on opposite sides of the arms race. The big powers in Europe had formed into two camps. Germany's Otto von Bismarck made alliances with Austria–Hungary in 1879 and with Italy in 1882. To counter this, France signed a military convention with Russia in 1892, and, despite differences over colonial interests, agreed the Entente Cordiale with Britain in 1904. France's dispute with Germany over Morocco in 1905 raised tensions between the superpowers.

In 1898 and 1902 'The Four' and Talwin Morris received publicity in the Munich magazine *Dekorative Kunst* and Mackintosh designed a dining room for its editor, Hugo Bruchmann. In Austria, the Mackintoshes and MacNairs took works to the 8th Exhibition of the Vienna

The Mackintosh exhibit at the Turin Exhibition of 1902.

Secession in November 1900, and Mackintosh's design for a House for an Art Lover was well-received there in 1901. John Keppie, art lover himself, was an understanding boss, allowing Mackintosh time to pursue these interests and the first two Kate Cranston projects as personal commissions, where another employer might have deemed them a distraction to his proper day job. However, by the time of the Turin Exhibition in Italy in 1902, Mackintosh had the responsibilities of marriage and a business partnership. He had abandoned any dreams of moving to Vienna to develop his career, and by 1905/06, Josef Hoffman, his friend there, had discarded a radical approach to design and had entered a classical phase. Movements like art nouveau were transient cosmopolitan styles for bourgeois sophisticates and held little interest for the upper classes, whose members had the money to commission work, but who also inherited homes, furniture and conservative tastes. Charles and Margaret's exhibition of items at the Kunstachau in Vienna in 1909 was one last, isolated attempt to regain the success of 1900/01.

On 30 March 1906, Toshie and Margaret moved from their rented city-centre flat to the more upmarket West End and purchased 6 Florentine Terrace (later renamed Southpark Avenue) for the sum of £925. The furniture and fittings from Mains Street were largely reproduced in the new home, perhaps because of personal financial constraints, or perhaps because Mackintosh was questioning his artistic direction and did not have new ideas. Having lost assistant Thomas Taylor in 1904, Mackintosh had interviewed and employed Graham Henderson, and he produced a perspective drawing for Auchenibert. Mackintosh drew his own versions, strange drawings in heavy black ink, quite unlike anything he had produced before or after.

In 1906, in addition to Auchenibert, Mackintosh had been working on Abbey Close Church's organ case, pulpit and font (the Paisley church has since been demolished), alterations to the Argyle Street Tea Rooms (the Dutch Kitchen), and Cloak Ploughman's Cottage in Kilmacolm. They were not great challenges. Fortunately, on 1 February 1907, John Honeyman, Keppie and Mackintosh were appointed for phase two of the Glasgow School of Art, and Mackintosh was the partner in charge. Just as his artistic direction seemed lost with architectural fashion changing around him, he found a new focus for it. This was his last chance to shine, and he was brilliant.

*An early Mackintosh sketch for Auchenibert, Killearn,
showing how he grappled with designing a house in Tudor style.*

Alexander McGibbon's sketch of Iona Cathedral in the early 1890s prior to restoration work.

CHAPTER 14

The restoration of churches and cathedrals

Honeyman altered a number of churches as congregations asked him to add to and improve their buildings. He had always had an interest in antiquity, but from the 1880s onwards, and especially in the 1890s when he had two younger men to let him concentrate on his own interests, he devoted more of his time to church restoration.

Honeyman may have had a conflict of interest between his role from 1866 in the City Improvement Trust, under the payroll of John Carrick, the city architect, and his position as Glasgow correspondent of the Society for the Protection of Ancient Buildings, set up in 1877 by William Morris to protect valuable old buildings. When asked by the SPAB secretary Norman Marks to comment on the proposed demolition of the Tron, St Enoch's and St George's churches, he wrote on 23 March 1879 that the 'destruction will be no great loss', only the Tron steeple being worthy of retention. It remains in Trongate today bereft of its church. In making these comments, Honeyman was merely reinforcing Carrick's strategy for redevelopment of the area.

In 1883 he was presented with the task of relocating James Smith's Old Parish Church in Govan, taking it down stone by stone and rebuilding it on another site. When it opened again on 30 August 1885, it was called Elder Park Church, the present Govan Old Parish Church being designed by Sir R. Rowand Anderson and built between 1884 and 1888. While Honeyman would have learned much about an older church during the dismantling and reconstruction process, particular archaeological interest arose from the Celtic stones present in the grounds. In 1893, Honeyman was asked to report on how these could be preserved. There are 30 sculptured stones at Govan Old Parish Church today, including one that had been purloined by James Smith in 1826 to take pride of place in the middle of his garden in Jordanhill. His house was eventually demolished in 1961 to make way for Keppie Henderson's Jordanhill College. The borrowed stone, the Govan Cross, returned to Govan via the Glasgow Art Gallery in 1928.

The new doorway and round window were part of Honeyman's alterations to Kilfinan Parish Church.

Kilfinan Parish Church dates from the thirteenth century. It is a small building measuring 18.9 metres from east to west and 5.3 metres north to south. Sir Coll Lamont added a wing in 1633. Having been extensively rebuilt in 1759, John Honeyman carried out restoration work in 1881 and 1882. He added a new pulpit, vestry and boiler room, and a new doorway and round window to the east wall. At the beginning of the twenty-first century the church has been restored again to ensure it withstands the worst of the weather off Loch Fyne.

St Andrew's Parish Church, East Links Road, Gullane, was not a restoration project, rather a new-build one, although it was inspired by the now ruined Church of St Andrew. Its appearance suggests that it is much older, and it has been given a category 'A' listing by Historic Scotland. Honeyman was obviously using his knowledge of old churches in this work, which was completed in 1887, with an entrance porch added by the practice in 1927.

In 1886 Honeyman repaired and reseated Kilmacolm Parish Church, and in 1890 he restored the thirteenth-century chancel for use as a vestry, now known as the Murray Chapel.

Glasgow Cathedral, 1890/91

As early as 1854 Honeyman wrote a pamphlet entitled *The Age of Glasgow Cathedral and of the Effigy in the Crypt.* In December 1857 he had the audacity to challenge a speaker at a Glasgow Archaeological Society meeting about the age of parts of the cathedral. The meeting adjourned to the crypt to continue the debate. Eminent architect J.T. Rochead chaired the event and was much impressed by Honeyman's views. The minutes of a later meeting of the society recorded that Honeyman illustrated a talk 'with the aid of diagrams [showing] the most striking characteristics of the varieties of Gothic architecture which were practised during the twelfth and thirteenth centuries'.

Papers were presented to the Glasgow Archaeological Society by Honeyman on 17 March 1881 and 15 November 1888 comparing details on various cathedrals such as Canterbury, Durham and Dunfermline to prove the various stages of development from the twelfth century. These showed the influence that the first bishop Achaius had due to his previous residence in

A Honeyman and Keppie sketch of alteration works to Glasgow Cathedral.

Italy, but disproved the contention that there was a French influence in the fourteenth century. Honeyman's knowledge of European as well as British buildings must have been extensive.

This commitment to the subject led him to campaign for proper guardianship of historic monuments, citing the transfer of Dunblane Cathedral in the 1880s to a local interest group as a successful way of ensuring improvements and ongoing caretaking. He still argued for central government funding for nationally important antiquities. On Glasgow Cathedral he wrote:

> I am almost afraid to say anything more about the Cathedral, lest you should think that you have heard enough about it lately; but I must plead that, after all, the cathedral is by far the most important ancient building within our province.

It was difficult to draw public attention to the building as it was in an unfashionable part of town, the more modern business and residential areas being much further west. As James Hamilton Muir's *Glasgow in 1901* stated: 'It is so far from our midst and so seldom in our thoughts, that of the citizens many have never seen it, and most have never stepped to the echoes in its marvellous crypt.'

Charles Rennie Mackintosh did not need to be persuaded of the value of Glasgow Cathedral, as he came from this part of town and sketched the building. Honeyman complained to the Ministry of Works in Edinburgh that students had to obtain written permission from them in advance if they wished to sketch the interior, and this discouraged visitors. Mackintosh possibly helped Honeyman when he was finally appointed to carry out improvements in 1890/91, and when Honeyman contributed a chapter to *The Book of Glasgow Cathedral*, edited by G. Eyre Todd in 1898, some of the illustrations, although anonymous, may have been drawn by Mackintosh. The alterations were fairly minor in nature, the published illustration signed by John Honeyman and Keppie being titled, 'Proposed rearrangement of platform in choir of Glasgow Cathedral'. Honeyman retained an interest in the cathedral to his dying days, his last paper on the subject being published in 1907.

Iona Cathedral, 1891 (proposals) and 1903–05

The story of Iona in modern times starts, like much of Scotland's recent religious history, with the Disruption of 1843. Donald McVean took half the congregation into the Free Church, while Alexander McGregor was appointed for those who remained loyal to the Established Church. McVean was unpopular with many for his strict principles, discouraging 'some barbarous customs' such as excessive intake of alcohol at funerals.

Following hard on this was the potato blight outbreak of 1846. This led to a decade of hardship, also characterised by clearance and emigration. Like Ireland, Iona had come to rely too much on the potato crop and had a density of population much too high for an agrarian community; in 1835 there were 521 on an island that can be walked around in a few hours. To make things worse, in 1847 John Campbell of Islay, factor to the fifth Duke of Argyll, raised rents by 50 per cent. In June 1847, 98 people left Port Ronain for overseas, each with a few belongings – proportionately as big a depletion of the community as had occurred in Mull one hundred years earlier after the Jacobite rebellion. It would be 1886 before the Crofters Act gave security of tenure to farmers.

Of the population of 247 in 1891, about 35 schoolchildren were boarded out from Glasgow. They were orphans (which often meant illegitimate) or abandoned, some perhaps with mothers in poorhouses, Magdalene Institutions or in service. This practice started in the 1860s and became more widespread in the 1880s. One wonders how the children coped with the Gaelic speakers on Iona.

In 1891 John Honeyman noted in his job book that he had carried out a report on re-roofing the choir, the central tower and south transept of the cathedral. We learn from correspondence of 10 October 1891 that this was unable to proceed, although a sketch of the proposed restored church appeared in *Academy Architecture* in 1901. It is believed that Charles Rennie Mackintosh and Herbert MacNair had accompanied Honeyman to Iona. Another assistant in the office, Alexander McGibbon, certainly did, because his detailed survey of the walls, defining their age from the thirteenth to the seventeenth centuries, was published in the *Builder* on 4 November 1893.

During the 1890s various people contemplated restoration of the abbey ruins and they were becoming something of a tourist attraction. In 1897 a regatta brought crowds to the island, and to coincide with Queen Victoria's Silver Jubilee in July of that year a telegraph service was installed from the mainland. Tourists could now send home 'wish you were here' telegrams.

While there was historical interest in St Columba, he had little spiritual significance for Presbyterians. In June 1897, on the 1,300th anniversary of his death, there were three separate events organised by Presbyterian, Episcopalian and Catholic churchmen on the island. In Ireland, crowds flocked to the saint's birthplace to take away bottles of holy water from his well, which had been specially reopened for the event. In Irish journals it was suggested that Iona be secured by the Catholic Church. While Scottish Protestants might have shown minimal interest in Columba, they would not be keen to let the Irish Catholics have his cathedral on Iona.

On 22 September 1899, the Duke of Argyll relinquished ownership of the abbey to the Iona Cathedral Trustees, an organisation linked to the Church of Scotland, with representatives from the four Scottish universities and Edinburgh and Glasgow Cathedrals. To avoid dispute among the locals and the increasing number of pilgrims and tourists visiting Iona, it was a condition that all churches be able to hold services there. Unfortunately, no endowment came with the gift, and public donations were sought. This process was delayed by the last Boer War, which also required public funds.

Early in 1902, David McGibbon and Thomas Ross prepared plans to carry out the work envisaged by John Honeyman's report of 1891. This pair were famous

Alex Ritchie was custodian of Iona Cathedral when Honeyman was carrying out alterations, while Euphemia Ritchie, who trained at Glasgow School of Art, taught locals the skills to set up a tourist industry in Celtic Art. Such was the pair's success that they had to outsource supplies, and soon 'authentic' Iona marble souvenirs were actually being made in Birmingham from Connemara marble.

for their encyclopedia of historic Scottish architecture, *The Castellated and Domestic Architecture of Scotland*, published in five volumes from 1887 to 1892. It is still in print and can be purchased in bookshops today. The encyclopedia was highly influential with architects of the time, Mackintosh basing a lecture on it to the Glasgow Architectural Association on 10 February 1891.

McGibbon and Ross may have been good at cataloguing historic buildings, but perhaps their knowledge of religious ones was limited, because controversy about the authenticity of their proposals quickly arose. In 1903 John Honeyman was called back to provide the necessary intellectual input, and he reviewed the work, despite his failing eyesight. The sketches that Honeyman used to illustrate a talk to the Scottish Ecclesiological Society in 1905 were made by John Keppie, who must have been his eyes. On 14 July 1905 a crowd of 300 attended the opening service in the restored cathedral. With John Honeyman's encouragement, Alexander Ritchie, local craftsman and cathedral custodian, developed a wider interest in architecture, joining the Glasgow Archaeological Society on 15 February 1906.

By 1907, Helen Campbell of Blythswood and her brother Walter had supplied a loan for further work, the former having raised money through women's guilds. £1,500 was available, but by this time John Honeyman was blind and unable to carry out the work. It is thought that he recommended Peter McGregor Chalmers instead. It says much for Honeyman's generosity and selflessness in pursuit of his client's ends that he recommended Chalmers as the best man for the job, despite personal animosity between the two. On 16 February 1899, John Keppie, in Honeyman's absence, had presented a paper on 'The Sculptured Stones of Govan'. Chalmers, Honeyman's

The restored Iona Cathedral.

assistant from the mid-1870s to 1887 when the work to Govan Old Parish Church was taking place, obviously thought that he was the authority on the stones and had been overlooked. There then followed heated correspondence with William Black, secretary of the Glasgow Archaeological Society, during which Chalmers accused Honeyman of misrepresenting him.

By 26 June 1910 the cathedral was fully restored. The east window was dedicated to Miss Campbell, and a teak board carved and painted in Celtic lettering by Alex Ritchie was placed below the south window.

Largo Parish Church, 1894

Thomas Rodger wrote in the nineteenth century:

> Strictly speaking there are two towns of Largo. There is the town situated on the shores of the bay and there is inland Upper Largo or the Kirktown, so called because the parish church (rather a pretty one of some antiquity and with a very good spire) is situated in it.

Largo Parish Church.

Lower Largo is the part most likely to attract tourists interested in the seafront, with its visitor centre dedicated to Alexander Selkirk, the real-life character who inspired Daniel Defoe to write *Robinson Crusoe*. If they do so they will miss the pleasure of a visit to a very pretty little church.

The John Honeyman and Keppie records indicate that alterations were carried out in 1894 for Sir John Gilmour of Montrave. The church history states that in 1894 and 1895 various architectural features were enhanced, including enlargement of the south transept, construction of a new vestry, re-roofing and the substitution of timber window mullions by more durable stone ones. Three new windows were also installed. All of this had to be carried out by someone sympathetic to parts of the building dating back to the seventeenth century.

Alexander Selkirk had been a parishioner of Largo, his parents being buried in the churchyard. He died of yellow fever off the west coast of Africa and was buried at sea. The church records indicate that his free spirit brought him into conflict with the strict Presbyterian Church Session. On 25 August 1695, 'Alex Selcraig was summoned for undecent behavier in ye church'. On 27 August, 'Alex Selcraig did not compear being gone away to ye seas: this business is continued till his return'. The records do not say what happened on his return, but on a voyage to the South Pacific in 1708 he fell out with the captain, who set him ashore on the island of Juan Fernandez, 400 miles from Chile. He remained there until he was rescued four years later.

St Michael's, 1894–96

West Lothian: An Illustrated Architectural Guide describes this church in Linlithgow as, 'perhaps the finest parish church in Scotland'; and so it should be, located as it is beside a royal palace. John Honeyman was called in to restore it back to its old glory and put right insensitive alterations from the early 1800s. An inspection in 1808 had revealed rotten ceiling beams that were in danger of imminent collapse, and in 1812 the timber ceiling was replaced with a plaster one due to oak being unavailable during the Napoleonic Wars. An old arch between the chancel and nave was removed and the internal walls were whitewashed. Huge galleries were built, and these required large holes to be made in the stone walls for support. Security measures were installed to deter grave robbers, the supply of bodies to anatomy lectures in Edinburgh being good business at that time.

Most of Honeyman's work from 1894 to 1896 undid this. In addition, the stone floor was replaced, central heating was installed and a new vestry was built on the foundations of the ancient sacristy. An oak communion table and pulpit were designed. The removal of the whitewash had to be carefully undertaken and new stone obtained from the Kingscavil Quarry when repairs were necessary, matching the existing stone as well as possible. There are Mackintosh sketches of St Michael's, suggesting that he may have assisted Honeyman in the restoration work. £6,200 had been raised for this from private donations and a bazaar.

The restored church was formally rededicated on 24 October 1896 by the Rev. Donald Macleod, minister of Park Church, Glasgow, who was formerly of St Michael's and chaplain to Queen Victoria. On Tuesday 7 September 1897, Honeyman showed the Glasgow Archaeological Society round the building. At the lunch thereafter at the

With industrial premises dominating the loch side, this Edwardian view of St Michael's at Linlithgow is much less picturesque than the same scene today.

Star and Garter Hotel, Honeyman expressed the view that, as a Scottish parish church, perhaps only St Giles' Cathedral in Edinburgh stood comparison to it. He stressed the importance of maintaining a good roof over historic buildings and looked forward to the urgent restoration of the old coronal spire on the tower. A modern interpretation of the latter was added, but not until 1964, when Geoffrey Clarke's gold anodised aluminium crown sought to reflect contemporary design rather than recreate the 1820 stone crown. Adviser Sir Basil Spence was concerned that only a lightweight structure was safe to place on top of the old tower.

Brechin, 1900–02

Restoration of Brechin Cathedral was initiated by the Rev. John Alexander Clark, who found eighteenth-century drawings and engravings indicating how the building had

appeared before insensitive Georgian alterations. Clark came from Glasgow and was a founder member of the Aberdeen Ecclesiological Society in 1886. Honeyman joined this society in 1890. His plans were submitted in September 1898 and were publicised to raise money for the improvements. Alexander McGibbon produced an artist's impression of the finished work, and subscriptions were received from local and exiled Brechiners. Restoration began in January 1900.

Restoration work underway at Brechin Cathedral.
Nowadays stonemasons would normally carry out carving work in the comfort
of their heated workshops, but in previous times it was done in situ.

By Saturday 22 September, sufficient work had progressed for a memorial stone to be laid. The afternoon was observed as a holiday (presumably everyone worked a six-day week), and there was a grand Masonic procession from the city hall to the cathedral:

> The deputation from Grand Lodge alone was the largest and most influential that had assembled outside headquarters, and the gathering of Masons was probably the largest ever seen out of Edinburgh or Glasgow.

James Hozier MP, the Grand Master Mason of Scotland, laid the memorial stone. Only £1,900 of the required £20,000 had still to be raised, with a bazaar planned to attend to this.

The plaster ceiling was removed to reveal an old clerestory intact. Concrete foundations were inserted to support the walls, and during the excavation some carved stone Celtic coffin lids were discovered, employed as makeshift foundation bases by the 1806 builders who obviously gave no regard to their antiquity. The early English choir was in ruins and had to be rebuilt.

Internally, the unsightly galleries were removed, as was the plaster on the nave wall. Henry Holiday designed new stained glass windows. The seats and walls were panelled in oak, electric light was installed, including the fitting of electric lamps to a 1615 chandelier, and a hot-air system heated all areas. Honeyman's eyesight became increasingly poor as the work progressed, and he used plasticine (the word used later by Alex Smellie, although it was probably described as 'moulding clay' in those days) to show the shape of stonework he wished built. The cathedral reopened on 23 April 1902.

While the works were being carried out at the cathedral, the practice received a commission from Alexander Philip for a new house in Brechin, called The Mary Acre. It is a handsome, category 'B' listed house, which one might guess from the outside was under the design control of John Keppie. However, there are certain internal features that have gained the property the local nomenclature of 'the Mackintosh House'.

The listing mentions fireplaces of art nouveau character, but a timber fireplace overmantle, stair newel posts, leaded cames on stair windows and a timber fireplace surround are all also suggestive of Mackintosh design. He certainly prepared drawings for the restoration of the cathedral, but the lack of coordination of the interior design of the house, and the relative crudity of the application of details, perhaps suggest that an assistant in Honeyman, Keppie and Mackintosh applied detailing prevalent in the office at the time. The house was designed in 1902 and built the following year. Unfortunately, at the time I was carrying out a search for record drawings, Montrose Library was in the process of sorting a mass of uncatalogued items. Their records did however indicate an application to carry out alterations in December 1906. Perhaps some day the full story will be known.

The end of a career

Brechin Cathedral and his involvement at Iona were John Honeyman's last projects. They were a fitting end to a career that was underlined by a studious approach to architectural style and a respect for the past. In 1905, when his restoration of Iona

John Honeyman's failing eyesight can be detected in this photograph taken towards the end of his career.

Cathedral was completed, he was 75 years old, virtually blind and had formally retired from the practice the year before. The University of Glasgow marked his retirement by awarding him an honorary Doctor of Laws in 1904. He had been elected an associate of the Royal Scottish Academy in 1892 and became a full academician in 1895. If not for his eyesight, and if he could have afforded the financial commitments involved, he might have accepted the offer of its presidency when Sir George Reid retired in 1902. Had he attained this position, a knighthood would have followed.

His son Herbert, even while at boarding school at Glenalmond, spent as much time with his father as possible, sharing his interests in architecture and archaeology. He helped him prepare papers on various subjects, the last of which, 'The Old Barony Pulpit', was written in 1912. In 1902 John Honeyman had asked John Keppie to give Herbert an apprenticeship, but he declined, perhaps because the practice could not support a potential third principal, but more likely because he did not believe he would be an asset to the office. Honeyman called in a favour from John James Burnet who accepted Herbert. James Shearer, senior assistant in Burnet's office described him as:

> An exceedingly shy young man who rarely spoke to anyone unless he was spoken to, spending his days in an odd kind of isolation . . . . The general impression made by 'HLH' on his associates was one of a youth in every way unusual, sensitive and somewhat old-fashioned for his years . . . . During his periods of idleness, he amused himself by embellishing the margins of his backing sheet with little drawings of tombstones with Latin inscriptions.

In 1911, John Keppie nominated Herbert for membership of the Royal Institute of British Architects, and he practised for much of the rest of his life in Northumberland, where he specialised in ecclesiastical and domestic projects. He joined the firm of Graham and Hill in December 1913, and, after being invalided out of the Royal Engineers due to illness in France in October 1918, he practised under the name of Hill and Honeyman. He wrote a number of books on architecture, archaeology and conservation, contributing to Nikolaus Pevsner's *The Buildings of England* series.

John Honeyman died of pneumonia at his home at Minewood, Bridge of Allan, on 8 January 1914. Patrick Honeyman had prepared his will in 1907, and it showed that he had no debts but only £20. 4s. 10d. in the bank. He owned no property, and other effects came to the value of £214. An insurance policy of £1,000 with the Life Association of Scotland was intended to provide for his widow Anne. She joined Herbert in Newcastle, and those who knew them remembered her as somewhat difficult and possessive, demanding much of her son. He cared for her with much patience until her death in 1936. After the Second World War he found himself a wife in Newcastle, Edith Sarsfield, and he spent the last five years of his life with her, dying on 23 November 1956.

There is less known about John Honeyman's other surviving son, John R.C. Honeyman, born in 1864 to his father's first wife. The only record of him that can be found relates to his attendance at the Glasgow School of Art as an architectural student from 1881 to 1884. He is not known to have practised thereafter as an architect. When his father died he would have been 50, while Herbert was only 28. In Honeyman's will, instructions were left for his estate to be divided between his surviving sons should Anne die, and an obituary refers to two surviving sons, so John junior must have been alive in 1914. Unfortunately, we do not know if the founder of our architectural practice has any descendants living today.

John Honeyman was buried in the Necropolis in Glasgow on 10 January 1914, at the grave where he had attended the funerals of his first and second wives, Ann (Rothesia) on 24 March 1864, and Margaret on 12 January 1881. They had only reached the ages of 31 and 44 when they died. John was 83. His third wife, Anne, was probably buried near Newcastle, but Herbert lies with his father at the Necropolis, interred there on 27 November 1956.

Honeyman would feel at home on a hill overlooking his native Glasgow, having contributed much to the architecture and social life of the city. He lies only a few hundred metres from his beloved Glasgow Cathedral, which intrigued him for much of his life. He is also only a few metres from the first known work of his assistant Charles Rennie Mackintosh, the funeral monument for his father's boss, Chief Constable Alexander McCall, who died in 1888. John Honeyman shares the cemetery with many of his clients, the creators of the Second City of the British Empire. In the very next lair to him lie clients Charles and Hugh Tennent, the Glasgow brewers, perhaps a little too close for comfort, even in death. David Walker's tribute to Honeyman sums up his architectural career: 'Everything he built had a quiet distinction, as scholarly, fastidious and above all as gentlemanly as the man himself.'

Alexander McCall's gravestone at the Necropolis in Glasgow is the first known work of Charles Rennie Mackintosh.

Honeyman and his family lie in an unmarked grave between these two Tennent family plots.

This photograph, published in a German magazine, gives a good view of the upper level detailing of the Glasgow Herald Building where Mackintosh was allowed some freedom to express himself.

168

CHAPTER 15

Newspaper buildings

The *Glasgow Herald* Building, 1893–95, 1898, 1913–20, 1927–29, 1935–37, and 1990–93

Before Keppie Design director David Collin retired in 2001, he made a concerted effort to catalogue a huge backlog of drawings of buildings kept from previous years. When a project finishes, an architect will be instructed to retain a selection of drawings in case problems occur and he is required to demonstrate that his design has been sound. Drawings are also needed if he is asked back to make alterations to the building in the future. At completion stage, architects are usually more interested in the next project they are designing, and are sometimes not as careful about selecting and cataloguing the old drawings as they should be. Those consulting them later will also have a tendency to return them to the archives in a less than tidy state.

In the late 1980s, with the interest in Mackintosh at its height, the Hunterian Museum and Art Gallery had taken the practice job books and the historic drawings it was interested in from Keppie Henderson to keep for posterity. This meant that in 2001 the archive contained mostly post-Second World War projects and only a small number of drawings prepared between the wars.

Part of a Mackintosh drawing of the Glasgow Herald Building found in the Keppie Design office rolled up in a bundle of old drawings in 2001.

However, in the very last bundle of drawings which David unrolled to catalogue, he came across alterations to the *Glasgow Herald* premises in Buchanan Street/Mitchell Street from the 1930s. Inside them were rolled up a number of working drawings of the building from the 1890s, and inside them drawings from the 1880s. It seemed that whoever was carrying out alterations from 1935 to 1937 (a period confirmed in the job books) had consulted old drawings from the practice's previous involvement in the building. Having thought that the practice had given away or sold anything to do with Mackintosh before 1990, it now had a set of original drawings for the *Glasgow Herald* Building.

It is difficult to tell how many of the drawings were by Mackintosh, although the elevations were undoubtedly in his style. They were possibly copies made by him to discuss with the builder on site, since there are notes scribbled on some of them. While the set of construction drawings is incomplete, the highest numbered is 213. In those days, all the drawings were usually prepared by the architect, including structural ones.

Today we think of the *Glasgow Herald* Building as the premises where the Lighthouse design and exhibition centre is. However this was the back or business side of the *Herald* premises that were entered by the public from Buchanan Street. Perhaps the young Mackintosh was only allowed the freedom to design the water tower and other features on the Mitchell Street part of the building because it was at the back and no one paid much attention to it.

If the Keppie practice originated in Victorian times and prospered from the entrepreneurship and social customs of the Victorians, the *Glasgow Advertiser*, as the *Herald* was originally known, had been established at the height of the Scottish Enlightenment when Glasgow was emerging as a major industrial and trading centre. If bad news sells newspapers, it could not have got off to a better start, since in January 1783 the finishing touches were being put to the Versailles Treaty which formally gave the American colonies their independence, thus bringing ruin to many of Glasgow's Tobacco Lords. The paper started publishing and printing from 65 Buchanan Street on 9 November 1868. It bought the site for £23,000 from M.M. Pattison, who had previously run a market behind the entrance from Buchanan Street featuring small shops arranged around a square with a large stone tank in the middle from which live fish were sold. John Baird was the original *Glasgow Herald* architect, but in 1879/80 James Sellars carried out a number of alterations.

The drawings in the Keppie archives from the 1880s do not bear the name of the author or the architectural practice. Since John Keppie had been James Sellars' assistant in the 1880s, these drawings may have been brought by him in 1888, or Honeyman may simply have obtained the old drawings from the *Glasgow Herald* to help Honeyman and Keppie carry out their work in 1893. Another link with the paper came via Honeyman's brother Michael, who was treasurer of the Commissioners for the Prevention and Repression of Juvenile Delinquency in the City of Glasgow in 1888 when Simpson MacHarg of the *Glasgow Herald* was its clerk. So the contact with the paper, and the commission for the design, could have come from three sources: Michael Honeyman, James Sellars via John Keppie, or my favourite hypothesis – directly from John Honeyman and his acquaintance with James Coltart Waters.

Waters' uncle was William Dun, who was cashier at the *Glasgow Herald* when Samuel Hunter was its editor in the early nineteenth century. The newspaper's circulation suffered because of Hunter's outspoken views on a number of subjects such as the Corn Laws and the abolition of slavery. He was particularly scathing about the Veto Act of 1834 whereby Church of Scotland parishioners were given the right to have a say in the choice of their minister rather than have him imposed by the local landlord (see chapter 2). In his editorial, Hunter stated:

> Be the patron king or subject, he cannot now count upon his right, unless under the sufferance of the parishioners, many of whom will be passive followers of some busy, intermeddling juncto. And prospective ministers will be exposed to the doubtful result of a humiliating canvass.

Hunter did not live to see the consequence of such reluctance to accept democratic principles – the Disruption. Luckily, Dun's skills as a cashier helped the *Glasgow Herald* to survive until George Outram became editor. Dun carried the newspaper's money in his coat pockets, notes and sovereigns in one and lesser coins in another, dealing with creditors and printers in offices, the street or taverns. His methods were successful but perhaps Glaswegians then were more law-abiding than they are today! William Dun amassed a large personal fortune, and in 1860 purchased the estate of Craigton and Culcreuch near his native Fintry, where his father had been a miller. He was a bachelor, and died in 1861. Although he had no children, family members – brother-in-law David Waters and nephew James Coltart Waters – were both fellow shareholders in the *Glasgow Herald*.

Craigton House, Fintry,
home of James Coltart Waters.

In 1861, James Coltart Waters approached John Honeyman to carry out alterations to the drawing room of Craigton House. More substantial alterations were carried out in 1868, a lodge was built in 1870, a balcony and washhouse were added in 1886, and the dining room was refurbished in 1889. The clients for the last of these were 'the Trustees of the late James Coltart Waters per P.S. Honeyman, writer, 88 West Regent Street'. The drawing room was further altered by Honeyman and Keppie in 1889/90 and illustrated in the *Builder* of 18 July 1890. Craigton House was demolished in the 1950s, and only the Dun family mausoleum, the stable block converted for residential use and Honeyman's gate lodge remain.

Alteration work to Culcreuch Castle in 1879 may have come from Dun family contacts, although the client named in the job books is Sir George Home-Speirs, and a framed document in the hallway today mentions Honeyman's brother Michael as a signatory to the building's purchase. This is now the Culcreuch Castle Hotel, and last time I visited it served a fine afternoon tea.

The last work to Craigton House was carried out in 1890, only a few years before Honeyman and Keppie were appointed to undertake major alterations to the *Glasgow Herald* premises. The two Johns may also have come into contact with the editor Charles Russell through the Glasgow Art Club. Russell promoted a number of artistic causes in the pages of his paper, most notably the campaign in 1891 to persuade the city fathers to purchase Whistler's portrait of Thomas Carlyle.

In 1893 John Honeyman and Keppie were commissioned to carry out alterations to the Buchanan Street section of the *Glasgow Herald* premises, and to redevelop the rest of the site back to Mitchell Street. Mackintosh's input to the design was probably limited, given his inexperience and the importance of the client, although he later described the design as his. As well as upper parts of the Mitchell Street building, including the water tower, he participated in the interior design of the part of the building between it and the Buchanan Street section. The design of the editor's room (1894) is probably largely by Keppie, but there are some details suggestive of Mackintosh's influence. In the manager's room (1894/95), he was given much more freedom to express himself, although the design concept was badly affected in 1898 when he had to erect a partition in it.

In a book by Alastair Phillips, written to celebrate the *Herald*'s bicentenary, he confesses that the newspaper did not do anything to preserve Mackintosh's work through the years, stating quite reasonably that before the 1960s Mackintosh was largely unrecognised in artistic circles:

> When internal alterations were afoot, the first things to go were his partitions with their high, narrow, undustable shelves. The pieces of his furniture which were consigned from office to office until they disappeared, were either uncomfortable, unstable, or both.

The editor's room at the Glasgow Herald Building.

The manager's room at the Glasgow Herald Building is full of Mackintosh design features, including the surviving table with its awkward lower stretchers.

Only a table and filing cabinet were left for George Outram and Co. to donate to Glasgow Museums and Art Galleries. Referring to the former, the bicentenary book says, 'it is this piece which may have first inspired dislike for his work; it is extremely difficult to find a place for one's feet under the table because of the lower stretchers'. Keppie Henderson continued to contribute to alteration work, initiated each time an editor decided that the business needed to be modernised or required a change in direction. A number of projects were carried out in the periods 1913–1920, 1927–1929 and 1935–1937.

In 1980 the *Glasgow Herald* moved out of the Buchanan Street/Mitchell Street premises to occupy the former premises of the *Scottish Daily Express* and the *Evening Citizen* in Albion Street where a new printing plant allowed the most modern of electronic technology to be utilised. Access for delivery vehicles was also much better at Albion Street. The building itself was less robust, and I was invited by the facilities manager to comment on how to deal with problems with the external walls. The elevations were listed because of the unique style associated with *Daily Express* premises in different parts of the country, but the cladding system required replacement because it was beyond repair. In the end, the *Herald* dodged the dilemma when, as part of the Scottish Media Group, it relocated its offices to the top of West Nile Street as an addition to the Scottish Television headquarters. The printing works moved out of the city centre to a site beside the M74 motorway.

One of the first projects the combined Scott Brownrigg and Turner and Keppie Henderson practice received in 1989 was at the old *Glasgow Herald* Buildings in Buchanan Street and Mitchell Street and Lane. The developer arm of Legal and General wished to redevelop the buildings to make them easier to let. Nothing transpired in the early 1990s because of one of the deepest recessions experienced since the Second World War, but proposals for offices above shops were eventually pursued on the Buchanan Street frontage, Glasgow obtaining a Warner Brothers store as one of the tenants.

A use for the rear of the building on Mitchell Street was more difficult to find, until a letter was received on 9 June 1993 from the steering committee for the bid for the City of Architecture and Design 1999, asking the practice for ideas in its support. We proposed that the old *Glasgow Herald* Building be converted for use as a centre for the event, and our sketch design for the building was part of the successful application. Habitat wanted to move from Bothwell Street to a high street location, and they might have helped sponsor the project, or at least their involvement might have helped subsidise the running costs. Perhaps naively, we thought that having instigated the project, we would be approached to carry out the work. We declined to take part in a selected design competition for the project, which became known as the Lighthouse.

Daily Record Building (67 Hope Street), 1900 and 1925–27 (*Evening News*), and 1937–39 (Associated Newspapers). *Daily Record* Building (20–28 Renfield Lane), 1900–04 and 1911–1923

In 1900, John Honeyman and Keppie carried out alterations to 67 Hope Street for the *Daily Record* and designed new premises for the newspaper in Renfield Lane. Mackintosh was responsible for the latter, which was completed in phases between 1901 and 1904. These projects probably resulted from the success of two titles launched by the owners of the *North British Daily Mail* in 1895. These were the *Daily Record*, the first halfpenny newspaper in the UK to carry pictures and to print ten text pages, and the *Noon Record*, a sports paper covering horse racing and football. In 1901, the *North British Daily Mail* and the *Daily Record* were merged, and the new premises designed by Mackintosh allowed the introduction of a Sunday paper in 1908, the *Weekly Record and Mail*, renamed the *Sunday Mail* in 1919. Various alterations were carried out to the Renfield Lane premises between 1911 and 1923, and for the *Evening News* at 67 Hope Street in 1925–27. At this time the latter was brought into the same stable by Associated Newspapers boss, Lord Kemsley. The *Evening News* was closed down after the takeover of the company by the Mirror Group in 1955. The *Noon Record* survived until 1968.

Mackintosh's second newspaper building was in a lane even narrower than the *Glasgow Herald*'s Mitchell Street. He adopted white, glazed bricks to reflect light into the 5.5-metre-wide Renfield Lane, a device which mainly benefited the building opposite. Only the occupants of this building can glimpse the quality of architectural detailing – especially on the upper levels – where green and red glazed bricks, in the shape of stylised trees, along with red sandstone lintels, contrast with the otherwise white facade.

Citizen Building, 1923–30

Major works were carried out in the 1920s for James Hedderwick and Sons who owned the *Glasgow Citizen* newspaper. James and Robert Hedderwick founded the *Evening Citizen* and the *Weekly Citizen* in 1842. James's sons, Edwin and Maxwell, took over. Edwin devoted himself to the newspapers, believing that he could not take other positions in public life in Glasgow and keep his editorial impartiality, unlike other prominent Glasgow men such as his cousin James, a stockbroker who at different times was chairman of the Glasgow Stock Exchange, president of the Glasgow Chamber of Commerce, director of the Royal Hospital for Sick Children, vice-chairman of the St Andrew's Ambulance Association and chairman of the Glasgow Royal Infirmary. Like John Keppie, James was a keen golfer and a member of both Prestwick and Western Gailes Golf Clubs.

Mackintosh's drawing of the Daily Record *Building in Renfield Lane, off Hope Street.*

DAILY RECORD BUILDINGS

Maxwell Hedderwick helped his brother until the business became a limited liability company in 1904. He was an innovator, obtaining telephones as soon as they were available, and was reputed to have been the first member of the public to make a call between Scotland and England. He was responsible for employing architect Thomas Lennox Watson from 1885 to 1889 to design the Citizen Building at 24 St Vincent Place. This is where the alterations by John Keppie and Henderson were carried out.

For many years Glasgow had two rival evening newspapers, the *Evening Citizen* and the *Evening Times*. However, advertising is one of the first things that companies cut back on in a recession, and in 1974 its owners, Beaverbrook Newspapers, announced that the *Citizen* would close after 132 years due to heavy losses. Sir Hugh Fraser's rival Outram Group paid £2.75 million for the title to ensure that the *Evening Times* would have a monopoly in the west of Scotland.

The Citizen Building, to which John Keppie
and Henderson carried out internal alterations.

*Pettigrew and Stephens' Manchester House, with its Mackintosh dome finial,
is in the middle of the picture, with the Willow Tea Rooms on the right.*

CHAPTER 16

Victorian and Edwardian shops, banks and tea rooms

The Ca'd'Oro, 1872/73 and 1988/89

In the early 1870s, John Honeyman received his first retail projects. Having been commissioned to carry out alterations to William Miller's house at Knockderry Castle near Cove on Loch Long in 1869, he altered his client's shop at the John McIntyre Corner, Glasgow Cross. Works took place to the 1850s cast-iron framed warehouse in 1874 and 1877. Honeyman often used cast-iron columns for galleries in churches to minimise restricted viewing, and the G. and J. Burns warehouse at 30 Jamaica Street (see page 18) in 1864 used a cast-iron frame to maximise the window wall. This was less innovative than its neighbour, the Gardner and Sons warehouse of 1856, although it was still a very fine design. However, the furniture warehouse for F. and J. Smith at the corner of Gordon Street and Union Street produced a flourish of decorative detailing in cast iron. At a cost of £11,000, like 30 Jamaica Street (sadly since burned down), it took its inspiration from Venice, although its arched, arcaded shopfronts and floral moulding are much grander than that of its former Glasgow relative.

It has been a Glasgow landmark for over a century, although its notability in local folklore came after it became known as the 'Ca'Doro' (original spelling), a corruption of the Venetian 'House of Gold' or Casa d'Oro. Use as a furniture store ceased in 1896, when it housed Mrs McCall's Victorian Restaurant, and in 1921 it became the flagship of the City Bakeries. At ground level it was fitted out with a marble shopping hall, quick lunch counter and businessmen's smoke room. Above this was a Venetian tea room, a musicians' gallery, a luncheon room, a business clubroom, dining rooms, and a banqueting hall. It was a favourite place to have weddings. J. Gaff Gillespie designed the alterations and Jack Coia (of Gillespie Kidd and Coia) added a rather inappropriate roof extension in the mid-1920s.

The Scottish Co-operative Society took

F. and J. Smith's warehouse at the corner of Gordon Street and Union Street subsequently became known as the Ca'd'Oro.

over the building after the Second World War, but it did not fare well and closed in April 1958. The Ca'd'Oro was split up to let to various companies, with Reo Stakis taking over the basement and two upper floors for restaurants, the El Guero, the Brasserie and the Tropicana. Clark's Shoes and Lillywhite Frowd's sports goods were at street level. A fire in 1987 gutted the inside of the building when plans were being prepared for redevelopment by Scott Brownrigg and Turner, just before the merger with Keppie Henderson. Partner Jim Fisher gave responsibility for the project to David Collin and Bill Rodger.

Client CIS Ltd. owned both the Ca'd'Oro and the adjacent 'Maison Centrale', and knew that they possessed something special, although the latter had severe structural problems and was demolished. The decision was taken to extend Honeyman's original building by two bays, rather than adopt the fashion of the time which was to form a facade out of reflective glass to show the surrounding streetscape. The mansard roof was removed to the original level. To prove the theory that John Honeyman's original intention in using cast iron would have been to obtain the effect of very fine masonry at low cost by the use of multiple castings from a single mould, a paint expert took scrapings of the various layers, going back to the original primer. The original paint was stone coloured. During his visit, the paint expert asked if he could see the old ballroom, but when he stepped into that once glorious space he seemed subdued, contemplative and quite at a loss for words. He eventually explained that the last time he had been in the building he was playing the piano accordion in a band. David Collin, himself an accomplished musician, had never met a sensitive accordionist before.

One unforeseen setback was the theft of significant numbers of stained glass windows from the building during the survey and research process. Despite the efforts of security staff, Glasgow's intrepid thieves risked their lives on dark, wet, rooftops to break in and attempted to strip the building of anything saleable. The stained glass is now believed to be in America.

It was expected that it would be necessary to bring horny-handed old craftsmen out of retirement for the specialist restoration tasks, but young and highly able men and women were found who were full of enthusiasm for a job they felt was worth doing well. Stonemasons, iron founders and stained glass artists all co-operated and readily shared their expertise. Sadly, Jim Fisher died only a few weeks after the restoration work was complete. A Europa Nostra award was received for the project.

Sauchiehall Street and Pettigrew and Stephens, 1896, 1900, 1902, 1910, 1915, 1938–40 and 1945

Most of the retail premises the Keppie practice worked on from 1880 to the First World War were in Sauchiehall Street, which took over from the Union Street/Jamaica Street/Argyle Street area as the fashionable shopping centre. In 1880 James Orr commissioned work to his shops in Union Street (untraced) and at 166 Sauchiehall Street (now the site of the Marks and Spencer building). Bailie William Miller probably reckoned that he needed an outlet in Sauchiehall Street as well as at Glasgow Cross, for Honeyman carried out £3,480 worth of work for him there in 1883 (again untraced). While alterations to Alex Hogg's premises at 60 Virginia Street took place in 1889, and lifts were installed in the Bank of Scotland in George Square in 1891, the first major retail commission was for Pettigrew and Stephens.

The style of this sketch of Pettigrew and Stephens' shop in Sauchiehall Street suggests that it was drawn by Alex McGibbon.

The shop was founded in 1888 on the corner of Sauchiehall Street and West Campbell Street. Andrew Pettigrew took control of the retail business when his partner W.H. Stephens died and in 1896 commissioned a complete redevelopment of the site as far back as Bath Street, including 140 Bath Street, where the Honeyman and Keppie practice had previously been based. Manchester House, as it was called, contained large plate-glass windows, a grand marble staircase, and was topped with a large dome. While John Keppie was in charge of the design, Charles Rennie Mackintosh contributed to the detail of the dome and the tea rooms. Mackintosh's assistant, William Moyes, confirmed that his boss had been responsible for internal showcases and some internal wall decoration at the Pettigrew and Stephens building. Some people have asserted that Keppie used Mackintosh's Chapter House dome design from 1890, but the resemblance is only slight. The opening in May 1901 was a grand affair which helped to cheer people up after Queen Victoria's death and celebrate the occupation of Pretoria during the Boer War.

Further alterations were carried out to Pettigrew and Stephens from 1920 to 1925, but department stores became less fashionable after the Second World War. A developer purchased the Sauchiehall Street site along with the adjoining Copland and Lye store so that the whole city block could become a modern shopping mall, now the Sauchiehall Street Centre. The old buildings were demolished in 1972, although the Mackintosh lantern and finial from the top of the dome was saved, restored and displayed at the 1988 Glasgow Garden Festival. The crude brick building was a poor replacement for the Victorian one, and it tried to cash in on the renewed Mackintosh interest of the time with 'Mockintosh' motifs in the food court. David Walker recalled meeting retailer Sir Hugh Fraser a few weeks before he died and being told how poorly he regarded the aesthetic and practical aspects of the new building, denying all responsibility for it. When a client of Keppie Design purchased the building in the late 1990s, the whole of it was turned into shop units. A new frontage was designed for the Healthlands Leisure Club in 1998 to try to enliven the Bath Street facade.

Other shops designed in Sauchiehall Street included numbers 309 to 313 for James Simpson, cabinetmaker (designed 1904, built 1906, £13,592); number 518 for T. and R. Annan and Sons, photographers (1903–05, £6,040, and 1912); numbers 137 to 145 for a Dr Walker, part of which was acquired by Stuart Cranston in 1907 for the

While Pettigrew and Stephens' Manchester House has been replaced by an ugly 1970s development, the dome finial was saved prior to demolition and can be viewed in the sculpture garden at the Hunterian Art Gallery at the University of Glasgow.

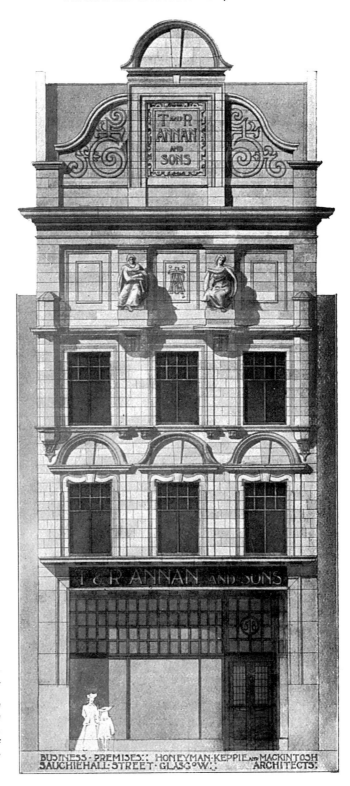

A drawing showing new premises for photographers T. and R. Annan and Sons in Sauchiehall Street, published in the 1904 edition of Academy Architecture.

McConnell's Building at the top of Hope Street, opposite the Theatre Royal.

The former Glasgow Savings Bank building on Gallowgate at Parkhead Cross.

Wellesley Lunch and Tea Rooms (1904/05, £13,685); and number 233 for Henry and Carruthers, ladies tailor, milliner and mourning specialist (1904, £1,160). The practice knew the Annan family well from commissioning them for portraits. Mackintosh had his own portrait photographed in 1893 by Craig Annan, who had taken over the business after his father, Thomas, died in 1887.

By 1904, Mackintosh was a partner in his own right pursuing his own projects, and, apart from his influences on the Annan showroom design, these buildings show nothing of his preferred style. Examples of Keppie's work separating from Mackintosh's are the City Improvement Trust tenement (1906/07) on Hope Street opposite the Theatre Royal (McConnell's Building), and the Savings Bank at Parkhead Cross (1908). Both are traditionally styled buildings with ornate detailing. Both have flats above commercial premises with rooftop drying areas on access balconies or the flat roof of the commercial premises below.

John Keppie had been president of the Glasgow Institute of Architects, and perhaps like John Gordon before him, who had also been president prior to obtaining the Bridge Street and Bridgeton Cross Savings Bank commissions, this position may have helped secure the work. Neil Duff had just completed the Shawlands branch, and since his father's surveying firm had been appointed to cost the Parkhead Cross project he assumed he would receive the commission. Keppie obtained it instead.

Tea rooms

In the eighteenth century the British of all social classes developed a passion for tea – sweet tea. This encouraged two triangular, global trade routes: one in the western hemisphere – from Britain to Africa to pick up slaves to take to sugar plantations in the Caribbean, with sugar coming back to Britain; and one in the east – from Britain to India to pick up textiles and opium which were used to pay for tea from China. The immorality of this trade was first recognised on the western route when, in 1834, slavery was legally abolished and UK taxpayers paid £20 million compensation to slave owners to set 700,000 slaves free.

The British public chose to ignore the effects that the (officially illegal) opium trade was having on Chinese society. When the Chinese objected, the Opium Wars started. The military technology of the British was overwhelming and when the Chinese sued for peace in 1841 they were forced to open five ports to free trade and to cede Hong Kong to Britain. However, gradually tea began to be grown in India and Ceylon and with different types of tea becoming available the commonplace drink acquired connoisseur status.

One of the tea specialists was Glaswegian Stuart Cranston, son of George Cranston who ran the city's Crown Hotel. A regular guest at the hotel was Arthur Dakin, a rep of London tea importer Twining, and he obtained young Stuart a job with a tea dealer. In 1871, at the age of 23, Stuart set up his own business at 44 St Enoch Square and later moved to 76 Argyle Street, on the corner of Queen Street. Although Dakin had instilled in Stuart the romance associated with China and its tea, Glasgow grocer Thomas Lipton stocked tea from India and Ceylon, and in order to be competitive Stuart had to offer a range of teas for potential customers to taste. To make his tea tastings more attractive, he also offered bread and cakes. The Glasgow tea room was born, eight years before such a place existed in London or anywhere else.

Middle-class women now had somewhere respectable to meet when shopping. With the suburbs spreading outwards, city businessmen did not have time to go home for lunch and those wo could not afford, or did not have the status, to join a club could pick up a snack in the middle of the day. With the temperance movement gaining ground, tea rooms were respectable for men as well as women.

Stuart's sister, Catherine (or Kate as she was better known), was not content to be the usual woman behind the scenes – she was too good a businesswoman. In 1878 she opened the Crown Luncheon and Tea Rooms at 114 Argyle Street, named after the family hotel. This was the year of the City of Glasgow Bank Crash, but by the mid-1880s her business was booming and in 1886 she opened new premises in Ingram Street.

Like many upper-class ladies, Kate Cranston had old-fashioned tastes, as her style of dress in this photograph shows. Nonetheless she realised the attraction of modern design to the fashion-conscious bourgeois who flocked to her tea rooms.

In 1888 she refurbished her Argyle Street tea rooms and for the job hired designer George Walton, brother of 'Glasgow Boy' artist Edward Walton. J. Taylor in the *Studio* magazine later wrote that with this appointment 'Decorative art may be said to have entered on the new phase at Glasgow'. This was to become known as the 'Glasgow Style'.

In 1894 Kate Cranston purchased 91–93 Buchanan Street to provide tea and luncheon rooms as well as smoking and billiard rooms for men. She chose Edinburgh

The Mackintosh murals in Kate Cranston's Buchanan Street Tea Rooms.

architect George Washington Browne and recalled George Walton for the interiors, but she also commissioned Charles Rennie Mackintosh to design wall murals, which met much critical acclaim. When expanding her Argyle Street premises she asked Mackintosh to design furniture. By 1900 she was extending the Ingram Street Tea Rooms, and with Walton now in London, Mackintosh carried out the complete interior design. His new wife Margaret contributed to the work. The predominantly white walls of the Ladies' Luncheon Room would have been a welcome relief from a dreich day in smoggy Glasgow.

Kate's next venture was a tea room at the 1901 International Exhibition beside the new art gallery and museum in Kelvingrove Park. However, it is not known if Walton or Mackintosh played a part in its design, although the latter designed Pettigrew and Stephens' stand there.

Hints of Mackintosh influence can be seen in the windows on the left at Pettigrew and Stephens' tea rooms.

At the turn of the century, Glasgow's department stores were adopting the 'American System' whereby customers were allowed to walk through the shop without being pressed to buy anything. One of the facilities offered to encourage customers to visit and stay longer was the tea room, and Pettigrew and Stephens' new building by Honeyman and Keppie, Manchester House in Sauchiehall Street, contained one when it opened in 1901. Mackintosh's Glasgow Style leaded glass was somewhat at odds with the more classically styled general interiors, and even the later tea room refurbishment of 1909 had a mixture of styles. Mackintosh was obviously not given the same freedom by the conservative owners of the department store that he had with Kate Cranston. The design was, however, popular, *Glasgow Today* reviewing it and commenting that the weary shopper could:

> rest awhile in the lounge so artistically designed, panelled in pale satinwood, upholstered in soft grey and white, so tranquil and agreeable to tired eyes, yet with its brilliant Turkey carpets and cosy green furniture so cheerful and bright a place for a chat.

To respond to the shift of retail focus to Sauchiehall Street, Kate Cranston secured the lease for number 217, next to Daly's department store. This time Mackintosh could design the whole building, exterior and interior. Like Hill House, in Helensburgh, from the same era, Mackintosh had the satisfaction of controlling every aspect of the project, including the costumes of the waitresses. The Willow Tea Rooms were opened on 29 October 1903. The *Evening News* declared them the 'acme of originality'. The *Bailie* wrote that the: 'Salon de luxe on the first floor is simply a marvel of the art of the upholsterer and decorator.'

Kate Cranston took the limelight when such praise was meted out. English architect Edwin Lutyens hurried to her establishments when he visited Glasgow, going straight from the train to 'these queer, funny tea rooms', like most visitors for the overall experience – 'good value, quality and art'. The designer was rarely mentioned, which must have been frustrating to Mackintosh who was now a partner in the practice and duty-bound to bring in work in his own right. His next project for Kate was the Dutch Kitchen at Argyle Street (1905/06), followed by the Oak Room (1907) and the Oval Room and Ladies' Rest Room (1909) at Ingram Street. By 1910 there was the suggestion of an element of job creation for her favourite designer, a recession being in full swing. The Chinese Room and Cloister Room at Ingram Street followed in 1911, the same year that Kate commissioned two tea rooms for the Scottish National

By the time the Willow Tea Rooms were designed, Kate Cranston was allowing Mackintosh the opportunity to detail all aspects of the project.

Exhibition. Mackintosh designed the White Cockade, and his wife Margaret the menu card. Margaret's sister, Frances, designed the menu for the Red Lion Tea Rooms.

Even after Mackintosh had left Glasgow, during the war years, Kate continued to try to give him work. Despite the restrictive Cake and Pastry Order of April 1917, which made ingredients for a proper afternoon tea impossible, Kate continued to build the Dug-Out (designed by Mackintosh in 1916) in the basement next to the Willow. The name and the black walls and ceiling were probably not appropriate for a public coming to terms with the horrors of trench warfare, but perhaps they reflected the depression of Mackintosh himself. A few weeks after the Dug-Out was completed, Kate's husband, John Cochrane, Provost of Barrhead from 1902 to 1907, fell ill and died. Kate moved from Hous'hill to live in the North British Railway Hotel in George Square (now the Millennium Hotel). The tea room empire was declining.

The Willow Tea Rooms closed in 1919 when Kate retired. Developer Arrowcroft Group purchased it in 1978 when the occupant, Daly's, moved to the new Sauchiehall Street Centre, which replaced Manchester House. At that time, Geoff Wimpenny of Keppie Henderson started a detective hunt, looking for drawings, photographs and physical evidence of how the building looked in 1903 so that it could be recreated. The reinstated Willow Tea Rooms was completed in 1980 and one can take tea and cakes there today.

A former manageress of Kate's ran the Ingram Street Tea Rooms after 1919 until she herself retired in 1930, four years before Kate died. The new owner built over the Mackintosh interiors, but they were later saved by Glasgow Corporation for display at the art galleries.

Mackintosh decorated the music room in Hous'hill, Kate Cranston's home in Nitshill, 1904.

Geoff Wimpenny's assistant, Les Adams, has just prised off a wall panel with his umbrella in the Willow Tea Rooms premises vacated by Daly's to reveal a Mackintosh fireplace.

Alex McGibbon must have stayed up late to prepare this illustration of the practice's unsuccessful competition design for Manchester Municipal Technical Schools. The hexagonal tower at top left seems to appear from nowhere – a Mackintosh late addition?

CHAPTER 17

Architectural competitions
and architectural styles

To someone commissioning a building, holding a competition may seem a good way of choosing an architect and arriving at an ideal design as the competitors strive to come up with an unexpected creation that will magically fulfil the brief. What could be better or more fun? John Honeyman did not enter many design competitions, however, and many experienced architects look on them with some cynicism. Nonetheless, those seeking to prove themselves use competitions to develop their ideas and promote them to potential clients. A review of some of those carried out between 1889 and 1913 gives an insight into the development of design aspirations within and outside the practice.

John Honeyman sometimes judged competitions like those for Lesmahagow Church and Midlothian County Buildings. As a council member of the Royal Institute of British Architects in 1880 (he was president of the Glasgow Institute of Architects the following two years), he tried to use his influence to ensure a successful outcome for the Glasgow City Chambers competition. His thoughts, expounded to the organisers, are as relevant today as they were then:

Honeyman judged the design competition for Lesmahagow Parish Church. This picture shows the Masonic ceremony of laying the keystone. Note the timber and cable pulley system used to hoist pieces of stone into position.

The design of such an important building should be entrusted to an able and experienced architect. How can the greatest number of men of this class be induced to compete? Some people seem to think that the offer of a few large premiums, however objectionable the conditions may be in other respects, will draw designs from the most eminent members of the profession – an utter and ridiculous mistake.

Such an offer will, no doubt, draw designs:

From a few *men of experience*, who happen to have nothing else to do;

From *speculative architects* who go in for competitions right and left, and somehow make a living by it;

> From *pushing architects* who calculate on success through unblushing
> mendacity and the assiduous application of personal influence;
> From *embryo architects*, who have done nothing, or next to nothing.

Attempting to defend the members of his profession, Honeyman expressed concerns that too much design work might be requested of the participants, that there was no guarantee that the winner would receive the commission, that there might be no impartial adviser to adjudicate the designs, and that the budget for the building might be inadequate. His main bone of contention was the amount of wasted design time given free by the participants. As he said:

> In dealing with any other profession, the shrewd businessmen of Glasgow
> know better than to employ inferior men in cases of importance or difficulty;
> they seek the best advisers and pay them handsomely. Architects desire and
> deserve the same consideration, and architects of good reputation will not
> submit to any different treatment.

He might have saved his breath. Inevitably, many 'men of experience' are enticed to demonstrate their abilities in competitions for prestigious projects, and all but a few waste their time and money. Honeyman did not enter the Glasgow City Chambers competition in 1881, but 110 others did, and this despite being a rerun of a flawed competition the previous year. It was also a little odd that first and fourth prizes were awarded, but not second and third ones. John Carrick, the city's Master of Works, had issued prescriptive floor plans for the proposed building determined by the internal politics of departmental hierarchies. This meant that the competition was largely a style contest for the elevations. He judged the proposals himself along with Charles Barry junior.

While Honeyman had entered some church design competitions, the introduction of John Keppie and Charles Rennie Mackintosh into the practice led to several competition entries. The first of these was for the Sydney Houses of Parliament in 1890. There may have been a relationship with James Campbell, a Sydney architect, whose assistant Alexander McRae came to work at Honeyman and Keppie from 1894 to 1896. Although only two competition entries were successful during this period, the Glasgow School of Art and Jordanhill School, competitions are a challenging relief from the often mundane design work in the office, and Mackintosh in particular used them to develop his thinking.

The Alexander Thomson Scholarship

Mackintosh studied at the Glasgow School of Art from 1884, and continued to do so after he joined Honeyman and Keppie in 1889. Evening classes were poorly attended by architectural assistants, and to encourage them the Glasgow Institute of Architects awarded cash prizes for drawings and designs. The GIA discouraged innovative solutions by students, believing it important for them to demonstrate what they had learned from their elders and betters. Mackintosh attained much success in these and other competitions, culminating in his winning of the Alexander Thomson Scholarship in 1890 for a public hall. The prize of £60 was equal to the annual salary of two other assistants in the practice in the early 1890s, Messrs Mitchell and Fulton, each of whom were paid £60 per year. Mackintosh used it to fund a study tour to Italy.

His scholarship-winning drawings for the public hall were sent, together with a design for a science and art museum, to South Kensington, the Glasgow School of Art then being administered by the Department of Science and Art in London. In the autumn of 1891 Mackintosh was awarded the national silver medal. There was a French influence to the design, which may have come from John Keppie's Beaux-Arts training in the Paris atelier of Jean-Louis Pascal from 1885 to 1886, or from one of Mackintosh's tutors at the art school, John James Burnet. The latter had also spent time with Pascal from 1875 to 1877.

The examiners were not without criticism, saying that the design 'has many good points, but the effect of the larger features above smaller ones is disagreeable'. The *Builder* of 1 August 1891 was more scathing, picking Mackintosh's design to harangue the Department of Science and Art:

> We can only observe that if the department can secure no higher standard than the things to which they award prizes, they had better give up teaching architecture at all. There is a silver medal given to a Glasgow student, for instance, for a design for a classic building, which is bad in every way, clumsy and heavy in design and defective in drawing.

This was the first public criticism Mackintosh received, although he probably paid as little regard to architectural critics then as most architects do today. With the publicity he was receiving, he was establishing himself within professional circles.

The practice hedged its bets with different design solutions for the Glasgow Art Galleries competition, this submission being classical and ornate.

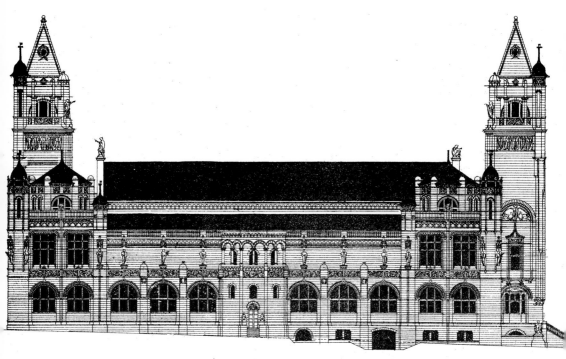

Front Elevation.

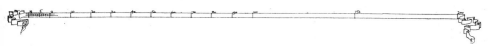

GLASGOW ART GALLERIES, FINAL COMPETITION
DESIGN BY
MESSRS. HONEYMAN & KEPPIE, GLASGOW.

The Glasgow Art Galleries, 1891/92

In 1892 Mackintosh contributed with John Honeyman and John Keppie to three designs that were entered for the art galleries design competition at Kelvingrove. Two of them were selected for the shortlist of six, and the practice was hopeful of obtaining a highly prestigious commission. They were extremely disappointed when London architects Simpson and Milner Allen were appointed. Like the Glasgow Municipal Buildings contest twelve years earlier, the competition was basically a style contest, the accommodation being strictly prescribed. The office tactics had presumably been to cover all angles by designing three styles of building in three entries. In the same year the practice entered the competition for the Manchester Municipal Technical Schools, but was not placed in the final shortlist of four. The hand of Mackintosh is detectable in the detailing of one of the art gallery schemes and in the sculpture and turrets of the Manchester scheme.

192

THE GREAT HALL.

The final scheme for the Glasgow Art Galleries contains a bright central hall with large rooflights, simpler and more modern detailing, and more flamboyant friezes on the upper walls. The elevations (opposite) were drawn by Mackintosh.

Mackintosh's design for a railway terminus is one of several unbuilt projects of his which have been modelled by Jamil Ozturk's Glasgow workshop, and which were displayed in an exhibition at Keppie Design's offices in 2003.

Railway Terminus, 1892/93

Judges in design competitions might be looking for a French Renaissance museum, an Italian Renaissance chapter house, or a Gothic railway terminus. But, perhaps for the first time, with the outcome of the railway terminus competition, Mackintosh might have realised that this approach was not necessarily correct, and that design integrity may be more important. William Emerson, the honorary secretary of the Royal Institute of British Architects, commented that the general standard of the competition schemes for the railway terminus was low, and awarded the prize to A. T. Bolton. Emerson's comments were interesting, for they preceded the 'form follows function' principles of the Modern Movement from the 1920s onwards. 'If the subject be a station, the principle feature of which is an enormous roof in one span, why mask it or altogether conceal it? If the design does not look like what it is intended for, you may depend on it that it is wrongly conceived.'

Like most other competitors, Mackintosh had placed a two-storey block containing offices and apartments in front of the arched station roof, masking it from view at the front. The building was decorated with unnecessary ornament and quasi-ecclesiastical window details. He learned the lesson well, for in a paper given to the Glasgow Institute of Architects in February 1893 he stated:

> Old architecture lived because it had purpose. Modern architecture, to be real, must not be an envelope without contents . . . . How absurd it is to see modern churches, theatres, banks, museums, exchanges, Municipal Buildings, Art Galleries, etc., etc., made in imitations of Greek temples.

Paisley Technical School, 1895

Having been unsuccessful with the Royal Insurance Building competition in Glasgow earlier that year, the practice submitted two entries for the Paisley Technical School competition. They were placed second and third. J. and P. Coats, Honeyman's clients for the Paisley Art Gallery and Library in 1870 and 1882, donated the site and £3,000 towards the cost. Paisley man Professor Archibald Barr (of Barr and Stroud engineers) was in charge of the project and nine architects from Paisley and Glasgow were invited to take part in the competition.

The winner was Paisley architect Thomas Graham Abercrombie, or perhaps his employee, William Kerr, who had joined Abercrombie from Burnet's office. Abercrombie helped Barr draw up the specifications for the building and his knowledge of the project

The unsuccessful Honeyman and Keppie scheme for Paisley Technical School.

would have been an advantage, even if the contest were fairly judged. 'TG', as his friends knew him, was a keen rugby player, co-founded the local Boys' Brigade company, and rose to the rank of captain in the 2nd Renfrewshire Rifle Volunteers. The local boy had triumphed. He had also been John Hutchison's architectural apprentice a few years before Mackintosh held the same post. Abercrombie's building later became the Gardner Building, 28–40 George Street, part of the University of Paisley.

The Glasgow School of Art, 1896

Mackintosh's masterpiece deserves the next chapter to itself, although as an architectural competition also merits mention here. Given the lack of funds available for the project and the inability of the sponsors to offer premiums to the runners-up, this was not a prestigious competition, and contemporary journals paid no attention to it. By 1899 only the first phase had been completed, and the incomplete building would have looked odd and incongruous, doing the reputation of Mackintosh and the practice little good. By the time the second phase of the building was complete in 1909 the competition had long since been forgotten, and a recession was about to start, leading to a lack of architectural opportunities.

Glasgow International Exhibition Competition, 1898

A competition was held in 1898 for an industrial hall, a machinery hall and a concert hall for the Glasgow International Exhibition of 1901. It was won by local architect

195

James Miller. Mackintosh submitted the Honeyman and Keppie scheme. On a sheet containing an alternative design for the concert hall were plans for a bar, dining room and a bridge.

The site at Kelvingrove was the same as the one on which John Keppie had worked for James Sellars at the first International Exhibition in 1888. Mackintosh's designs were much less ornate than Miller's. Glasgow's exhibitions throughout the years have been known for their flamboyance, and to the organisers the Spanish Renaissance style of the Miller scheme probably fitted the bill better than Mackintosh's more restrained approach.

House for an Art Lover, 1901

To all but the winner, architectural competitions are highly frustrating, especially if an exciting commission is lost. It is perhaps better to treat them as exercises in learning and experimenting. Unexecuted schemes retain a certain allure, as they are not tarnished by the practicalities of project execution, and are often purer expressions of artistic intent. From 1900 to about 1906, Mackintosh, along with Margaret Macdonald, and to some extent the MacNairs, received critical acclaim in various parts of continental Europe, and the *Haus eines Kunstfreundes* represented a chance to escape completely from the local politics and jealousies of a Glasgow or British competition.

Modern movements rebelling against academicism and tradition had emerged in Europe, centred around artistic groups called the Munich Secession (founded in 1893 and partly taking its inspiration from an exhibition by seventeen of the 'Glasgow Boys' at the Munich Art Society in 1890), and the Vienna Secession (founded in 1897). Charles and Margaret Mackintosh exhibited in Vienna in 1900, and the next year they entered the House for an Art Lover competition. The judges hoped for a radical reassessment of modern architecture, but were sufficiently disappointed not to award a first prize. The Mackintosh entry was disqualified because it contained the wrong number of illustrations, but was regarded highly enough to be publicised along with two other schemes. Thomas Howarth's book contrasts second-placed English architect Baillie Scott's design with Mackintosh's. The former was a concoction of quasi-Dutch gables, Franco–Scottish turrets and Tudor timber panels and windows, the equivalent of a Eurovision Song Contest entry. Mackintosh's non-conventional approach attracted much more interest, and won a special prize of 600 marks; despite this he may have been disappointed that the widespread publicity the design received did not result in any significant commissions.

Although the proposal was prepared very quickly and was never intended to be built, that did not stop engineer and Mackintosh enthusiast Graham Roxburgh from trying some 90 years later. Having saved and refurbished Honeyman's Craigie Hall, with Keppie and Mackintosh interiors, he set about raising money and building *Das Haus eines Kunstfreundes* in Glasgow's Bellahouston Park. His intention in 1988 was to have the building ready for Glasgow's year as European City of Culture in 1990, but sponsors were discouraged by the recession of the time. Only after the Glasgow School of Art decided to locate its postgraduate school in part of the building did the project become viable, and it was completed in August 1996. As well as a pleasant place to spend a Sunday afternoon, it is a popular venue for weddings. Some do not regard it as 'real' Mackintosh. Roger Billcliffe wrote:

Mackintosh gave the judges his concept of the ideal domestic structure for an enlightened and committed client for whom cost was not a hindrance. Architecture, however, is ultimately about more than this; great architecture tests an architect's responses to the restraints which real life presents before him. This is why the Glasgow School of Art, Scotland Street School and the Hill House brought out more in Mackintosh through the problems they set him and the solutions he achieved.

Liverpool Anglican Cathedral, 1903

In 1885, Sir William Emerson won a competition for a new Liverpool cathedral with his Byzantine design, capped by a large dome. The selection committee was having difficulty purchasing the land identified for the building and had second thoughts about how the winning scheme would look beside the adjacent neo-classical St George's Hall. It abandoned the competition and launched a new one on another site in 1903. Sir William made the most of his position as president of the Royal Institute of British Architects to protest about the conduct of the competition committee, and declined to enter the second competition. The committee determined that the new cathedral be designed in Gothic style, which was controversial since it revisited the Gothic-versus-classical debate of the 1880s.

The two advisory architects, G.F. Bodley and R. Norman Shaw, chose a select group of architects to submit designs in April 1903. The controversy was to continue when Giles Gilbert Scott won. According to the committee, in his plans were found 'that power combined with beauty which makes a great and noble building'. He was a 22-year-old who had not yet completed his apprenticeship, but he was the son of George Gilbert Scott and grandson of Sir George Gilbert Scott, possibly the most prominent British architect of the 'High Victorian' period, and designer of the University of Glasgow. The 1924 guide to the cathedral stated that 'with the instinct for compromise which is the Englishman's outstanding characteristic,' 75-year-old competition assessor George Frederick Bodley agreed to work with him, developing the design. This he did until his death in 1907. Bodley's sister was married to Giles Scott's great uncle and the latter had a business relationship with Bodley's father in the church furnishing business of Watts and Co. The final design presented in 1910 bore little resemblance to

An early Mackintosh sketch of Liverpool Cathedral.

the competition-winning scheme and seemed to contain elements of other entries, including the one from Mackintosh, which was not shortlisted.

The great Gothic expert, John Honeyman, was close to retirement, but the practice apparently fancied its chances sufficiently to submit two entries. Only Mackintosh's design drawings remain, displaying the new practice name of Honeyman, Keppie and Mackintosh. There must have been some reason for them to choose this particular competition to enter. Honeyman probably knew of Bodley's relationship with the Scott family. He had supported Sir George Gilbert Scott's Gothic design for the new University of Glasgow buildings at Gilmorehill when others in the city like Alexander Thomson had been advocating a classical approach.

Mackintosh also had Liverpool links through Herbert MacNair, who had gone there in 1898 to be Instructor in Decorative Design at the School of Architecture and Applied Art, remaining until about 1906. He possibly thought that Professor Reilly, head of the Liverpool school, might be an ally, but instead later inferred that Reilly had stymied his competition entry, forced his friend MacNair out of his teaching post, and affected Mackintosh's ability to obtain work in London. In a letter to his wife Margaret from Port Vendre in France in 1927 he wrote:

I have waited patiently for 20 years to get one back at Reilly – and during those 20 years I have never said one word about him to any outsider. Now I can get a few nails in his nasty stinking cheap coffin! I am not vindictive – far from it – you know how much I want to paint well – but I think I have one stronger passion and that is to make Reilly a really discredited outsider before I am finished with him. When I get him on the run I will drive him like a fiend until he is a raving lunatic.

Looking back in later life to the early 1900s when he was in his thirties and in his prime, Mackintosh probably saw the Liverpool Cathedral competition as a lost opportunity to develop his career outside Glasgow. Liverpool also lost out, obtaining in 1960, when it was finally complete, a Gothic building more in tune with late-Victorian thinking than with the early twentieth century romanticism that Mackintosh was proposing.

The Mitchell Library Competition, 1905

As president of the Glasgow Institute of Architects at the time, John Keppie was appointed assessor of this competition, along with the city engineer, A. B. McDonald. As people in this position before and after have resolved, he would have endeavoured to ensure that the terms and evaluation of the competition were as fair as possible. The conditions were issued on 25 August 1904. It would be open to all architects, the winner would be commissioned at a fee of 5 per cent of the construction cost, and the runners-up would be paid premiums of £100, £75 and £50.

Keppie produced a detailed brief that defined the purpose of the building, the area required by different departments and functions, space standards (for bookcases and passageways), the requirements for natural and artificial light, and for heating and ventilation. With the Mackintosh extension to Honeyman's Paisley Library in 1904, Keppie would have recent knowledge of the subject. The budget was £40,000, and the entrants had to demonstrate on a four-page cost breakdown that their scheme could be achieved within this. The desire to ensure that the needs of Mr Stenhouse, the city librarian, be met and be deliverable, were tempered by a wish not to be over-prescriptive: 'it is not expected that the accommodation indicated can be supplied exact to the letter in every detail'.

To retain anonymity there were strict rules about drawings not bearing any distinguishing marks, and a defined list of drawings was to be provided, each of them 27 inches square. 'Coloured elevations, framed drawings or additional drawings will be immediately destroyed.' Keppie even specified the colours that different types of accommodation had to be shaded on the plans. Apart from stating that the building should occupy the whole of the site bounded by Berkeley Street, Kent Road, North Street and the St Andrew's Halls (James Sellars's masterpiece whose front elevation survived a fire and now forms the back of the Mitchell Library), the entrants were free to design the building as they thought fit: 'The style of architecture is left to the discretion of the architect.' Some guidance was given to the approach expected: 'the desire of the Corporation is that the building shall depend for its architectural character and effect on good proportion, rather than on elaboration of decorative detail'. There was a presumption that the main entrance would be at, or close to, the corner of North Street and Kent Road, since there was no public square for a grand central entrance on North Street to face. Luckily the winning architect chose to change this in his final design, and with the M8 motorway opening up the vista in the 1970s we can now enjoy the front of the building in its full glory.

The Libraries Committee meeting on 14 February 1905 recorded that 76 designs had been submitted and the city chamberlain announced that £26,000 had been received from New York, being the second instalment of Andrew Carnegie's gift to the city towards the new library. In June, Keppie presented his report, with 42 entries having merited consideration and seven on a shortlist. A cost consultant had been appointed in April to review the schemes and concluded that the budget had to be exceeded to obtain the required building, all entries being valued between £40,000 and £50,000. Design 32, at a cost of £44,479, was recommended by the assessors, although the fourth-placed scheme was favoured by Bailie Shaw Maxwell who presented a motion to have it placed first. Perhaps, despite all the efforts to retain anonymity, he had discovered that Design 55 was by architect J.R. Rhind, who was locally based, having returned from a spell in Montreal, but was originally from Inverness. The motion failed and another local architect, William Whitie, won. He had already designed Springburn District Library, and was to design the Metropole Theatre beside St George's Cross a few years later. The style of these buildings may have been influenced by the work of J.M. Dick Peddie's office in Edinburgh, where Whitie had been apprenticed.

The style of the architecture may have been left to the architect, but the somewhat pompous Baroque manner and elaborate detailing – despite the contentions of the brief – indicated what the city fathers and John Keppie were looking for in a major civic building. Mackintosh was precluded from entering of course, but this would not have been a good vehicle with which to promote his radical view of architecture.

John Keppie worked with William Whitie to include various changes required by Glasgow Corporation. A heating system by William Key, 'ventilation and warming engineer', was incorporated. The Libraries Committee finally signed off the design in February 1906 at a cost of £52,850. In later years, according to architects Alfred Lochhead and Sandy Wright (in conversation with David Walker), Keppie teased Whitie mercilessly at the Glasgow Art Club to the effect that Design 32 was of such high quality that he assumed it had been by someone else.

Jordanhill Demonstration School, 1912/13

Graham Henderson had joined the practice in May 1904 and John R. Hacking in April 1905, and with a slowing down of commissions in 1911 they decided to enter a competition for Manchester Library and Art Gallery. Their design was premiated (a term meaning to be shortlisted in an architectural competition), winning a prize of one hundred guineas (£105). The next year the competition for Jordanhill Demonstration School was announced (a school for teacher training) and the practice decided to enter it. Thus started a 60-year relationship with Jordanhill College.

By 1900, the provision of teacher training was as confused as the school system itself, which saw working class and lower middle class children attending elementary schools run by school boards or by the churches, the latter mostly Roman Catholic but some Episcopalian. The wealthy, and a few bursary winners, went to private schools. Much teacher training took place within the schools themselves, alongside two Presbyterian colleges and a Roman Catholic one, and with the University of Glasgow also providing a course. When the school leaving age was raised to fourteen in 1901, it became clear that the system would have to be regularised and improved to cope.

The Scotch Education Department wished to centralise control and in 1905 it set up four provincial committees to enlarge and improve existing facilities for teachers. The Glasgow committee set an objective of building a new college and demonstration school, although it wasn't until 1911 that it purchased 45 acres of parkland at Woodend, Jordanhill. The history of the college, *Teaching the Teachers*, quotes:

> In respect of sanitary conditions, quietness and environment, the Woodend site easily comes first . . . . The factor of environment is also one of great significance, especially in the case of the best type of student. At the student stage, when character and habit are in the making, suggestions from without, ethical and aesthetic, exercise a formative power which it would be unwise indeed to overlook. Environment is the half of destiny; and it is difficult to believe that a student living for three or four years in such an environment . . . as can be created at Woodend would not look back on his College with the same pride, loyalty and affection that the public school boy of the best kind bestows upon his old school.

Six local firms of architects were invited to enter a design competition for the college, a demonstration school and a hostel for women students. One of these was Honeyman Keppie and Mackintosh. H. and D. Barclay were awarded the college (they had previously designed the Royal Glasgow Technical College, now part of the University of Strathclyde), Honeyman Keppie and Mackintosh won the demonstration school, and Andrew Balfour designed the hostel. The eighteenth-century Jordanhill House was to be used for housewifery, cookery, laundry and music practice. Perhaps, with the lack of work available, the judges felt it their duty to share the project between three practices.

The college, later named the David Stow Building, accommodated 1,200 students, and Honeyman, Keppie and Mackintosh's school was to provide space for 800 pupils at primary and higher grade levels. Classrooms were larger than normal so that students could view model lessons and take notes. The school built up a reputation for excellence that quickly led to demand for houses in the area. Responsibility for the design competition in the practice was initially given to Mackintosh, who was assisted by

Graham Henderson and James Diggle. However, by this time Mackintosh had become disillusioned due to a shortage of work and a lack of artistic challenge. Given the straightforward designs that succeeded in the Jordanhill competition, the college did not appear to be welcoming innovative ideas anyway.

As his biographer Thomas Howarth put it:

At one moment he could be exultant, proud and confident; then after a meeting with a client or committee less indulgent than Miss Cranston – and there were few Miss Cranstons in Glasgow – either he would be consumed with rage or be plunged into despair. Suggestions and advice he began to interpret as criticism, as a reflection on his ability and good judgement, and he became more and more intractable. . . . Even in his student days he had not been a temperate individual and he now turned frequently to drink, and in consequence began to lose interest in the practice. We are told by those who worked with him that his lunch hour often lasted from 1 o'clock to 4.45 p.m., then he expected the draughtsmen to stay on late into the evening. At times his directions became vague and purposeless.

Mackintosh is recorded as representing the practice at a Glasgow provincial committee meeting in July 1913. According to Graham Henderson: 'His preliminary sketches were unworkable, and some of his corridors terminated in mid-air.' This was a highly important opportunity for the practice at a time of deep recession when large projects were hard to come by. John Keppie helped Henderson submit the proposals, and the demonstration school was won. Mackintosh withdrew from the practice soon after, although the partnership was not formally dissolved until June 1914.

John Keppie signed the formal appointment for Jordanhill School on 18 May 1914, on behalf of Honeyman and Keppie Architects. It was witnessed by Andrew Graham Henderson and James Duncan Diggle. Keppie sent a cheque for £250 to Mackintosh as his share of the competition award.

Jordanhill School.

Overleaf: *A 1914 floor plan for Jordanhill School.*

201

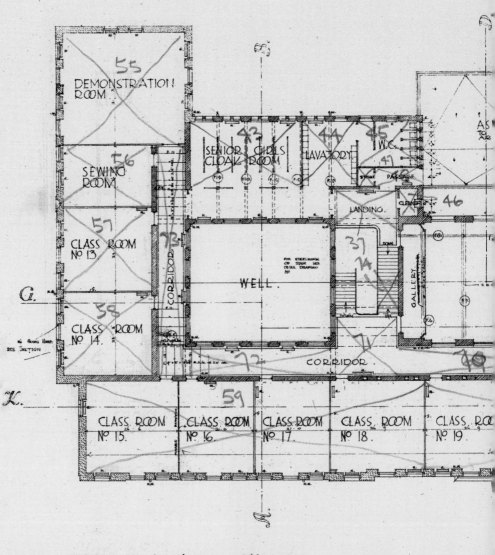

DEMONSTRATION SCHO

JORDANHILL *for*

Provincial Committee for the Training of Teac.

Plan of First Floor

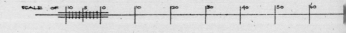

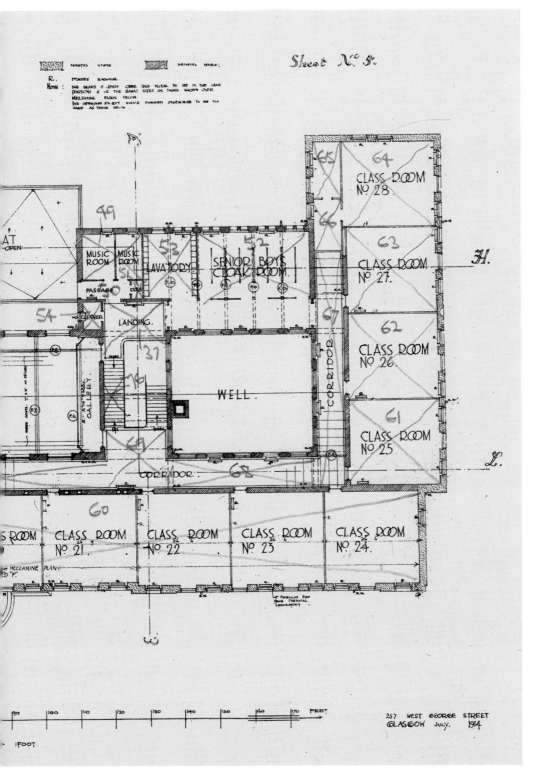

Sheet N° 5.

257 WEST GEORGE STREET
GLASGOW JULY. 1914

Phase one of the Glasgow School of Art completed.

CHAPTER 18

The Glasgow School of Art and the Mackintosh legacy

Recognised as world-class architecture, the Glasgow School of Art is Mackintosh's masterpiece. If the practice had not been appointed for the project or if phase one had been badly carried out, Mackintosh would probably not have been chosen to design Hill House, Helensburgh, and he might have gone down in a footnote of a textbook as a quirky designer, interested in art nouveau, whose designs for Kate Cranston's tea rooms were typical of the period in Glasgow. He may have been recognised as a talented artist, but would almost certainly not have become a partner in an architectural practice.

The contention has been that Mackintosh designed the art school himself, but that Keppie, as the partner in charge, took credit for it at the time and marginalised his assistant. The truth is somewhat more complex.

The Glasgow International Exhibition of 1888, on which Keppie had assisted Sellars in the design of some buildings, had made a handsome profit, and it was decided to put the proceeds towards the construction of a new art gallery and museum at Kelvingrove. Also originally in the plans were a music hall (the organ in the main gallery was the compromise when cost-savings were made) and an art school in the basement. Honeyman and Keppie submitted three design competition entries in 1892, two of which were shortlisted in the last six. They were extremely disappointed when London architects Simpson and Milner Allen were selected. The commission would have catapulted the practice to the top level of Scottish design, having already demonstrated its versatility with the concepts it had produced in its entries, including one with some non-traditional elements by Mackintosh.

At the time, the School of Art was a branch of the South Kensington Department of Science and Art, and it was crammed into a section of the McLellan Galleries at the corner of Sauchiehall Street and Rose Street. A plan of the galleries from an exhibition in 1874 shows the extent of space available as four rooms occupying the east half of the first floor and two rooms on the second floor. The basement of an art gallery at Kelvingrove would not have been much better than its existing location, and the governors of the school decided that they should build a separate building.

In 1893 the head of the school, Francis Newbery, and chairman of the governors, pottery manufacturer James Fleming, visited the schools at Birmingham and Manchester to gain an appreciation of the accommodation required. By March 1896 the governors had raised £21,000 towards the project, with £14,000 to be spent on the building. Newbery realised that this was not a large sum of money, and in his brief of June 1896 asked for a 'plain building'. The winner of a design competition would obtain the commission at a fee of 5 per cent of the construction cost.

By August, all of the competitors were in agreement that the required accommodation could not be provided within the budget, and the submission date was extended from 15 September to 1 October to allow them to propose what could be provided for the money. Honeyman and Keppie were appointed on 13 January 1897 for the first phase of the building, and construction work took place from late 1897 to December 1899. It had to be complete before the end of 1899 to obtain a £500 grant from the South Kensington Department of Science and Art, which would cease to have the ability to make such an award thereafter. The second phase had to wait until further funds became available. This was designed between September 1906 and May 1907, with construction taking place from 1907 to 1909.

It has often been speculated that Francis Newbery made sure that his protégé Mackintosh designed the building. He was one of three judges who would all have been sympathetic to Honeyman and Keppie in their loss of the controversial art galleries appointment in 1892, as well as realising their disappointment in coming second and third the previous year in the Paisley Technical School competition. Perhaps this was the consolation prize. The whole competition was a low-key affair, unreported by the press at the time. The counter to this is that Francis Newbery had to obtain approval from his masters at South Kensington, although they merely confirmed the recommended choice and were more interested in the practical, engineering aspects of the design. They were no doubt content that Mackintosh was backed up by the resources and skills of an established office.

The timing of the competition gives another clue to Newbery's tactics. The most inconvenient time to launch a major competition is in June, just when everyone is about to go on holiday, and for Victorian architects this could mean several weeks in Britain or abroad on sketching tours. At the best of times competitions are a major inconvenience to the director of a design studio. They divert resources away from fee-paying work into speculative ventures. It is often felt better not to submit at all than to present a half-hearted design or risk underperformance on other clients' projects.

Perhaps Newbery merely wished a friend of the art school to win the competition. Of the eleven firms which submitted design entries, two were from governors of the school who resigned so they could enter, J.J. Burnet and W.F. Salmon, and four were from practices associated with Honeyman and Keppie. A.N. Paterson contained Charles Whitelaw who had left Honeyman and Keppie in 1891 (Donald Stoddart and George Paterson followed him there). Others were W.J. Conner and Henry Mitchell, the latter leaving Honeyman and Keppie in 1894, and Alexander McGibbon who left in 1890. The last of these was known more as an architectural illustrator than a designer in his own right.

Why did Newbery not delay the competition to the autumn when he might receive better, more considered proposals? Perhaps he had persuaded the entrants to treat the competition as a summer exercise for the up-and-coming talent in their offices; or perhaps because he had arranged for 'The Four', Mackintosh, MacNair and the Macdonald sisters, to get their big break in London at the Arts and Crafts Society exhibition later that year, and Mackintosh needed time to prepare for it. The art school design competition may have been a 'fix', but architects who enter competitions suspect that there is often a hidden agenda.

The first phase of design and construction went smoothly. It was generally assumed that John Keppie, as the partner in charge, merely dealt with the administrative aspects of the project. Apart from the contention by Mackintosh's biographer, Thomas Howarth, that Honeyman played a significant part in the arrangement of the floor plans, Mackintosh is traditionally credited as designing the art school by himself. More recent research suggests that the design of the building was a team effort, as one would expect of a project of this importance to the practice, with each partner and his assistants playing to their strengths.

From an art historian's point of view, there can only be one architect credited with a building design, the one who is responsible for the aesthetic concept and the integrity of the visual form. In practice, a whole team of people is involved. Nowadays there are specialist cost consultants, structural engineers and mechanical and electrical advisers, but these disciplines barely existed in Victorian times. All design skills lay within the architect's office, with possible outside help from craftsmen and builders. It is not as if Victorian buildings were necessarily simpler than their modern counterparts. The art school was to be on the side of a steep hill (perhaps this is why the site was readily available to the commissioners). This complicated the structure and required retaining walls. The need for large windows for the studios on the north side of the building also potentially threatened the integrity of the whole design if not addressed properly.

The other challenge for any large public building was how to ventilate it without letting in industrial pollution. Those who cannot remember Glasgow before the 1960s

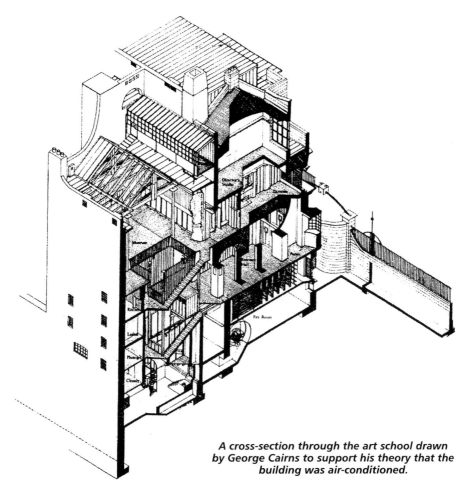

A cross-section through the art school drawn by George Cairns to support his theory that the building was air-conditioned.

The large basement tunnels were part of the ventilation system for the School of Art.

when the Clean Air Acts came into force may not realise that for most of the year (apart from the two weeks of the Glasgow Fair when the factories closed down) a thick smog engulfed the city centre. This turned buildings jet black within a few months of completion. The effects on the inhabitants of Glasgow were respiratory conditions and eye infections, and flecks of soot and industrial grit blown in through the windows of the art school would not have been desirable as they would have landed on paintings and drawings. It was to this task that John Keppie turned his attention to design what some people reckon was the first planned air-conditioned building in the world. Phase one of the art school was completed five years before Frank Lloyd Wright's Larkin Building in Buffalo, which Reyner Banham in his book *The Architecture of the Well-Tempered Environment* contends was the first to employ air-conditioning.

John Keppie and the builder of the art school obtained the necessary knowledge from two sources. To source ventilation fans large enough to move the air through the system of horizontal and vertical ducts in the building they went to the B.F. Sturtevant Company of Cincinnati. Its catalogue showed ways to fit systems of warm air heating and filtering to buildings. Keppie's work on the Victoria Infirmary in Glasgow with James Sellars was also invaluable. It was unusual for hospitals of the time because a large number of people actually got better in it. Its ventilation system was exemplary, leading to good air quality in the wards and quicker patient recovery.

One of the workmen's governors on the infirmary project, William Key, was subsequently seconded to help with the new Birmingham General Hospital, and the architects for this, William Henman and Henry Lea, further refined the Victoria Infirmary's ventilation principles at the Royal Victoria Hospital, Belfast. Key took out a patent in London in 1892. Compiled in 1891, it described a true air-conditioning system, adjusting both air temperature and humidity using water sprays or blocks of ice in the air stream for cooling, and steam coils for heating. The water sprays, along with rope filters, cleaned the air of pollutants from the outside air supply.

The specification for phase one of the Glasgow School of Art contained water sprays and rope filters. The phase two specification called for the filters to be replaced by a more modern version consisting of animal hair placed between perforated brass plates within a cardboard surround. One wonders if Keppie was infringing William Key's copyright, or if he even knew of its existence (he certainly kept in touch with Key as he obtained his services for the Mitchell Library). Perhaps the running cost of maintaining air-conditioning was too great in the aftermath of the First World War, but in 1920 John Keppie and Henderson installed a piped water and steam radiator system in the art school, with no provision for cooling and only natural ventilation from opening windows.

When it opened in 1899, phase one of the School of Art was not declared a great triumph. Pictures of the time show the limited impact made by the half-finished building.

Since the design had been exhibited at the annual exhibition of students' work in February 1897, it had attracted controversy because of its associations with art nouveau. An oblique reference was made by writer and artist Muirhead Bone when commenting on contemporary Glasgow architecture: 'Some few things here and there show a weedy, "arty" influence, and in certain places the strange idea seems to obtain that the vegetable is the architect's pattern.' A sarcastic comment was made by Sir T.D. Gibson Carmichael at the first annual public meeting of the school's supporters, where he, 'confessed surprised to hear from Mr Fleming that they were absolutely satisfied with the new premises . . . . It was the first building he had ever heard of where the architects did exactly what they were told (laughter).'

John Keppie had been an examiner at the art school, along with William Leiper and John Lavery, for the Haldane Bursary in session 1890/91. Perhaps to help ensure that the practice was retained to carry out phase two of the school, or more likely because of his prominent position in the art scene in Glasgow, Keppie became a member of the governors of the Glasgow School of Art from 1904, was vice-chairman from 1926 to 1931 and was chairman from 1931 to 1937.

In 1901 the art school was allowed to grant its own diplomas. In deference to the Paris Ecole des Beaux-Arts, at which both J.J. Burnet and John Keppie had trained, Professor J.L. Pascal was asked to help select someone to become the first Professor of Architectural Design. Pascal sent Eugene Bourdon, whose work with Charles Girault in Paris, and his experience in New York, was sufficiently impressive to warrant the post. The Glasgow School of Architecture was established in 1903, with the first student intake in the session 1904/05. The need for more accommodation then became urgent. On 27 September 1906 the governors appointed a building committee consisting of Burnet, Salmon (both unsuccessful competitors for phase one) and David Barclay. They determined that more accommodation was required, leading to a higher west

Alex McGibbon's sketch shows the end gable of phase one
as it would have looked prior to 1907.

wing and an extra level of studios on the roof of phase one. This required another fire escape stair.

Sir James Fleming, Lord Provost of Glasgow and chairman of the governors, was responsible for raising funds, receiving sums from Honeyman Keppie and Mackintosh clients Blackie and Kate Cranston. The practice even contributed £100 itself in January 1906, and the following June Mackintosh reduced the charge for the design of furniture for the director's room from £780 to £325. This was a good investment, with the formal appointment for phase two coming on 1 February 1907.

Mackintosh was now a partner and, as such, was not under the supervision of John Keppie. This, and the change in brief, gave him the opportunity, as a mature designer, to revisit the design and produce more sophisticated west elevation and library proposals. However, the building committee was concerned that Mackintosh might not be careful with their limited funds. Glasgow is a small community where bad news travels fast, and the overspend on Scotland Street School was still being resolved. At the same time, any architect knows that no matter how much he has modelled the design, by sketches, physical models (or nowadays by computer visualisations), there will inevitably be surprises or second thoughts as the building work progresses, and the experienced client will have a contingency sum hidden. Mackintosh was the same as any other architect, before or since, who seeks that extra 10 per cent which transforms a building from a fundamentally sensible and practical concept into something that little bit more special, and as a result there were conflicts with the building committee.

John Keppie probably had no direct involvement with phase two of the art school. However, he would lobby governors at the Art Club. Mackintosh did not join the club, and it was probably more appropriate that he was not a member during the design of the art school. There was a difficult balance to be achieved between criticisms that phase one had been too plain, and a budget that had been inadequate from the start. Keppie knew that additional funds could be obtained, as they had been when phase one went over budget during his control of the project. He was right, because the overspend on phase two was cleared within one year of completion.

Nevertheless, to keep himself in the clear, one governor had written to Mackintosh on 5 February 1908:

Referring to my informal conversation with your Mr Keppie in the Art Club today, it is right that the views of the governors should be put before you formally. Six of the governors inspected the newly erected sub-basement Porch and Entrance in Scott Street and were surprised to find that the work was carried out in an extravagant manner and not in accordance with the plans and estimate which was submitted and signed. I beg to intimate that we must decline all liability for any increase of cost.

Mackintosh had problems achieving deadlines during 1907, some of them being challenging enough without his other busy workload. In February 1907 his assistant William Moyes decided to emigrate to Australia and it was November before the plans were prepared and approved by the local authority. On 5 February 1908, when the building committee called him to account over increased costs, his father was dying. Some savings were made, for example by dispensing with the sculptures on the west facade. The new building was finally opened on 15 December 1909 to qualified praise at the time.

The completion of the Glasgow School of Art marked the end of an era. Between 1910 and 1913 only six or seven new projects could be attributed to Mackintosh, and none of these was of any consequence. The 1909 Finance Act, and David Lloyd George's 'People's Budget', practically halted property development. Increment duty was introduced on builders' profits and new feu duties were created. Mackintosh withdrew from the practice in the second half of 1913, although the partnership was not dissolved until June 1914. Other practices, such as Salmon and Gillespie, were dissolved around the same time for the same reason.

As well as a downturn in workload, the mood of the time had changed. As biographer Alan Crawford put it: 'Progressive architects adopted a stricter, more impersonal discipline, for which classicism was the appropriate language. Mackintosh was out of date.' It may seem strange to us today that John Keppie's McConnell's Building opposite the Theatre Royal or the Savings Bank at Parkhead Cross might have been regarded at the time as more fashionable than a Mackintosh design.

The completed west end of the art school.

Born in New Zealand and educated at Allan Glen's School in Glasgow and the University of Oxford, Graham Henderson (*c.*1882–1963) became the new star of the office. Mackintosh interviewed and appointed him. He was a talented draughtsman who in 1911 with John Hacking submitted a competition design for the Manchester Library and Art Gallery, and in 1913 came close to winning the competition for Langside Library in Glasgow. His designs won the Jordanhill Demonstration School competition in 1913, and the Glasgow Cross redevelopment the following year.

It is difficult to know which projects in Mackintosh's last few years with the practice were designed by him, or at least were under his control. The main commissions at this time were Mossdyke, Kilmacolm (1913/14), and Auchenbothie Mains (1913–16), both for Major H.B. Collins, Pinehurst, Bearsden (1912), tenements at Hospital Street/ Rutherglen Road (1912–15) for Glasgow Corporation ('B' listed but demolished in 1981), plus alterations to the *Daily Record* Building, Annan's offices and Hill House.

In 1914 Francis Newbery painted a group portrait of the building committee of the Glasgow School of Art and on the left of it he added Mackintosh, who had become a director of the school as the representative of the Glasgow Institute of Architects. Mackintosh is seen as an isolated figure at one side, with Newbery at the other looking at the viewer as if disinterested in the business at hand. In July 1914, the Mackintoshs went on holiday to Newbery's villa in Walberswick, Suffolk, and a few weeks later the

This drawing of Queen's College in Oxford shows how good a draftsman Henderson was prior to his right arm being badly wounded in the First World War.

First World War broke out. There was no longer much chance of new architectural commissions and they did not return to live in Glasgow. As Margaret Mackintosh later told a friend, 'I induced Toshie to just stop on and get the real rest cure that he has so badly needed for quite two years'.

John Keppie did not hear from Mackintosh after he left Glasgow in the summer of 1914 until he received a letter from him dated 28 December. Keppie wrote back on 31 December:

Dear Mackintosh,
I was glad to get your letter of 28th and find from it that you were working at Walberswick. I had almost given up hope of hearing from you and must confess you are not distinguished as a correspondent. I heard from Newbery that you were in Suffolk. He has been very unwell with nerves and is not likely to be back at the School for some time yet . . . . I am going off to Kirkcudbright for the week and will be bringing in the New Year as usual with Hornel. I hope that things will go well with you next year and with my good wishes for the season to you and Mrs Mackintosh.

Faithfully yours,
John Keppie.

This is a cordial letter, with Keppie clearly concerned that he had not heard recently from his colleague of the previous 24 years. He was obviously not at all bitter about the break-up. With the war not having been over by Christmas as some had predicted, everyone was entering uncertain times. Keppie was not quick to erase Mackintosh from the practice records, a drawing submitted to Glasgow Corporation for building approval in 1919 still bearing the nomenclature 'John Keppie and Mackintosh'. This may have been an old drawing resubmitted, but perhaps the post-war era, for those who survived it, would have allowed a fresh start, and Keppie may have been keeping the option open for Mackintosh to return to Glasgow.

Much has been written about splits between Keppie and Mackintosh, but they worked together for many years and they relied on each other as complementary talents. From 1901 to 1912, Mackintosh introduced £4,934 worth of work into the office against

Tenements on Rutherglen Road (right) designed by the practice.

Keppie's £16,303, while the profits were shared out at £5,467 and £7,069 respectively. John Keppie valued Mackintosh's ability to take on projects he had sourced through business or social contacts.

It is tempting to compare the careers of Mackintosh and his American contemporary, Frank Lloyd Wright. They were born within twelve months of each other. Wright entered the offices of Dankmar Adler and Louis Sullivan just over a year before Mackintosh joined John Honeyman and John Keppie, although Frank Lloyd Wright was more fortunate in that the Chicago office was primarily focused on commercial projects and was happy for him to develop the residential side just as the suburbs were burgeoning. His 'Prairie Style' was the result. The careers of both seemed to be over around 1910, Mackintosh's because of a recession, Wright's because of a professional crisis of confidence which led him to desert his clientele, wife and family, and run away with a client's wife to Germany.

While Wright continued to obtain a small but steady workload from 1911 to 1918, including the Imperial Hotel in Tokyo (perhaps the equivalent project for Mackintosh

Francis Newbery's 1914 portrait of the art school governors.

would have been Liverpool Cathedral, had he won the competition), the real difference between the two was Wright's longevity. He regained world prominence during the 'traditional versus modernism' debate of the 1920s and 30s, his Taliesin atelier contrasting with the European Bauhaus, and he became an architectural force again with Fallingwater, Pennsylvania and the Johnson Wax Building, Wisconsin, both built in 1936 and subsequent icons for post-war architects. His Guggenheim Museum in New York was not completed until he was 89 years old.

Mackintosh died aged 59 and his last 25 years were architecturally sparse. Designs such as that for a shop and office block in an arcaded street of 1915 suggest that he could have reinvented himself to respond to a post-1918 world, but whether he could have done this from a Glasgow base is unlikely. President of the Glasgow Institute of Architects, George Boswell, wrote in 1931:

> The shifting fashions of architecture, as exemplified by much of the building practised on the Continent, find little favour here, though, in point of fact, a Glasgow architect, in the person of the late C.R. Mackintosh, was the leader of the Modernist Movement, and 20 years ago he erected buildings in Glasgow, which are regarded today as ultra modern. That the movement has not attained to the extravagance seen in some foreign countries redounds to the credit of Glasgow's common sense.

However, the biggest difference between Wright and Mackintosh was evident in the two men's characters. Wright came from an unsettled family background, was an arrogant self-publicist and had the confidence to independently set up ventures such as his own practice and the two Taliesins. Mackintosh enjoyed the fellowship of family and the comforts of home, which he did not leave until he found his soulmate in Margaret Macdonald. He operated within the framework of an established architectural practice

SHOP AND OFFICE BLOCK IN AN ARCADED STREET

where he could leave the business side, and the socialising with prospective commercial clients, to John Keppie. When he left it, and left Glasgow, he lost this support mechanism, and, even if he had lived longer, it is difficult to see how his architectural career could have been revived. John Keppie and Charles Rennie Mackintosh complemented each other for most of the period they worked together. At the time Mackintosh was under the shadow of Keppie. It is different today.

John Honeyman

John Keppie.

C. R. Mackintosh

Signatures of the practice's first three partners.

This design by Mackintosh would not look out of place in a sleek modern shopping development, and suggests that he could have developed his architectural career further given the opportunity and a longer life.

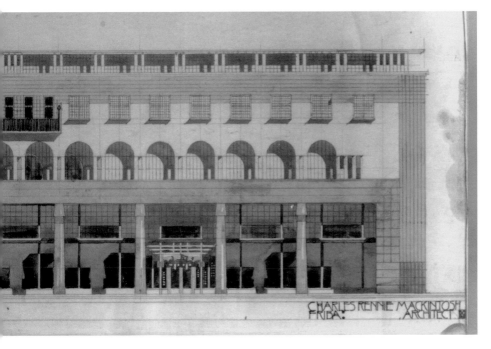

The Mercat Building forms an imposing end to the streetscape in this photograph, although today many surrounding buildings have disappeared and left it somewhat exposed.

216

CHAPTER 19

The inter-war years

During the First World War John Keppie kept the practice ticking over with bits and pieces of work from old clients like the *Glasgow Herald*, Mavor and Coulson, and Pettigrew and Stephens. There were also a few residential projects. Graham Henderson came back early from the war with an injury from being shot in the right elbow in 1916. He convalesced in Rouen and at Bangour Hospital. The surgeons wished to amputate the arm, but he persuaded them to spare it so he could at least steady his golf club with it. He had to learn to draw with his left hand. Keppie had obviously been keen to retain Henderson as he had paid him £216 per year in 1914

John Keppie photographed after the First World War.

and 1915 while he was in the army. In 1917 he was receiving a partner's share of £145 (as against Keppie's £556). Three other employees received small sums during the war – James Diggle, David McGibbon and Archie Paton. No sums are noted as being paid to Alex Smellie, but he did return, albeit slightly deaf after being injured in a train crash in Palestine.

The inter-war years coincided with an unsteady economic period, especially during the Depression of the 1930s. The plentiful supply of projects that existed before 1909 did not return, and the conservative style of architecture prevalent in the country reflected the lack of confidence of the time. Elsewhere in Europe there might have been a debate between the modernists and the traditionalists, but for most architectural practices pragmatism prevailed. Clients were to be cherished, especially old ones like the Glasgow School of Art (the Assembly Hall, 1927–30, now the students' union, the installation of a new heating system in 1920 in the Mackintosh building, and repairs in 1927–33). Keppie founded two scholarships in 1923, the John Keppie Scholarship in Architecture and the Scholarship in Sculpture, and became chairman of the school in 1930. Other established clients were the *Glasgow Herald* (alterations, 1913–20 and 1927–30) and Pettigrew and Stephens (extension onto Bath Street, 1920–25, and their Bothwell Street warehouse, 1920–25).

Other commercial projects included offices for the City of Glasgow Friendly Society

The Bath Street extension to Pettigrew and Stephens' premises.

at 200 Bath Street (1920–25), a building for the Scottish Co-operative Society at Wallace and Clarence Streets (1920–23, now demolished) next to their headquarters, an extension to Watt Brothers on to Bath Street (1929–32), and the most prominent of these, the new Sauchiehall Street Bank of Scotland (1930–32) at the corner of Blythswood Street. Keppie had the opportunity to employ his favourite sculptor on this, Benno Schotz. The offices attached to the building are today called Keppie House. A major refurbishment of the Kenilworth Hotel took place at 78–90 Argyle Street/5–9 Queen Street, this building being demolished for a new commercial development (1986/ 87) for the Legal and General Assurance Society by Scott Brownrigg and Turner, just before they merged with Keppie Henderson.

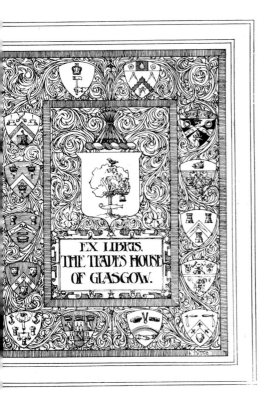

This book plate was found among materials collected by Graham Henderson around the time of the 100th anniversary of the practice, and was probably prepared by John Keppie for the Trades House.

The 1930s Keppie Henderson Watt Brothers' extension and the 1980s SBT Keppie Fisher House guard opposite corners on Bath Street.

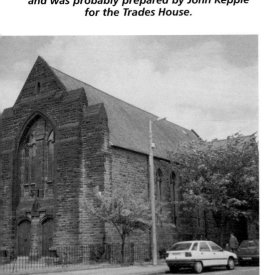

St Enoch's Hogganfield was built to serve the expanding suburbs to the north-east of the city.

The design of Croftfoot Church, in the southern suburbs of Glasgow, broke away from traditional Scottish forms.

Keppie Henderson's Bank of Scotland Building (1930–32), located at the corner of Sauchiehall Street and Blythswood Street.

New clients led to groups of projects. Alterations to the British Linen Bank at West George Street (1926/27) prepared the way for others at the bank's branches in Gorbals Street (1931), Clarkston (1931/32), Queen Street (1934), Thurso (1936), Gordon Street (1936/37), Dennistoun (1938), Lanark (1938–41) and 165 West George Street (1939–41). These all appear to involve alteration work, the single new-build project being an infill next to a church in Wick (1933–35). Kodak shops were enjoying an expansion in 1929/30, and they were fitted out at 46 Buchanan Street, Glasgow, Grainger Street, Newcastle, and Lord Street, Liverpool.

Keppie received work from his friends at the Glasgow Art Club (1922/23) and the Trades House in Glassford Street, where he had been a former deacon. Just before the First World War he obtained roof timbers from Glasgow Cathedral and designed chairs that were made and carved from them by James and John Grant. They reside in the Trades House saloon today, the windows in this room also having been designed by Keppie. In 1927 he refaced the exterior and in 1929 converted two shops at ground floor level into the present reception room.

Church projects continued, although mainly alteration work – the First Church of Christ Science at 7–11 Clifton Street, Glasgow (1924/25), Port Glasgow Parish Church (1924), Langside Parish Church halls (1926/27), St Matthew's, Perth (1927/28), Campsie Parish Church (1928), West Parish Church, Greenock (1928), Trinity College, Glasgow (1939–41), and manses at Govan Parish (1928) and Carmunnock (1929). The only new-build projects were St Enoch's, Hogganfield (1927–31) and Croftfoot Church, Glasgow (1934–36). The contrast in styles could not be greater, the former built in red stone and very much of the Keppie era, the latter a brick building and much more modern.

Domestic projects continued, including those at Blanefield for John Hay (1918–20); Kelvinside for William Keaton (1919–21); Brisbane House at 9 Rowan Road, Bellahouston, for Sir Robert Bruce (1920–26 and 1929); Harvieston, 23 Leslie Road, Pollokshields, for Hugh Mcfarlane (1926 and 1929); three separate houses at Whitecraigs (1927–29); St Brelade's Bay, Jersey, for Benjamin Lang (1928/29); a house at Prestwick for Mrs Isabella Watt (1928/29); Easter Culbowie, Buchlyvie, for W.P. Drummond (1930–32); and Viewmount, Bridge of Weir, for John A. Biggart (1938). Larger projects included the Kelvin Nursing Home at 15 Park Terrace (1928–30 and 1935), and convalescent seaside homes at Dunoon (1930).

1939 saw a burst of activity for a new type of building – air raid protection shelters. All of the practice's retail and office clients commissioned them, as well as schools at Laurel Bank, Cloberhill, Temple, St Mark's Elementary, Tollcross and Shettleston.

Jordanhill Demonstration School, 1913 to 1922

The appointment for Jordanhill School stated that John Keppie 'shall prepare a complete set of plans, shewing in addition to the buildings the exact position of all drains, chimneys, shafts, ventilators, water pipes, gas pipes, electric wires and other details'. There were few environmental or electrical engineers to call on for help in those days, so architects often specified all these items. The fee was 5 per cent of the construction cost, with half of this being paid by the end of 1914 when it was expected that building would be well under way.

Jordanhill School.

The outbreak of war in August 1914 caused a slowdown in construction at Jordanhill due to a lack of skilled labour and a shortage of materials. Costs increased for the same reasons. By the autumn of 1915 the walls had only been built to a third of their intended height. The roof was not erected until the end of 1916.

On 4 March 1918, before the school was complete, the Admiralty requisitioned it:

> for the purposes of adapting the School for the purpose of housing workmen employed in the production, storage or transport of War Material and of housing such workmen therein . . . . The War Department shall give up possession of the School to the Committee not later than six months after the date of the signature of the treaty of Peace between Great Britain and Germany.

Before the War Department could fully adapt the building to its purposes, peace broke out. John Keppie earned £766 up to 17 May 1919 on inspection duties, and construction work received a boost. However, it was 1922 before all the buildings at Jordanhill were officially opened.

Glasgow Cross, 1914 and 1923–31

In the nineteenth century, Glasgow Cross was seen as the heart of the city, the City Chambers in George Square not being completed until 1890. Until the late twentieth century it was still the place to congregate to bring in the New Year.

During Victorian and Edwardian times, the constricted nature of the junction of High Street as it met Glasgow Cross caused severe traffic problems. The destruction of the Tontine Hotel by fire in 1911 prompted a radical reassessment of the Cross, and Honeyman and Keppie's scheme for the site, submitted in July 1914, won Glasgow Corporation's competition. Graham Henderson is attributed with the design of the buildings finally erected. He had played a part in the winning of the 1913 competition for Jordanhill School, and these two projects would be seen by Keppie as the basis for rebuilding the practice after the war.

To relieve congestion, it was intended to demolish the Tolbooth (except for its steeple). The drawings which appear in the *Builder* of 9 April 1915 show a convex building still attached to the steeple by an archway through which pedestrians could walk, releasing more space for vehicles to pass on its east side. This solution still did not address the traffic issues sufficiently, and after considering relocating the steeple across the road to the Gallowgate/London Road confluence, the masterplan proposal was changed to include two symmetrical buildings either side of High Street at the Cross, their concave shape allowing more space for traffic to pass either side of the steeple. Only the building on the west was built, the one on the John McIntyre Building side succumbing to the financial stringencies of the 1920s and 30s and a lowering in status of the area with the move westwards of the commercial centre of the city.

One other part of the masterplan was completed. The 1915 drawing shows the Mercat Cross located beside the Tolbooth steeple. This was not the original cross but a modern interpretation of one removed from Glasgow Cross in 1659. The new proposal envisaged a location for the Mercat Cross between where Gallowgate and London Road meet Glasgow Cross, a move finally realised by Edith Burnet Hughes in 1930, with a new building behind it by John Keppie and Henderson which became known as

In this proposal, the new building at Glasgow Cross is convex with an archway to help support the Tolbooth Steeple. The final design was concave, with the steeple standing in isolation on a traffic island.

the Mercat Building. This is a grander building, with statues on each facade by Alexander Proudfoot, Archibald Dawson and Benno Schotz. In his book *Public Sculpture of Glasgow*, Ray McKenzie describes these three as 'the most important sculptors of their generation in the west of Scotland' and Benno Schotz as 'a protégé of the architect John Keppie'. He created a bust of Keppie in 1922 as an appreciation of their friendship. McKenzie recounts an episode from Schotz's autobiography:

Shortly before beginning work on carving his figures, he took the precaution of measuring the blocks the builders had installed on the facade, and discovered that they did not project as far as the architect had specified, and were therefore unsuited to the figures he had modelled. The distinguished London sculptor William Reid Dick advised John Keppie to insist that the builder

223

replace the blocks. 'Oh no', he is said to have replied, 'Benno will slightly redesign the figures to suit the stones.' This he accordingly did, as did Dawson, a fact that may account for the noticeably cramped appearance of the figures' legs. Proudfoot, on the other hand, was unaware of the changes required. When his full scale models arrived on site, it was found that the legs projected beyond the surface of the block, so that extra pieces of stone had to be added to accommodate the knees. The joints are clearly visible.

The work started in 1923, with demolition of the Tolbooth building and stabilisation of the steeple being completed in 1925. Next was construction of what was termed 'Building A', designed from 1923 and completed in 1927. The Mercat Building was referred to as 'Building B', designed from 1928 and completed in 1931. There is no note of a design for a 'Building C' to complete the composition, which remains incomplete today.

Mavor and Coulson, 1912, 1927–30 and 1934

Industrial projects are seldom glamorous. The buildings are by nature functional, the clients focused on the industrial process, and the investment is primarily in this. The product is the showpiece, not the building that helps produce it and which will be changed and adapted over the years. The architect's skill is in understanding the needs of the industrial process and the people involved in it, and translating these into an efficient building. In return the architect will receive fairly lucrative commissions, and if he satisfactorily carries these out will be invited back to make alterations to respond to changes in the business activities.

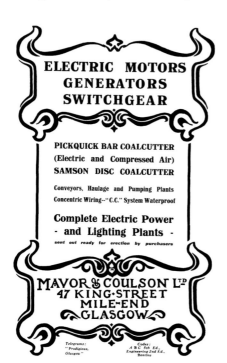

The practice carried out work for Mavor and Coulson between 1912 and 1934.

In 1861 John Honeyman designed £3,391 worth of alterations at Mirrlees and Tait's engineering works at Scotland Street, Glasgow, the most expensive project of his early career by some margin. He was back in 1872 making further alterations. If many nineteenth-century industrial projects were associated with the use of steam power, the practice's association with the company of Mavor and Coulson from 1912 to 1934 was the result of the development of electricity.

Henry Alexander Mavor was born in Stranraer in 1858, but moved to Glasgow when he was four years old. He trained as an electrical engineer at the Glasgow College of Science and Arts and continued his studies at the University of Glasgow after he started working. He became a partner in Muir and Mavor in 1883, having been responsible in 1878 for the electric lighting of, and electrical supply to, Queen Street station, Glasgow's main post office, the municipal buildings and other city centre buildings.

Glasgow Corporation used its statutory powers to bring this electricity supply company into public ownership in 1892. A new company, Mavor and Coulson Ltd., was set up, working to introduce electric power into coal mines. Henry Mavor's brother Samuel joined the business, having installed electric lighting in various cities in Britain and Ireland while working for Crompton and Co. in London. In 1887, between leaving Crompton and joining his brother, he developed his ideas in the Far East on board the Japanese cruiser *Jakachiao Kan*, which sank the Russian warships *Variag* and *Rurik* during the Russo–Japanese War of 1904/05.

At the same time as John Keppie was governor of the Glasgow School of Art, Henry Mavor was governor of the Glasgow and West of Scotland Technical College, and the two of them joined forces to develop courses for the education of architects. Mavor was also an officer with the Lanarkshire Rifle Volunteers. His brother Sam was a member of the Glasgow Art Club.

While Honeyman, Keppie and Mackintosh were designing their first commission to alter the works of Mavor and Coulson at 47 Broad Street, Mile-End, Glasgow, in 1912, the Mavor brothers were developing an alternating-current dynamo for powering ships, first demonstrated on the Gare Loch on 31 May 1911 by the ship *Electric Arc*. The electricity was generated using a six-cylinder petrol motor, giving a higher speed from 35 horsepower than a 45-horsepower steam engine did. The enhanced efficiency arose from the ability to run the propellers at varying and lower speeds than when the engine – whether steam or petrol powered – was connected directly to the propeller shaft. At lower speeds the fuel economy was improved by up to 50 per cent. Initially, Swan Hunter on the Tyne adopted the system, as did some American shipbuilders, the USA battleship *California* being powered by it. The British Admiralty eventually appreciated its advantages and Honeyman and Keppie received commissions throughout the First World War to design extensions and alterations to the Broad Street factory.

Henry Mavor died in 1915 and his obituary stated that: 'unlike many of the leading industrialists of Clydeside he built no neo-baronial castle at Rhu and not even a villa in Pollokshields'. He lived most of his life in West Regent Street in Glasgow, bringing up his family there and for a short time in East Kilbride. His son, Osborne Henry Mavor, was better known under the nom de plume James Bridie, writer and driving force in setting up the Citizens Theatre.

It was in East Kilbride that John Keppie and Henderson designed a new factory for the company from 1927 to 1930, extending it in 1934. Expansion at Broad Street was still taking place at this time.

Beattie the Baker, 1921–39, 1945, 1950–55 and 1960

The first project noted for William Beattie involved alterations to his house, Craigend, near Milngavie, in 1905 (designed 1903/04). £7,835 was spent on east and west gate lodges, hothouses and various other external improvements. The job books also indicate designs for a Trades House in Milngavie from 1909 to 1919 with William Beattie as the client. This has not been traced. However, work to Beattie's many bakeries provided the practice with a constant supply of work for many years.

From the 1870s bread-making became mechanised, with the standard 2lb white

William Beattie and his bakery business were both important clients of the practice.

loaf being mass-produced. A multitude of small bakers disappeared, but so did unhygienic practices such as kneading dough by trampling it underfoot. John Montgomery was the first Glasgow baker to wrap loaves individually; others transported trays of unwrapped bread through the polluted streets of Glasgow which were covered in horse manure. William Beattie designed much of his own machinery at the Dennistoun Bakery to standards of hygiene set by the Bakery and Factory Acts. He was a council member of the Glasgow Institute of Fine Arts for many years and this may have brought him into contact with John Keppie. On 15 November 1906 Keppie proposed him for membership of the Glasgow Archaeological Society, although his address at the time was Parkhall, Dalmuir.

It was at the Dennistoun Bakery that various alterations were carried out from 1921 to 1934. Works are recorded as taking place at 38 Wesleyan Street from 1936 to 1937 and to stables at Aitken Street, Dennistoun (1938/39). The work was well-suited to Alex Smellie, since it involved factory premises where his engineering skills and architectural planning made him a one-man-band design team. Assistants after the Second World War referred to him as a loner, and one can imagine him alone in his office in Woodside Place, which was a rabbit warren of rooms created from two old terraced houses. Post-war work reflected the expansion of Beattie's, from extensions at Drumchapel (1945 and 1954/55) to new bakeries at Kings Cross Road, Dundee (1950–53 and 1960) in an unemployment black spot, and Edinburgh (1960). It was not glamorous work, but it paid the bills.

The daughter of the master of works at Beattie's, Mr Silver, worked as a maid at Balmoral in the 1950s when Graham Henderson was designing the Queen Mother's house at Birkhall.

Golf clubs

One of Mackintosh's biographers stated that John Keppie was the long-distance driving champion of Glasgow. I have not been able to confirm this, although I did

Killermont House, which Glasgow Golf Club member John Keppie converted to a clubhouse when the club moved there in 1904.

find a medal score that had Keppie going round Glasgow Golf Club in the spring meeting of May 1902 in 90 shots less his three handicap. Perhaps the weather was bad that day, or a troublesome client was taking his mind off his game. He was captain of the Glasgow Golf Club in 1909. The club moved to the Killermont Estate in 1904, and John Keppie converted Killermont House for the use of its members. When major alterations were planned for the house from 1931 to 1933, the practice was appointed to carry them out. John Keppie and Graham Henderson had prepared various options from 1923 to address the poor condition of the building. The club eventually approved £7,570 worth of reconstruction work and rejected another proposal by Keppie for a £20,000 new building in its stead. The committee minutes of 22 December 1930 approved £6,000 for work at Killermont and the club's second course at Gailes. The extension at the latter was removed to build new changing rooms in 2001.

The interior of the Pollok Golf Club house locker room.

Works to Pollok Golf Club house took place in 1926 and 1933. It had been used as a recuperation facility for wounded soldiers during the First World War, and the practice carried out extensions for the members. The gents' changing room (the only changing room as it does not allow female members) has interior decor and roof trusses which suggested to one Mackintosh enthusiast that a lost design by him had been uncovered. Perhaps an old one had been recycled, but it is a very attractive space.

The original 1906 Whitecraigs Golf Club house, which was extended by Keppie Henderson to much the size it is today.

Graham Henderson was a member of Pollok Golf Club, but it is not clear how the practice came to obtain the commission for Whitecraigs clubhouse from 1935 to 1937. Perhaps one of the three clients the practice had designed houses for in the area at the end of the 1920s had been a member.

The last years of King John

With Graham Henderson in charge of the office, and Alex Smellie becoming a partner in 1930, Keppie could work at his own pace. He spent a lot of time at the Glasgow Art Club, sitting in a prominent position where he could see everyone coming and going.

His nickname there was 'King John'.

During the 1920s he enjoyed the company of Benno Schotz. As Schotz recalled:

Every Saturday afternoon we would both go out to sketch. We would walk along the Forth and Clyde Canal, or we would take a tramcar to the outskirts of the city and walk from there. When we found something which Keppie considered suitable, we would sit down, make ourselves comfortable, and draw. For me, the outings were of immense importance. Usually I had to draw what Keppie chose, but this did not worry me, so long as I drew. It helped me to loosen my hand and my line. On the way back to town we would stop for a cup of tea, and it became an unwritten rule that he would pay one Saturday, and I the next. He kept good accounting, and if I was not quick enough he would say 'Benno, it is your turn'. We continued these outings for years, even for some time after I was married, until my wife began to protest that it was not fair to leave her alone on Saturday afternoons, considering that she herself was busy all week in her dressmaking shop. She was right, but Keppie, being a bachelor, remained unconvinced.

Those of us who have fallen heir to John Keppie's sketches cherish them.

On 25 January 1925, Schotz strained himself lifting a heavy clay bust and started to vomit blood. A friend rushed round to the ambulance base at the corner of West Regent Street and Blythswood Square, and he was taken to the Royal Infirmary. John Keppie heard about the accident and came in to visit the next day. He knew the chief of the ward and had Schotz moved from the Nightingale ward (of open-plan design with about fourteen men in it) to a private room, where he remained for seven weeks until he was better. 'I had peace and quietness, except that the nurses would come in and tickle my toes. What a fine bunch of girls!'

From 1924 to 1926, John Keppie was president of the Royal Incorporation of Architects in Scotland. By the mid-1920s he had become a council member of the

John Keppie could have travelled up to Gailes to play golf, as he was a member of the Glasgow Golf Club, but he joined the St Nicholas Club in Prestwick. He could walk to it from his house, and, unlike at the Glasgow Golf Club, women and children were welcome.

Royal Institute of British Architects, and in 1929 was appointed vice-president. In 1920 he was elected an associate of the Royal Scottish Academy, becoming a full member in 1937.

John Keppie probably retired from the business in 1937. The certificate of registration of April 1939 certainly confirms Andrew Graham Henderson and Alexander Smellie as the sole partners of John Keppie and Henderson, 181 West Regent Street. From 1905 Keppie and his sister Jessie had lived at 16 Hamilton Park Terrace, just off Great Western Road in the West End of Glasgow. In 1939 they gave their address to the Glasgow Art Club as Haddington Park, Prestwick, a large semi-detached villa on the road down to the railway station and the shore. The family had always had a house there. In 1892 Keppie had designed a bell tower for Prestwick North Church (completed 1896), noticeable by its stonework being a different colour from the rest of the church. Mackintosh received a good financial package when he became a partner from 1902 to 1904, and one of the items of office expenditure at the time was life membership of Prestwick St Nicholas Golf Club, suggesting that Keppie had made this a benefit of the partnership agreement. By 1937 Keppie was 75 years old and probably past managing a full round of golf. His obituary in the *Ayr Advertiser* stated that his health had been poor from around 1938.

Thomas Howarth visited the Keppies at Prestwick on several occasions. At the time, no one knew which buildings had been designed by Mackintosh, which were the result of collaboration, and which were by others in the office. Keppie was not helpful: 'unfortunately conversation about the early days was not easy; John Keppie did not have many charitable things to say about his former partner'. It is a pity Howarth tells us no more about what he learned on the visits. His only interest must have been Mackintosh, and to Keppie his erstwhile partner was involved in only a part of his distinguished working life.

By this time Keppie was an old man. Employee Archie Doak remembered coming into the office in the 1930s on a day off to pick something up and being confronted by Keppie in the hall: 'Who are you? What do you want?' was the demand and Doak replied 'I work here Mr Keppie, it's my day off.' Keppie had not recognised a member of staff who was not wearing the regulation wing collar. Staff members were also encouraged to wear green waistcoats and yellow ties. According to Alex Smellie's daughter Margaret, in his later years Keppie was somewhat wandered and eccentric, and it is doubtful that Howarth would have been able to obtain any sort of balanced view from him on events of 40 years before. Margaret was not particularly complimentary about the interview they had with Howarth. Her father was concerned that he had interpreted from his comments that Mackintosh was a drunkard, which, despite the troubles in his later years in Glasgow, he certainly was not.

After Keppie died in 1945, Jessie contacted Howarth and sent him photographs of the Immortals for an exhibition he was setting up at Glasgow School of Art. It is strange that he did not use them, and it was many years before they were discovered again in the school's archives, possibly bequeathed by Jessie. She had certainly retained affection for Mackintosh, even though he had chosen Margaret Macdonald in her stead. Jessie visited the Mackintosh memorial exhibition in 1933 with John Keppie and Benno Schotz and purchased one of Mackintosh's watercolours. A grumpy old man might not have wanted to talk to Howarth about a troublesome business partner, but an old lady cherished the memories she had and held on to these personal mementos of happy times with friends.

One of Jessie's photographs may give a clue as to how she felt about Mackintosh's transfer of affections from her to Margaret. The composition is obviously stage-managed. Mackintosh is the centre of attention, with maids of honour dressed in white, two of them forming an archway over him. On the right, Jessie and Margaret are dressed in the same colour, the former looking over her shoulder to her friend, whom she had probably introduced to Toshie some years before. The mischievous smiles on the faces of the two do not suggest the animosity others have attributed to their love of the same man.

In 1949, in response to a Howarth letter, Jessie wrote:

Probably the last photograph to be taken of John Keppie.

I have read with great interest your letter on Charles Rennie Mackintosh in yesterday's *Herald*. I knew him so well in his early days and always felt that architecture was to him the most important thing in his life. I could never understand how Glasgow got the name of not appreciating his work as I think no young architect ever got so many of his own ideas carried out – or was so much admired – by so many clients: with

Jessie Keppie treasured this photograph of the Immortals, which reminded her of happy days when she was young.

the war intervening while he was still at the zenith of his work he had to be content with the lighter phase of his capabilities, otherwise we might have had many more of his beautiful buildings. I think your letter was most enlightening and very fair. And I am waiting with interest to see your book. Believe me.

John Keppie died on 28 April 1945, and his sister on 10 October 1951. His estate was valued at £40,931. 3s. 6d., and hers at £48,915. 19s. 6d. Graham Henderson received a letter dated 5 May 1945 from Maclay Murray and Spens informing him that Mr John Keppie RSA, FRIBA had bequeathed him the sum of £2,000, 'for the respect and regard I have for him and as a memento of the pleasant and to me satisfactory relationship I have always had with him'. John is buried in a prominent corner plot in Prestwick and Monkton Cemetery beside the runway of Prestwick Airport, along with Jessie (1868–1951), and the headstone commemorates two other sisters, Mary Quillins Keppie (1858–1923) and Jane Keppie (1860–1924), and John's brother-in-law John Henderson (1863–1918).

The Keppie family grave.

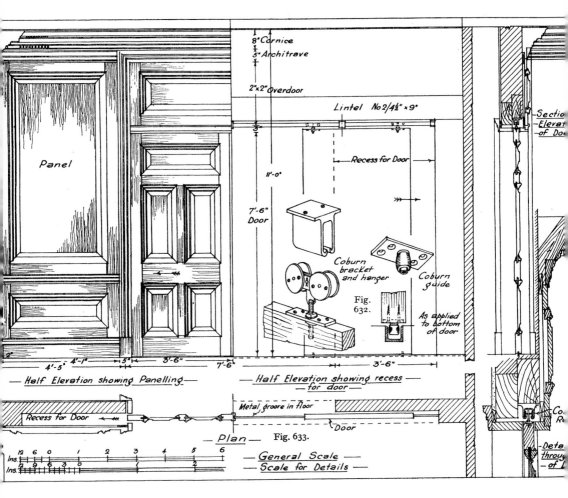

8" Cornice

⅜" Architrave

2"×2" Overdoor

Lintel No 2/4½"×9"

Panel

Recess for Door

11'-0"

7'-6" Door

Coburn bracket and hanger

Coburn guide

Fig. 632.

As applied to bottom of door

Sectio
Elevat
of Do

4'-5"   4'-1"   5"   3'-6"   7'-6"   3'-6"

— Half Elevation showing Panelling —   — Half Elevation showing recess —
for door —

Recess for Door

Metal groove in floor

Door

Co
Re

— Plan —   Fig. 633.

Deta
throu
of L

12 6 0   1   2   3   4   5   6
Ins.

Ins.

— General Scale —
— Scale for Details —

Until the 1960s and 70s architects consulted textbooks like Mitchell's Building Construction which were based on the use of traditional trades and skills.

232

CHAPTER 20

The practice from 1945 to 1979

Lieutenant Colonel A. Graham Henderson FRIBA, president of the Glasgow Art Club, returned to the practice in 1945. He was president of the Royal Incorporation of Architects in Scotland from 1945 to 1947. Alex Smellie had looked after the business during the war, as well as being a fire watcher from his home in Newlands. John Keppie had died, and Henderson and Smellie were in their sixties, but with the country's hopes of building a new land 'fit for heroes' they set about establishing a practice to meet new challenges. Smellie brought his daughter in to help for a few months over the summer of 1959, but she ended up staying for 24 years. Prior to the war, the office had moved from 181 West Regent Street to 26 Blythswood Square, and after the war 196 West Regent Street was purchased. With an increasing workload, 21 Woodside Place was bought in 1952, with number 20 added the following year.

Lieutenant Colonel Graham Henderson.

By 1946 the country had become used to the central government control that had been in place since 1940, and shortages ensured that this situation continued for the next decade. In this environment, state control of the rebuilding effort was a natural consequence and with a new Labour government broader socialist principles could be tested. Schools had been taken under the control of the state with the Education Act of 1872, and at the beginning of the twentieth century state-subsidised public housing became commonplace, much to the detriment of private social housing developers who could no longer compete. It took until 1948 for healthcare to become socialised with the creation of the National Health Service.

Industrial development was sponsored by public agencies, but these still used private-sector developers like Taylor Woodrow. The practice's involvement in this area and other public sector initiatives – schools, further education and healthcare – are

Joseph L. Gleave.

given their own chapters. This chapter covers the other work carried out during this period.

In the years to 1979, the nature of the practice was largely defined by healthcare and education projects. Joseph Lea Gleave became a partner in 1949 to develop healthcare in particular. The practice then became known as John Keppie and Henderson and J.L. Gleave. Gleave asked Professor John Needham at the architectural school in Dundee to 'send me your best student' each year, and Ian Plenderleith, John Boys, Matt Neilson and Alastair Lamond came from this source. In 1955 the certificate of registration shows the partners as Andrew Graham Henderson, Alexander Smellie, Joseph Lea Gleave, Thomas Russell Scott, Geoffrey George Wimpenny and Richard Rudolph Chitham De'Ath. The circumstances surrounding Gleave's departure in 1958 are given in chapter 24, the practice reverting to the name of Keppie Henderson and Partners after that year.

After the austerity of the late 1940s and 1950s, the economy experienced a series of ups and downs and gradually slipped behind those of defeated countries such as Japan, West Germany and even Italy. Industrial relations were poor and strikes by seamen in 1966, dock-workers in 1970, and miners in 1971, 1972 and 1973 caused the prime ministers of the time to declare states of emergency. At one time the country only had enough electrical power for businesses to work three days a week, and the government had to go cap in hand to the World Bank as public borrowing had got out of control. Public sector projects stuttered, and the lack of economic certainty, combined with high taxation, discouraged private-sector investment. To some extent a practice such as Keppie Henderson was cushioned from these effects as large public sector projects, once started, gained their own momentum, and scale fees based on a percentage of capital costs combined with high rates of inflation could result in a windfall payment when the final account was prepared.

Geoff Wimpenny's textbook from 1939, *Mitchell's Building Construction*, is still in our office. It was written in a different world where traditionally designed buildings were built by craftsmen. However, from 1950, architecture developed a utopian vision intended to sweep the bad old world away, and this, combined with new industrialised construction techniques that substituted for a shortage of labour, led to the wholesale introduction of modernism into design. Unfortunately, new techniques and materials, a lack of skills and public funding that was thinly spread, led to many poor results and a general public disenchantment with modern architecture. Radical modernism seldom blended well with adjacent historic buildings or a traditional townscape. Architects who saw bold concrete structures in dry, sunny countries copied them in the UK, where the weather conditions ensured a grey drabness. Modern flat roofs and wall panels leaked, 'movement joints' failed to work and walls cracked, floor screeds failed, large window walls created unpleasant internal environments and concrete spawled

234

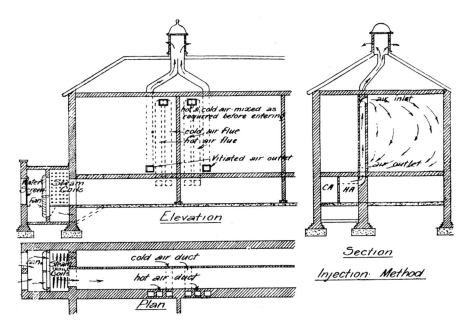

Mitchell's Building Construction *allowed architects to make rule-of-thumb designs, in this case for a ventilation system, which in today's bureaucratic, litigious and more sophisticated world require the input of specialist engineers.*

(broke away from steel reinforcements as they rusted within it). But such was the confidence of the creators of the 'brave new world' that such issues were regarded as minor setbacks, and this insensitivity, and perhaps arrogance, led to a fall in the prestige of the architectural profession.

Architects become very passionate about using peer-approved architectural style, and in the past great theoretical debates have arisen about Gothic versus classical, free style versus established, modern versus classical, or modernism versus postmodernism. However, most of society is more concerned that all three principles of the Roman architect, Vitruvius, are applied: that buildings display 'commodity, firmness and delight'. Some architects in the 1960s and 70s compromised the first two to impress peers with the third characteristic. Many buildings that looked good in magazines and won awards when they were brand new did not stand the test of time. This is why Keppie Design today is somewhat ambivalent about peer awards.

Social and assisted housing

The Scottish Council for the Care of Spastics was formed in 1946. In those days, someone with cerebral palsy was called a 'spastic', and someone with Down's syndrome, a 'mongol'. However, in 1996 the Scottish Council for Spastics became Capability Scotland, with the motto: 'Turning disability into ability', and the Disability Discrimination Act (1995) has made it unlawful to treat disabled people less favourably than other people for a reason relating to their disability. As a result, access audits are now an integral part of the design of buildings. Victorian public buildings would often have grand public stairs at their entrances which paid little regard to disability issues,

Stanmore House, near Lanark, was being used as a boarding school for boys before it was converted into a residential school for handicapped children.

A Hanover Housing Association development close to Crow Road in Glasgow.

and many post-war buildings were little better.

In the 1960s Keppie Henderson was obliged to employ at least one disabled person as the staff complement had risen above 50. Graham Henderson's daughter and her husband worked with the Crippled League and they had a special interest in disabled issues. Pat Murray was hired as a receptionist for the practice on 13 March 1961, and every morning she was lifted up the front steps of the Woodside Place office in her wheelchair by two strong lads. Henderson himself suffered disability after a stroke in 1961, and his chauffeur, Peter, would pick up Pat each morning. Her disability arose after a smallpox scare in 1950, when, as a fifteen-year-old, she was administered a faulty vaccine. She retired on 22 September 1989.

When it opened in October 1957, Stanmore School was the first residential establishment for physically disabled children in Britain. Ten years later, Keppie Henderson designed a purpose-built home for the school just outside Lanark, called Stanmore House. Next, in June 1980, came the Rashielee Hostel in Erskine, renamed Westlands, and then a hostel and day centre called Wallace Court in Elderslie, which opened on 19 March 1990. It has accommodation for 25 people, fifteen single flats and five shared, each with en suite facilities. Catering for children and adults with cerebral palsy, its clients have access to occupational therapy, physiotherapy, and speech and language therapy.

The Hanover Housing Association also provided assisted housing at Wallace Court in Elderslie, Bloom Court in Livingston, in Dunblane, Laurel Street in Glasgow, in Drumchapel and at Church Street, Broxburn. The last such project the practice carried out was at Eldon Street in Greenock for the Margaret Blackwood Housing Association. It had a long gestation period during the 1980s, with no fees payable until the project obtained financial approval for public funding. The costs of redesigning the project until a solution was affordable eventually became financially unviable for the practice, although in the early 1990s many architects still carried out housing association work on a speculative basis with the certain knowledge that the low, competitive fees available for such work would inevitably lead to a loss.

Peter McCann House, on Bell Street, was named after a Lord Provost of Glasgow, and was commissioned by the corporation as a model lodging house for homeless people, providing an alternative to the Great Eastern Hotel. Rooms had to be designed to be as small as possible for single-living accommodation.

Retail and commercial projects

In the 1960s there was a consumer boom, the first since the recession of 1910. Keppie Henderson was involved in the expansion of Littlewoods stores in Glasgow, Aberdeen, Edinburgh and Kirkcaldy, and by 1970 the practice's first shopping mall was being designed in Rutherglen, where partner Geoff Wimpenny lived. By the standards of the American-inspired malls of the 1980s, the Rutherglen mall now looks rather insignificant, and today retail outlets in inner suburbs like this are at a disadvantage compared to those in city centres or at out-of-town developments. In 2004 the prospect of the M74 extension making Rutherglen more accessible to a wider population could lead to a reassessment of this status.

Before the Conservative government's private-sector revival in the 1980s, being a commercial developer was extremely difficult. Keppie Henderson secured work with developer Ladbrokes in Glasgow, and for Ravenstone Securities built an office block at 219–221 West George Street, Glasgow, and shops and offices at 174–176 High Street, Perth. Geoff Wimpenny was the partner in charge of the Motherwell Bridge and Engineering offices. GKN commissioned alterations to their Glasgow offices, and such was the success of these that the practice was asked to design a new GKN headquarters in Birmingham. GKN chief architect, Kenneth Gryce, decided to carry out the site supervision himself, and Keppie Henderson had to accept its fee being reduced from 6 per cent of construction cost to 4 per cent accordingly.

Birkhall, c.1955

Graham Henderson became the first Scottish-based president of the Royal Institute of British Architects. Perhaps because of this position, he was invited to design the conversion of the Queen Mother's house at Birkhall on Deeside. It sits on a promontory overlooking the River Muick and is bowered in old varieties of roses, the favourite flower of the late Queen Mother. The Birkhall Estate dates from 1715 and was purchased by Queen Victoria and Prince Albert in 1849 for their son, Edward.

After her daughter succeeded to the throne, Queen Elizabeth the Queen Mother made Birkhall her home. Situated just outside Ballater, it was not far from Balmoral.

237

Birkhall, near Ballater, was purchased by Queen Victoria and Prince Albert in 1849. After her daughter came to the throne, Queen Elizabeth, the Queen Mother moved to Birkhall and had Graham Henderson design an extension for her.

Graham Henderson carried out the conversion and added a south wing. With only one good arm, he had a chauffeur called James and on two occasions their car slid off icy roads and into a ditch on its way north. The Queen Mother was most sympathetic, and was ready with a large whisky each time they arrived. Henderson met the Queen at Birkhall and again when she came to visit Vale of Leven Industrial Estate.

Past presidents of RIBA were normally awarded a knighthood, and Henderson was extremely disappointed to be an exception. He said he would have been happy with an MBE. Staff who worked with him offered stories to explain this. One is that he upset Prince Philip at some point; another that when a young architect criticised Henderson's design in front of the Queen Mother, he took exception and made a scene. Perhaps being born outside the UK had some relevance, and Bill Sprague, the RIBA secretary at the time, wondered if it was because he was not London-based. We shall probably never know. He certainly thought of himself as having the proper pedigree. His daughter gave me a copy of his family tree that he had traced as far back as 1260 to Dom. Gullielmus de Dunlop.

Glasgow Sheriff Court, 1970–86, and 2001

As early as 1932 it was identified that the sheriff court building in the Merchant City was too small and had no room to expand. The 1841 county buildings and courthouses in Wilson Street originally contained the county offices as well as courts until the City Chambers were completed in 1890. The whole city block in Wilson Street eventually became the courts building. Management consultants were appointed in 1965 by the Court House Commissioners and they recommended that a new building be constructed containing four criminal jury courts, eleven general purpose courts, a diet court (a court to debate points of law), an appeal court, two juvenile courts, a civil court and a criminal custody court.

As there was no space large enough in the city centre to provide for what was needed, the commissioners looked south of the river where the Gorbals was being comprehensively redeveloped, or rather obliterated. The area had deteriorated during the 1930s recession and the post-war era, earning a reputation for its slums and *No Mean City* image. The chosen site for the courts was located between one which would later contain the Glasgow Central Mosque and Carlton Terrace, which was terminated at its eastern end by a church designed by David Hamilton. The church was sufficiently decrepit and insignificantly small in townscape terms in relation to the new building that Keppie Henderson partner Dick De'Ath refused to consider its retention. The Scottish Development Department reluctantly accepted this fait accompli.

Keppie Henderson were appointed as architects in 1970. In 1972 the client body changed from Glasgow Corporation to the newly formed Property Services Agency of the Department of the Environment, which was charged with providing accommodation required by the government. Then, on 1 April 1975 the sheriffdoms of Glasgow and Strathkelvin were combined and took over responsibility. Each time the client changed, so did the requirements. Work did not commence on site until March 1979, and then only to divert sewers which would have been in the way of the building. Proper construction work did not start until June 1981, with the 'topping out' ceremony being carried out on 28 September 1983 by Michael Ancram MP, then Minister for Home Affairs and Environment at the Scottish Office. Construction work was finished in January 1986, with fitting-out work and furnishings following on, so that sittings did not commence until May 1986.

In contrast with other public buildings of the era such as schools and hospitals, the budget allowed the best of materials. There was granite cladding from the Isle of Bornholm in the Baltic Sea, Hoptonwood limestone from Middleton Quarry in Wirksworth, and Cat Castle Quarry in Lartington was specially reopened to obtain sandstone. The interior was lined with wenge hardwood from Zaire, American white oak, Japanese sen ash, and, most expensive of all, English brown oak was used for the shrieval chambers. In those days people were only starting to ask if hardwoods came from renewable sources. Since it was considered important that there should be continuity of the grain pattern of the wood, each log had to be assessed to ensure

Glasgow Sheriff Court.

239

The main public concourse in Glasgow Sheriff Court.

Prisoners frequently used to be crowded into these cells all day for what was often a short visit upstairs to a court to plead 'guilty' or 'not guilty' pending trial. A video link with Barlinnie Prison now allows this to happen remotely, reducing the need to transfer prisoners across Glasgow.

that it contained enough timber for a particular room or court.

All this granite and sandstone created a very heavy building, and 707 concrete piles were driven over 20 metres down to sit the foundations on and stop the courts sinking into the 33-metre deep soft alluvial muds and deposits beneath the site.

Key to the planning of the building was the segregation of various groups of people. After entering the reception area, potential jury members are taken to one side of each criminal court, and witnesses to the other. Prosecution and defence witnesses wait in separate rooms. The judges and other officials enter from the back via a stair from their underground car park or upper-level chambers, and the accused are taken directly from the basement cells up a stair to the dock in the centre of the courtroom.

In 2001 Keppie Design returned to Glasgow Sheriff Court to extend the shrieval chambers, and the same year the practice was appointed to redevelop Dumbarton Sheriff Court, which was in a very unsuitable Victorian building. Cross circulation meant that witnesses and jury members could accidentally meet, and prisoners had to be taken outside to enter the court by a different door, often using the same corridor for access as the magistrate. Occasionally, inappropriate liaisons occurred, and the rights of defendants were compromised. The reconfigured building solved this.

The Glasgow and Strathkelvin Sheriff Court is also a highly serviced building. All courtrooms are air-conditioned, with computerised controls for ventilation, energy, fire detection, and security systems. The latter are linked to infrared and microwave detection, and over 50 cameras are interconnected with video recording systems. Gas-fired boilers are backed up by diesel-electric powered ones.

A limited competition for artwork for the building, organised by the Glasgow School of Art, was won by Jake Kempsell in 1985, and in the atrium space he carved a low bas-relief in stone incorporating the scales of justice, the Glasgow coat of arms and St Mungo, Glasgow's patron saint.

The courts are sometimes open to the public on Doors Open Days, and the tour of the various parts of the building is fascinating. Despite the fact that some of its occupants are by their nature not well-behaved citizens, and it is one of the busiest courts in Europe, it still looks as good as it did when it opened almost 20 years ago. This cannot be said for many buildings of its era.

Jake Kempsell's bas-relief commissioned for Glasgow Sheriff Court.

The Vale of Leven Industrial Estate opened in 1948 on a 40-acre site on the Strathleven Estate.

CHAPTER 21

Rebuilding Scotland's industry

After the First World War, the traditional heavy industries of the west of Scotland – shipbuilding, mechanical engineering, steel production and coal mining – went into decline. In 1937 Scottish Industrial Estates was set up to promote light industrial development, and architect Edward Wylie (his practice later becoming Wylie Shanks) was appointed to coordinate the design of industrial developments. This explains the similarity in style of industrial estates of the era like those at Hillington and Newhouse.

In 1946 a site was acquired by Scottish Industrial Estates at Vale of Leven, an area suffering from the decline of traditional industries. Keppie Henderson obtained the architectural work for the new industrial estate, a massive boost to set the practice on a sure footing after the Second World War. Blocks 1 to 3 were designed and built from 1946 to 1948, W. and J.R. Watson being the builder, and the massive sum of £299,381 was the final cost. Watson's also built Block 4 for Westclox, but Angus MacDougall was appointed to build Block 5 for Burroughs.

Great success was achieved in attracting companies to Scotland during the 1950s and 60s, but the fluctuating fortunes of the country's and the world's economies led to decline in the 1970s and 80s. The days of government participation in the provision and ownership of industry had passed, this not being compatible with the free market approach pursued by the Thatcher government from 1979. In 1985 the Scottish Development Agency set up a partnership with private developers City Link Developments with a view to carrying out an £18 million redevelopment of the Vale of Leven Industrial Estate, but in June 1990 it eventually sold it to Caledonian Land as part of a package of Scottish industrial premises amounting to 7 million square feet and 365 acres of land which cost a total of £105 million. The Vale of Leven element amounted to nineteen lettable units totalling 168,000 square feet.

Caledonian Land was a joint venture between London and Edinburgh Trust and Lilley Construction, the latter itself succumbing to the recession of the early 1990s. SBT Keppie was employed by Caledonian Land to prepare a masterplan

The Vale of Leven Industrial Estate was a great success, attracting over 2,000 jobs. This footbridge linked the estate to Renton.

In the 1980s the government recognised that new, high-tech industries required a different type of premises, and revised town planning use-classification allowed business parks to grow up around cities. In Glasgow, these were initially regarded as a possible threat to the city centre office market because of their access to good parking, close to motorways. Only a few small developments were therefore built, like this one at Hillington.

for Hillington Industrial Estate, but only a few sites there were developed during difficult economic times. Some infrastructure works, a small shopping centre and two low-cost industrial units were designed by SBT Keppie, along with an office development on a site purchased by another private developer, London and Clydeside. The recession of the early 1980s was followed by a boom in the second half of the decade, and the biggest boom in the boom and bust cycle of the post-war period led to what seemed like the biggest bust in the early 1990s. Caledonian Land gradually sold off many of its assets in parcels and rested on the secure rental income of the remainder.

Westclox, 1953, 1956 and c.1988

Muir Glen was born in Glasgow, and was educated at Kelvinside Academy and Loretto School before qualifying as a chartered accountant. In 1937 he was employed by the General Time Corporation in the USA with the intention of opening a factory to make clocks in Britain. War intervened, but after serving as a major in the Royal Artillery and being awarded an MBE, he became managing director of the new Westclox factory in Vale of Leven.

Initially, clock parts were imported from the USA, but by 1952 all components were being made in Scotland, including newly invented luminous dials. Extensions to the factory were completed by Keppie Henderson in 1953 and 1956, Melville Dundas and Whitson and Angus MacDougall being the builders. Some of the 500 employees went on exchange programmes to the firm's Canadian factory. 60 per cent of the staff were women, which was controversial since men returning from the forces expected priority for jobs, and the employment of women was seen as denying them work and reducing labour costs for the firm. However, this was the main reason American companies were setting up plants in the UK, since labour costs were half those in America. By 1972 the factory was making 2.5 million clocks and watches each year with one third being exported, despite the threat of the British market being flooded by cheap products from communist countries behind the Iron Curtain.

Block 6 at Vale of Leven was used to make pocket watches, which were fashionable for a short time in the 1950s. Pilkington took it over in 1968 to develop fibre optics, infrared glasses and optical crystals for use in lasers. For a short time, after the purchase of Barr and Stroud, glass was melted at Vale of Leven for extruding into fibre-optic cables, but it soon proved cheaper to import the material from Germany and Japan.

This part of the business was sold off in 1990. A few years before this, Keppie Henderson had carried out alterations to Pilkington Electro Optic Material, as the Vale of Leven concern was called.

Westclox bucked the trend in the 1960s and 1970s when a mixture of decaying traditional industries, industrial unrest and militantism, and class-motivated management was the norm. In 1973, when Minister of Industrial Development Chris Chataway visited the factory to be presented with the 50-millionth alarm clock made, managing director John Santos stated:

BIG BEN WON'T TAKE Z$Z_{Z_{Z_Z}}$ FOR AN ANSWER

A 'Jock Clock' made by Westclox.

Firms considering starting operations in Scotland should disregard critics who castigate the region and come and look at the record for themselves. Scotland is not a cemetery for industry. General Time established a completely new light engineering industry in the west of Scotland in an area of traditional heavy engineering where light engineering was relatively unknown over 25 years ago. We strongly disagree with such Jeremiahs and know there are many others like us who are satisfied with the environment and are operating successfully here.

One of the markets Westclox alarm clocks were exported to was the Republic of Ireland, and due to their reliability and simplicity of construction, 'Jock Clocks', as they were known, were a favourite of the IRA for adapting into bomb detonators.

In October 1974 the Westclox factory was visited by Neil Armstrong, the first man on the moon, and Patrick Moore, astronomer and television personality. This was to publicise the company's first range of quartz digital and analogue watches, technology which had been developed during the space race. The watches claimed 'unparalleled accuracy to within 60 seconds a year'.

The future had seemed bright up to 1974, but no one could have predicted the world economic crisis which took place that year, and which affected even the most efficient companies. For a few years the USA had been encouraging Middle Eastern countries to increase their oil prices to make American-produced oil more competitive. American oil companies who had stakes in Middle Eastern oil would also profit from this. Unfortunately, the OPEC oil producing countries of the Middle East thought this such a good idea that they went out on their own and raised prices so much that in the first six months of 1974 the cost of living of the OECD countries – Canada, USA, Japan, France, Germany, Italy, and the UK – rose by an average of 14.8 per cent. The UK economy, which had already been in decline, went into free fall.

Westclox struggled against a depressed world economy and changing technologies until 1980 when three batches of redundancies took place. Margaret Thatcher had come to power the year before with a mandate to stop government support for failing industries and to curtail the power of militant trades unions. At a conference at Aviemore to discuss the Scottish economy in 1974, Peter Jay, then economics editor at *The Times*, had predicted the bitter medicine:

Only if the governments of the major industrial countries, which are also for the most part the great democracies, are willing to countenance years of mass unemployment, without taking any fiscal or monetary counteraction, will it be plausible to expect any secular or long-term abatement of inflation.

In 1987 there was a plan for £1.25 million worth of investment in Westclox, by then called Tulley UK, for diversification into the manufacture of bathware goods. Clock manufacture stopped in 1990 when 145 of the 230 remaining staff were made redundant. At the time, Marie Hopwood, representative of the Amalgamated Engineering Union, said:

In here it was a family, not a company. If the management needed anything, the workers bent over backwards and worked all the hours to get things out. Some of the people leaving here are in their 40s and there is little chance of them getting a job now – they have no prospects.

In April 1990 the factory was sold to a UK company, Turnkey, which continued into the twenty-first century to make components for IBM.

Burroughs Adding Machines

For the first six months of operation in the UK, Detroit-based Burroughs worked out of an old printing works at Bonhill. They moved into a new factory in January 1950, and Keppie Henderson designed a 150,000 square-foot second factory at Vale of Leven for them in 1953 at a cost of £122,412. A newspaper report of the time stated that, in the early days:

The parent company shipped to this country the calculator, blue prints, records, tools, machinery, and everything required for making an adding machine. The latter term is a better description of the machine made in the Vale of Leven because it is capable of adding, subtracting, dividing, multiplying, and taking percentages, some in pounds, shillings and pence, and others, according to the market for which they are designed, in francs, marks, rupees, or other currency.

Two types of machines were made, 'a non-printing calculator which gives the answer on dials and one which prints out answers'. These machines were enormous in comparison to today's palmtop personal computers, but they were a miracle product of the new post-war scientific age. The workforce built up to 3,000 in Scotland, eventually making all 1,800 parts for the adding machines or calculators.

In 1958 Keppie Henderson designed a new factory in Cumbernauld for Burroughs. Graham Henderson was officially in charge of the project and had specified a classical portico at the entrance door, but Geoff Wimpenny and assistant Matt Neilson took over and modernised the design. This became an anchor employer for the community, which was designated a new town in 1956, and the workforce peaked at 3,000. Suffering the same fate as much of the rest of British industry in the 1970s, redundancies started to take place by 1976, with only 1,600 staff left the following year, by which time the Cumbernauld factory had started making electronic machines. The consequences

The Queen visiting the Burroughs factory at Vale of Leven on 16 April 1953.
Burroughs' president, John S. Coleman, stands on the far left.

were worse at Vale of Leven, which closed in 1977 when the last 360 staff were made redundant.

The Cumbernauld plant survived, latterly under the ownership of Unisys, until 1989 when Japanese firm OKI purchased the factory. It did not need such a large facility for its operations, and as Burroughs had obtained land for possible expansion when it first negotiated the purchase of the site, Keppie Design prepared drawings for OKI to move into a smaller, purpose-built factory, the rest of the site to be used for a retail park. Sir Robert McAlpine was appointed to build the factory in 2004.

Polaroid

From 1964, and throughout the 1970s, Keppie Henderson designed a number of buildings and alterations for Polaroid. The company had always manufactured instant cameras and films, and survived longer than most of its competitors. Technological

247

change allowed it to diversify into sunglasses and polarisers, graphics imaging, secure identification systems, and the software, hardware and media systems that have been part of the digital revolution.

At the beginning of the twenty-first century it still had over 700 employees at its 370,000 square feet of accommodation at Vale of Leven. With the bulk of hardware production now in low labour-cost China, the Scottish plant concentrates on high value products and research and development. More than 400 of the employees take part in continuous improvement programmes, which constantly look for ways of speeding up design and development so that the company continues to be at the forefront of the marketplace.

Organon

At the same time as Vale of Leven was being developed, Keppie Henderson was designing a factory for Organon at Newhouse. Again the client was Scottish Industrial Estates and the builder W. and J.R. Watson. The cost was £97,931. Several alterations and extensions followed in the 1960s and 70s.

Taylor Woodrow Industrial Estates

The Dixons Blazes Industrial Estate was constructed in the late 1960s and early 1970s, but retained the nickname of the steelworks that had been cleared from the site. William Dixon came from Newcastle in 1771 to set up the Little Govan Colliery in Govanhill on the east side of Cathcart Road, Glasgow. His son founded the blast furnaces on the site which gave the works its name. The new estate sought to provide opportunities for light industries and distribution businesses, and contained premises for Rawlplug, the Pneumatic Tent Company, CES, Avon Tyres, Silver Roadways and Marshall Wight.

Taylor Woodrow also owned Rutherglen Industrial Estate. Warehouses were located here in 1971 for Whitbread (the 133,000 square-foot Rutherglen Beer and Spirit Distribution Warehouse), A. Goldberg and Son, and a 20,000 square-foot warehouse for battery manufacturer Electric Power Storage Ltd. The Whitbread brands stored in Rutherglen were Tankard and Trophy draught beers, Whitbread pale ale, Heineken lager, Mackeson stout, Braemar Scotch whisky, Corrida sweet Spanish wine and Black Rose demerara rum. As a publicity stunt before opening their new Rutherglen premises, the battery company flew an Austin 1300 car to the North Pole with one of their Exide batteries in it, and after a week of freezing conditions were able to demonstrate that it worked perfectly.

At Birkenshaw, near Uddingston, there was a depot, workshop and offices for Onward Road Transport, a warehouse for Stilwear, and a distribution depot for Kipling Cakes. A direct appointment came from Goodyear Tyres. Most of the occupants of premises built for Taylor Woodrow suffered from the ups and downs of the economy in the following 20 years, and the sites have been largely redeveloped since.

Opposite: *Motherwell Food Park.*

The food industry

In 1983, to encourage employers into in an area suffering from the decline in traditional industries, the Scottish Development Agency set up the Motherwell Food Park on a 26-acre site in Bellshill. It had development area status and attracted maximum regional development grants. Loans and preferential rates could be given because the park was located in a coal and steel closure area. After working with the SDA on various proposals, Keppie Henderson designed buildings for food park occupants United Biscuits and Geest. A laboratory provided SDA client companies with services for new product development, quality control and food analysis. A food brokerage company could link companies with supermarket groups at home and abroad, and a marketing company could help with launching new products. Sales literature from the late 1980s stated that:

> to date, well over 100 companies have taken advantage of the centre's current services and facilities, and this success – together with a growth in demand for market intelligence, trade development and practical advice – offers exciting prospects for the future.

Its own future as an initiative did not last long as the park was sold off to the private sector in the early 1990s.

The practice worked with Geest for a number of years, and was about to extend its Garrion Bridge unit for ripening bananas in the early 1990s when a hurricane in the Caribbean destroyed the crop. Geest plc sold Geest Bananas in early 1996.

The central public space in Mearns Primary School on the south side of Glasgow, one of the first Public Private Partnership schools by Keppie Design.

CHAPTER 22

Twentieth-century schools

Although Scotland Street School (1904–06) and Jordanhill School (1913–22) were built in the twentieth century, their design philosophy was grounded in the Victorian era. St Ninian's Primary School at 2150 Great Western Road was built as Cloberhill Elementary School for 1,000 pupils in 1929/30. It was awarded the RIBA bronze medal for its originality. The two-storey classroom wings were linked to the central offices and gym block by wholly glazed stairwells. Open corridors (later closed in) gave access to classrooms with retractable screens so that they could be opened to the outside in good weather.

An established and successful architectural practice is generally rather ambivalent towards architectural awards. Doing something different may attract attention, but will only be of value if the innovation is appropriate. One of the factors which drew critical acclaim to Cloberhill was the facility to open classrooms to the outside air, a dubious notion considering Glasgow weather during term time. The best judges of Cloberhill were not John Keppie and Henderson's architectural peers of the 1930s, but the generations of schoolchildren and teachers that have passed through the school since.

Cloberhill heralded the largely glazed, open-plan designs of post-Second World War schools. The earliest of these were Whitby Junior and Infants' School (1948–52) and Whitby County Modern School (1951–54) in North Yorkshire. These early post-war schools with facing brick walls and pitched roofs look more domestic in character than the 1960s flat-roofed boxes

Cloberhill School, Knightswood, is now called St Ninian's Primary School.

Keppie Henderson designed both primary and secondary schools in Whitby, the former of which is illustrated here.

St Benedict's RC School, Glasgow.

St Gregory's RC Secondary School, Carntyne Road, Glasgow.

St Gregory's School, Glasgow.

with glazed wall-panel systems. St Benedict's RC Primary School, Glasgow, which opened in 1959, had brick walls, but with large sections of glazed panelling and a roof which sloped down across three storeys. It was one of three primary schools designed by the practice in Drumchapel.

St Gregory's RC Secondary School, on Carntyne Road, Glasgow, opened in 1960 and cost £700,000. This made the full conversion to the new aesthetic of predominantly flat roofs and modular panel walls with occasional brick feature panels – an approach Joe Gleave had first used on Vale of Leven Hospital. Keppie, Henderson and Partners had been appointed around 1955 for the St Gregory's project, which was planned for 1,200 pupils seeking a full range of junior secondary and senior secondary courses for ordinary and higher certificates. Like many secondary schools of the time, it contained a swimming pool.

The *Glasgow Herald* described Cranhill Secondary School, the day after its official opening on 17 January 1961, as 'the most ambitious school building project to be completed in Glasgow since the war'. John Boys was the project architect. At a cost of around £500,000 (the final account was probably much higher) it accommodated 1,350 pupils. It sought to help make up for the dearth of social facilities in the post-war housing estate, with the swimming pool open from 9.00 a.m. to 10.00 p.m. for pupils and local clubs. The pool was flanked by a spectators' gallery and two gymnasia, one with a rock-climbing wall. The local community could use the dressing rooms next to the gym for outside sports on the football, rugby and hockey pitches, while the school library was described as having 'gay modern decor' and could be accessed outwith school hours. The assembly hall was designed as a fully equipped theatre to seat 540 people, and was linked to the entrance hall by a picture gallery. The partners of Keppie Henderson were members of the Glasgow Art Club, and to support local artists works were commissioned for presentation to schools at their opening ceremonies.

Commissioned in 1954, Lightburn Secondary School was the largest school of this era. Joe Gleave was the partner in charge, with Ian Plenderleith and Tom Scott assisting. When completed by builder Melville Dundas and Whitson in 1956 it cost £1,120,689. Ian Plenderleith went on to design Fleurs Avenue School (1960–63), a comprehensive school for 1,350 boys and girls. By the time it opened, it had been renamed Bellahouston Academy.

Inside Bellahouston Academy.

Bellahouston was a difficult building to design. Only a quarter of the site could be built on due to old mine workings, and the remaining area at the north end was steeply contoured – in effect a small hillock composed largely of soft clay. To avoid differential settlement between the areas of clay and sandstone, the concrete frame spanned concrete piles that were driven down as far as eight metres until they hit rock. This part of the site was also beside the main Glasgow to Ayrshire railway line, and as well as ensuring that classrooms were located on the other side of the building a baffle wall was built and trees planted to deflect noise. An unusual feature was the use of beech veneered wall linings in all the classrooms instead of the usual painted plaster walls, which would soon become dirty. Staff rooms and administration offices had walnut veneers. The extra quality in these areas was afforded by taking the finishes out of circulation spaces and merely painting the brickwork.

In the 1960s a number of primary schools were constructed to similar or standard designs in various parts of Glasgow, each costing just over £100,000. So standardised were these becoming that the Glasgow City Architects Department formed a research and development group in 1968:

> The overall objective is the acceleration of the building programme by the development and application of improved methods to the processes of briefing, design, construction and equipping, enabling buildings of appropriate design quality and cost to be produced more quickly.

Fine words, but the main product of the exercise was the standardisation of building elements by 'a vocabulary of dimensionally coordinated, interchangeable components and assemblies'. The metric system was about to be introduced, and everything had to be considered within 100 millimetre planning grids. It was no surprise when buildings turned out looking like boxes made up of geometric blocks. Keppie Henderson and Partners were the private-sector contributors to the exercise, working with City Architect

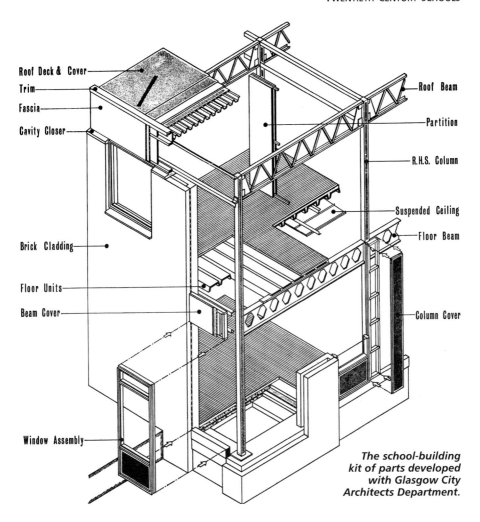

Roof Deck & Cover

Trim

Fascia

Cavity Closer

Brick Cladding

Floor Units

Beam Cover

Window Assembly

Roof Beam

Partition

R.H.S. Column

Suspended Ceiling

Floor Beam

Column Cover

The school-building kit of parts developed with Glasgow City Architects Department.

A.G. Jury, and W.E. Finlayson and E. Aldred of his department. By 1971 two standardised schools had been completed, four were under construction and two were about to start.

This was the technical and architectural response to the problem of providing the schools the politicians were demanding while coping with tight budgets and short timescales. Around the same time, Glasgow Corporation's Education Committee set up the School Building Study Group, presumably because they were concerned about the design of the schools built to date. It consisted of nineteen headmasters and headmistresses from the city's schools, and one of its remits was 'to make proposals to the Education Committee for inclusion in briefing instructions to be issued to architects'. When its short and succinct report began, 'Although the Group acknowledged the special qualifications of the architect in the planning of new schools' it was clear that a big 'but' would follow:

A move away from the modern box-like structure should be made . . . to be less institutional in character and more pleasant on the eye . . . . A somewhat irregular shape of building could be an advantage especially when this led to the formation of useful bays and sheltered corners . . . shelters should not be constructed away from the main building . . . use could be made of the overhang of the roof, and this would act as a classroom sunshade in summer as well as protection from inclement weather.

But this would have required sloping roofs, and they were no longer part of the architectural vocabulary, or perhaps more appropriately the prevailing architectural dogma.

Part of the vocabulary was large areas of glazed walls, justified in human terms as providing light environments for children. Unfortunately they also created hot environments in summer and, with huge heat losses in winter, were expensive to keep warm, never mind the condensation. The main reason for the widespread use of glass was the new production techniques developed by Pilkington in the 1950s. Previously, glass-making had been very expensive, involving much grinding and polishing of individual sections of plate glass, and consequently architects designed buildings with small windows or window panes. By the end of the 1950s, Pilkington were starting to perfect a continuous factory process where molten glass was floated on a conveyor belt, and large sections of glass were automatically cut off as they cooled. Pilkington made a fortune and architects obtained cheap glass in large panels.

A report by Strathclyde Regional Council on schools in September 1976 put the glare of sunlight and flat roofs at the beginning of its list of criticisms of school design. 'Flat roofs were greatly criticised, partly because they had a monotonous appearance and were not weatherproofed, and also because they were easy for children to climb onto.' The report did conclude that 'it is heartening to note that more design specialists are learning to think like teachers and more teachers and administrators are learning to think like designers'. Such a pity it was too late, with the economy in the second half of the 1970s taking a nosedive, and major public spending going off the agenda for the next 20 years.

Keppie Henderson did not only design schools for Glasgow Corporation. During the 1970s Renfrewshire commissioned St Margaret's School, Johnstone; in Dunbartonshire there was Kirkintilloch High School, Oxgang Primary, Kirkintilloch,

Oxgang Primary School in Kirkintilloch.

Blackcraig RC Secondary School, Cumbernauld, and primary schools at Bearsden, Dalmuir and Milngavie; and in Lanarkshire Blantyre Primary School and alterations to Wishaw High School and Our Lady's/St Joseph's RC High School, Motherwell. Thirty years later they mostly look shabby. Children are certainly expert at testing the robustness of building construction, sometimes to destruction, but the building programme set targets that were too short and budgets that were too cheap. Expenditure of only £3. 6s. was available per square foot. On several projects only softwood windows could be afforded and it was known that they would not last. The construction industry's response involved some untested factory techniques and new materials like woodwool slabs – strong, cheap and with good thermal insulation until the roof leaked and they turned into papier mâché. Flat roofs were not a good idea, given the cheap, easily punctured roofing felts that were originally used in their construction.

Poor maintenance was another factor. In 1998, Keppie Design was appointed to advise Glasgow City Council on its project to have the entire estate of Glasgow secondary schools upgraded using the government's Private Finance Initiative, including the Keppie Henderson buildings mentioned above. The public sector is not good at maintaining its property, maintenance plans and budgets being at the mercy of short-term public spending allocations. In 1998 there was a huge backlog of maintenance outstanding, and records had gone missing as the responsibility for schools had transferred from Glasgow Corporation to Strathclyde Regional Council and then to Glasgow City Council. One of the tasks for a PFI advisor is to calculate a 'public sector comparator' for the PFI proposal to be benchmarked against. Unfortunately, no one could define the true cost of an individual school since different elements of expenditure came under different global council budgets – education, parks, cleansing, etc. The PSC should take account of, and cost, all the factors and risks which would apply if the project were carried out by the public sector or if the status quo persisted; but how does one cost the health risks to girls who did not visit the toilet from 9.00 a.m. to 3.15 p.m. because the school lavatories were so badly maintained and were utterly revolting?

It was calculated that the public sector would take up to 20 years to effect the programme of works necessary, which would involve perhaps one or two new schools and the other 27 being refurbished. The successful PFI provider offered twelve new schools and had the work carried out in four years. One might question the standards of some of the provision, but the private-sector partner is contractually bound to maintain the buildings in good condition for 25 years. PFI delivers for politicians, and at the beginning of the twenty-first century is providing billions of pounds worth of schools each year in the UK. Keppie Design is very much a part of it, from Portree in the north to Ealing in London, the latter in joint venture with Seymour Harris.

The private school sector survived the socialist reforms of the twentieth century. During the 1940s and 50s, a series of small projects were carried out for Glasgow Academy – repairs to the gymnasium and dining hall, alterations to the assembly hall, a memorial plaque to commemorate the former pupils who fell in the war, and even a plan to help the school purchase the ground for playing fields at New Anniesland in 1948. By the beginning of the 1970s, state grants to private schools were stopped and they had to fully fund themselves. The High School of Glasgow could no longer charge fees and plans were drawn up for its closure. It was reborn as a private school but had to move out of the council-owned property at Elmbank Street in 1976. Keppie Henderson designed a new school at Anniesland beside the playing fields.

The Foulis Building at the Glasgow School of Art, which now has an extension on its roof.

CHAPTER 23

Further education

Jordanhill College

The military had helped complete the Jordanhill Demonstration School during the First World War (chapter 19), and they finally got their money's worth out of it when it was requisitioned from 1940 to 1944. The depleted student population of 626 and the pupils of the school were squeezed into the David Stow Building. On 5 July 1940, on behalf of the Sub-Area Quartering Commandant No. 2 (Glasgow), Lieutenant Colonel Heriz-Smith, Captain Mocatto and Major A.G. Henderson marched into the college to take possession of it.

During the Second World War, Graham Henderson had responsibility for requisitioned buildings in west-central Scotland. His daughter remembers accompanying him on some 'marching in' and 'marching out' inspections to determine the condition of premises before and after occupation by the military. It may have been the first time that an architect had requisitioned a building for military purposes that he had designed, and no doubt the contacts made with Jordanhill College stood him in good stead to obtain work from them in the 1960s. Representatives of Keppie Henderson toured Sweden and Finland for design inspiration, since building work there had not been significantly affected by the war, and they were particularly impressed by the work of architect Asprind Gunner.

Throughout the post-First World War period, the college was subject to severe financial constraints. The annual outlay on training was cut from £52,000 in 1920/21 to £38,000 the following year, and it did not creep up to £50,000 again until 1936/37. In the post-Second World War period, against the background of the baby boom, student numbers rose from 1,389 in 1952/53 to 1,953 in 1958/59. The school leaving age had been raised in 1947. Although the Kerr Building was opened in 1958 to house technical subjects and craftwork, the rest of the campus had only been designed for 1,200 students.

A report in November 1958 highlighted the problems:

> The students are required to work harder than ten years ago (for the equivalent number of students, the issue of books from the library has doubled in that time) but they are disturbed by bustle, lack of quiet and space. They stand in queues for food and for lavatories, and in free periods and lunch hours they have difficulty finding anywhere to sit, since common rooms and reading rooms are too small and the library seats only 60.

The official history of Jordanhill College calls the period from 1959 to 1976 'the Golden Years'. In 1959 the centralised and stifling controls of the national and provincial committees were abolished and the college obtained a more independent status. The board of governors better represented local interests, with members from local education authorities, the University of Glasgow and the Church of Scotland. Developments in education practice also demanded additional accommodation. Men were allowed to join the primary school diploma course in 1967 and specialisms were introduced – speech therapy, social work, and youth and community work.

The first phase of projects designed by Keppie Henderson and Partners was opened by the Queen and Prince Philip on Wednesday 3 July 1963. This included the provision of a gym, swimming pool, and a tutorial block and lecture theatre. The following day the *Glasgow Herald* described the college as 'the largest teacher training establishment in the Commonwealth'.

The gym was completed in February 1962 and had a fold-shaped roof to reduce noise echoing, supported by only four columns to give a free space of 36 metres by 20 metres for games. It was partly destroyed by fire in March 1964, but was rebuilt for the beginning of session 1964/65. The swimming pool measured 25 metres by ten metres and was opened in June 1963.

Jordanhill College gym, with its fold-shaped roof to reduce echoes inside the hall.

The tutorial block and lecture theatre was called the Crawfurd Building after a sixteenth-century owner of lands at Jordanhill, Thomas Crawfurd. It was built on the site of Jordanhill House (demolished by January 1961), whose last occupiers many years before were James Smith and his son, Archibald. The Keppie Henderson partners of the time would have been unaware of a link between Jordanhill House, the Smiths and their predecessor, John Honeyman. In 1884, Honeyman had been given the task of having Govan Parish Church taken down stone by stone and re-erected on another site. The original building dated from 1826 and had been sponsored and partly designed by James Smith of Jordanhill. Smith was at one time president of both the Glasgow Geological and Archaeological Societies, and a member of the Royal Societies of Edinburgh and London.

Govan's religious heritage stretches back 1,400 years to St Constantine who set up a base there. At the time James Smith was working on the church, he took a fancy to the remains of an ancient Celtic cross which he thought would look good as a centrepiece to his garden at Jordanhill. By the time Honeyman's work started it had gone. When Glasgow Corporation Education Authority purchased Jordanhill House from the Smiths in 1911 to rehouse its teacher training college, the importance of the stone was recognised and it was removed to Kelvingrove Museum for safe keeping. It was eventually returned to Govan Kirk on 28 September 1928, where it now sits in the transept.

Reminders of the Jordanhill Estate lie in the grounds of Jordanhill College today, including parts of the high brick walls of the walled garden behind the Smith Building,

Jordanhill College.

*The Sir Henry Wood Building
at Jordanhill College.*

itself named after the father and son. A five metre stone pillar that also stood in the garden was relocated to the car park beside the student residences to the west of the main Jordanhill buildings.

The next Keppie Henderson and Partners projects were the Smith Building containing science and maths departments, designed from 1966, and the Scottish School of Physical Education, designed in 1966 and 1967. Both were officially opened on 5 June 1970. The Scottish School of Further Education was designed from 1968 to 1971 and was opened on 14 September 1973, and the Sir Henry Wood Building, containing the much-needed main library, was designed from 1967 to 1971 and opened by the man himself on 15 March 1974. All of this construction work had taken place during his period as principal, from 1949 to 1971. Henry Wood was described as 'fundamentally a man of great warmth, superficially he often appeared withdrawn and aloof. A good listener, he preferred to speak briefly and to the point. The college quip about him was that he never used two words where none would do.'

The college merged with the University of Strathclyde in 1993, and by 2004 the part of the site containing the swimming pool and the Scottish School of Further Education had been sold off to developers CALA for housing. On 25 November 2003 the former gymnasium was gutted by fire. In 1996 it had been converted into a research centre with laboratories, and the life's work of Professor Myra Nimmo and four of her colleagues largely went up in smoke that night.

The Keppie practice missed out on the first prize in 1913 by not winning the commission for the main college building, later named the David Stow Building. However, by 1974 it had surrounded it on all sides and the student population was rising to a peak of 3,713. While the college will continue to develop to meet the needs of society, 'the Golden Age' of its expansion in the West End referred to in the Jordanhill College official history is certainly past.

The Glasgow School of Art

The first post-war work for the Glasgow School of Art took place in 1946. It was a very small alteration, but very significant, because it involved a new stair in the library. The client was Henry Alison, interim director following Allan Walton's departure to resume his professional career in London, having just been appointed to refurbish 11 Downing Street. In his history of the art school, Hugh Ferguson recounts former students who referred to Alison as 'a holy terror' and 'a wee bastard'. His pugnacity stopped Graham Henderson making inappropriate changes to the art school library.

Ferguson tells the story:

The Library balcony could be entered only from an external half-landing above, and to improve security and facilitate supervision, Henderson wanted to build a spiral staircase in the north-west window bay, for internal access. Alison thought this was an appalling idea, so he designed a little timber staircase (Alison's father was a joiner), and with the help of a janitor built it over the Easter vacation in 1946. That is the origin of the existing library staircase, which

The interior of the Glasgow School of Art library, which was refurbished by Geoff Wimpenny of Keppie Henderson.

was fitted with the removal of just one joist from the balcony floor to create the stair opening, and done so neatly and sympathetically that generations of students have gone through the school believing it to be part of Mackintosh's original design.

In later years, just after he had recreated the Willow Tea Rooms in Sauchiehall Street, Geoff Wimpenny made further sensitive enhancements to the library, including the lighting system that exists today.

Graham Henderson's close association with the Glasgow School of Art brought him into contact with Thomas Howarth in the 1940s when he was carrying out his research on Mackintosh. In 1946 Howarth moved to Manchester to become a lecturer in the city's school of architecture, but he regularly returned to Glasgow, following up research leads and trying to persuade a publisher that his book on Mackintosh would sell. It took until 1952 for it to published. In 1957, during his period as president of the Royal Institute of British Architects, Henderson paid a visit to Toronto, where he was asked if he could recommend a new director of the school of architecture there. Henderson spoke highly of Howarth and, after an interview in London, he was appointed, remaining there until his retirement in 1978.

The first major new-build, post-war project at the School of Art was the Foulis Building in 1963, on the corner of Renfrew Street and Dalhousie Street. It housed the departments of graphic design, interior design and industrial design, and was named after Robert and Andrew Foulis, who in 1753, at the old college in High Street, set up the first school of art in Britain to train professional artists. The first teacher was David Allan, the industrial designer for the Carron Ironworks near Falkirk.

From 1901 to 1979 the School of Art ran diploma courses in architecture, initially lasting four years, but from 1919/20 five years. It was a valued certificate because it allowed the holder to enter professional practice rather than being just a graduate trainee. However, some subjects were taught at the Glasgow and West of Scotland Technical College, which became the University of Strathclyde in 1964. It followed the

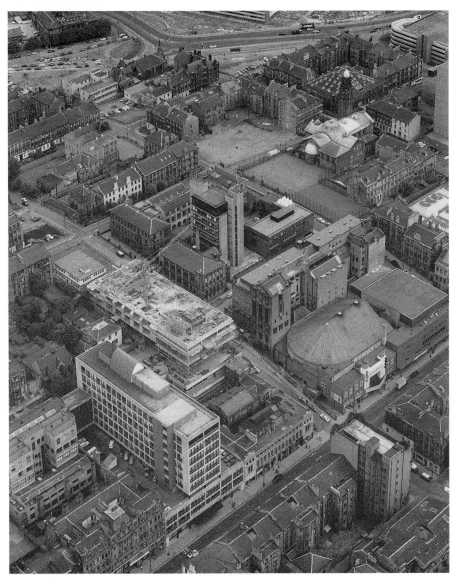

After many design revisions and rounds of cost-cutting, this picture shows the Bourdon Building finally under construction. The Newbery Tower has been completed.

Royal Institute of British Architects' pro-university training bias and had its own school of architecture, the Glasgow School of Art having no full-time architectural course. New director of the art school, Jefferson Barnes, reopened discussions that had previously taken place with the University of Glasgow with a view to offering architecture degree courses in partnership with them. Governors Jack Coia and Ninian Johnston assisted Barnes in the diplomatic effort. The new Mackintosh School was sanctioned by the RIBA, the Scottish Education Department and the university in March 1965, with the first intake of degree students finishing in session 1970/71.

However, a new building was required to house the school. Keppie Henderson was appointed in 1969 to design the Bourdon Building (named after Eugene Bourdon, Professor of Architectural Design at the beginning of the twentieth century), but it was plagued by problems and was not completed until 1979. Being so close to the Mackintosh building, and spanning Renfrew Street to form a western

The Glasgow School of Art Newbery Tower, with the 1930 John Keppie and Henderson Assembly Hall in front of it.

boundary to the campus, planning permission took a long time to achieve with many changes and modifications to the design. To save money, stone cladding was omitted and copper cladding became copper-covered felt. Exposed concrete was a poor alternative to stone, but was in accord with the architectural fashion of the time. The link over Scott Street to a new building to replace John Keppie and Henderson's Assembly Hall (1927–30) did not transpire, nor did masterplan aspirations to extend the campus down to Sauchiehall Street on the site where the Glasgow Dental School was built. Once the design for the Bourdon Building was approved, the oil crisis of 1974 hit the country, and the British government had to go cap in hand to the International Monetary Fund to underwrite its borrowing. Public funds were difficult to obtain but they were at last found. Barnes was upset when the architects in the school said it did not meet their requirements; he thought it a 'fine building'.

The Newbery Tower was the other new building of the era, being constructed from 1969 to 1970. It was of course named after Mackintosh's mentor, Francis Newbery.

Glasgow College of Food Technology

Too bulky and monolithic for its site, this could not be said to be one of the most beautiful buildings in the further education zone north of George Square. Built from

1970 to 1972, the £1.37 million building housed 2,020 students taking classes in catering, baking and confectionery, meat trades, the licensed trade, food processing and public health. Dr Dan Docherty, convenor of Glasgow Corporation Education Authority, and Bob Heatley, managing director of builders Gilbert Ash Scotland, took part in the topping-out ceremony in September 1971. Perhaps because of the problems with prefabricated concrete panels on previous projects, the walls are constructed of pink facing brick, which, without the appropriate detailing and articulation, adds to the monotony of the elevations.

The University of Glasgow

John Honeyman attended the University of Glasgow in the late 1840s, then at its old site to the east of High Street. The area was surrounded by slum housing, the clearance of which Honeyman later contributed to as a consultant to the City Improvement Trust. He was also one of the few Glasgow architects to support the appointment of Sir George Gilbert Scott for the new buildings at Gilmorehill and the adoption of a Gothic rather than classical style, the latter favoured by 'Greek' Thomson.

Since the first post-war project for the university was major alterations to Anderson's Medical College (1948–53), the relationships built on this could well have been the route by which further work was won. John Keppie brought the original project to the practice in 1888/89, having been working on the design when he was with James Sellars. The medical school had originally been part of Anderson's College (the forerunner of the University of Strathclyde), but when the latter was taken over by the Glasgow and West of Scotland Technical College there was no provision to teach medicine and the medical school became independent, the new building opening in autumn 1889 at a cost of £10,618. 4s. 9d. John Keppie and Henderson had been carrying out work to the building in 1936/37, and it was sensible for them to continue when the University of Glasgow took it over in 1947. Further alterations took place in 1956 and 1957, one of these involving the installation of an animal house for research; a feature now somewhat euphemistically termed a biomedical research facility.

In the same period (1949–51), alterations were taking place to the Bute and Randolph Halls and the Mathematics Department. The elevational drawing showing the colour scheme for the former was deemed sufficiently attractive to be framed, and still hangs in the Keppie Design office. In 1952, the university celebrated its 500th anniversary. Keppie Henderson designed new memorial gates on which the names of famous professors and students could be placed.

In the years between the wars, the student population fluctuated between 4,500 and 5,500. There was a peak immediately after the Second World War as servicemen and -women returned, and in the 1950s there were about 6,000 students. Gradual development led to more major projects, especially following the Robbins Committee recommendations in 1963 that 'courses of higher education should be available for all those who are qualified by ability and attainment to pursue them and who wish to do so'. By 1974 there were 10,000 students. Sir Frank Mears had prepared a masterplan for the Hillhead area in 1951 as the university bought up property for expansion, but it was difficult to plan ahead when government grants were only made a year at a time by the University Grants Committee. Normally about half of the money requested was granted, and of the £4.3 million spent between 1951 and 1960 the university had to raise 32 per cent of it itself, largely from commercial sponsors.

The final design of the James Watt Building illustrates the difficulties experienced by architects trying to juxtapose modernist architecture with older buildings.

In 1952 two storeys were added on to the 1901 Sir John J. Burnet-designed Engineering Building, and the Geography and Geology Department was extended in 1955–57. The James Watt Building was commissioned in 1955. Application for funding had been made in July 1952, but it was not until the foundations and structural steelwork had almost been completed in July 1956 that the UGC agreed to meet two-thirds of the cost. This replaced a building by Sir George Gilbert Scott, the design of which was based on the Abbot's Kitchen at Glastonbury. The project description was an extension of the engineering department, and this accounts for the location at the east end of Randolph Hall. The modern, functional building is an unfortunately close neighbour to the nineteenth-century Gothic buildings, although its bulk is largely hidden from University Avenue by the mature trees lining it. The south end, facing Kelvingrove Park, is clad in Portland stone on which is a large bas-relief by Eric Kennington depicting various aspects of science. The artist died in 1957 while the work was in progress.

The Biochemistry Department was commissioned in 1960 and built from 1963 to 1964 on top of Jack Coia's boilerhouse of 1951. In 1959/60, the Stevenson Physical Education Building was built, containing a gymnasium and swimming pool. Graham Henderson was personally responsible for the design. Adjacent to this, at the corner of Gibson Street, the University Union was extended in 1965.

In 1947 the university purchased the Garscube Estate off Maryhill Road and at one time was considering a completely new campus there. The veterinary hospital moved there in 1958, with laboratories and the veterinary school following later. Keppie Henderson designed the Hydrodynamics Laboratory and Astronomy Building from 1964 to 1967.

In 1958 Joe Gleave, along with Ivor Dorward, left the Keppie, Henderson and J.L. Gleave partnership. Gleave retained a planning consultancy role at the university, and when Frank Fielden became head of the School of Architecture at Glasgow School of Art in 1959 the two of them masterplanned the area where the library and Hunterian Museum and Art Gallery were to be located. At Gleave's recommendation, Fielden designed the refectory, later called the Hub.

After Gleave died, Dorward obtained projects from the university. These were the Mathematics Building (1969), alterations to the Senate Room (1969), the Boyd Orr Building (1972), an extension of the Engineering Building (1977), and the Geology Building (1980). From 1950 to 1980, Keppie Henderson and Partners and Dorward Matheson Gleave and Partners received the lion's share of the projects, half a dozen other architects being awarded only one or two commissions each.

Keppie Henderson seems to have fallen out of favour with the university in the late 1960s as Dorward Matheson Gleave and Partners obtained repeat commissions for the next ten years. The reasons could have been technical problems, or perhaps contractual ones. Flat roofs and swimming pools had a tendency to leak in those days, and floor screeds to crack. The economic boom and bust cycles led to price uncertainties and contractual conflicts with builders, projects often running over budget and deadline. The last project of this era carried out by Keppie Henderson was the Rankine Building in 1969 which looked clean and crisp when it opened, although today the concrete cladding panels are in a poor state of repair and the building looks grubby.

Almost all of the buildings constructed in the 35 years after the Second World War at Gilmorehill look crude, insensitive and dated to our eyes now, undermining the credibility of the 'brave new world' motives of post-war architecture. Perhaps insufficient money to fund the massive reinvestment in public infrastructure throughout the UK was largely to blame. The budget for Sir George Gilbert Scott's original building at Gilmorehill was around £350,000. Of this from 1865 to 1868, £120,000 was raised from Treasury grants and £134,000 from public subscription. Even this was not enough, with a gift from the Marquess of Bute and a legacy from Charles Randolph required to complete the Bute and Randolph Halls. To put this sum in perspective, the largest project Honeyman had been involved in up to 1870 cost £13,812, so it is not surprising that no Glasgow architect was trusted with the project. The enormous sum at Scott's disposal allowed him to design a top-quality building that the local population could be proud of. From the 1950s to the 1970s, estates officers had to make the best they could from such central government funds that were available. I wonder what would have happened if their budgets had been doubled, as Scott's had been, with public donations.

The Rankine Building at the University of Glasgow displays the fragility of almost all 1960s and 70s buildings constructed using industrialised building techniques.

Sir Frank Mears' masterplan was updated in 1963 by architects Wilson and Womersley, a practice that eventually became part of Keppie Design in 1996. One of the houses demolished as a result of this was that of Charles Rennie Mackintosh at 6 Florentine Terrace, which he occupied from 1906 to 1914. Having moved to London, he had sold it to William Davidson who had commissioned Windyhill, Kilmacolm. He continued to fill it with Mackintosh furniture and fittings until he died in 1945. The university showed great foresight in carefully preserving the contents, since Thomas Howarth's book bringing Mackintosh to public attention did not appear until 1952. The contents are now in a recreation of Florentine Terrace at the Hunterian Museum and Art Gallery. Also on display is the salvaged Mackintosh finial from the dome that topped Pettigrew and Stephens' Manchester House in Sauchiehall Street.

The maternity unit at the Southern General Hospital in Glasgow.

CHAPTER 24

Hospitals

One could argue that the practice's first healthcare project was a fever ward in the 1859 Campbeltown Poorhouse, but in those days this was more an isolation facility than one for treatment. The first major hospital project was for a lunatic asylum in Paisley at Riccartsbar, designed in 1872 to replace an earlier building of 1854. It was opened in 1876 and could accommodate 120 patients.

Planned in a figure of eight, the two secure courtyards segregated men and women without the need for prison-like boundary walls. The one place they came together was at the chapel in the middle. The section through the dormitory block is interesting. While coal fires are shown in elevation, these must have been a danger to many patients, so a system of hot-air-ducted ventilation was supplied in addition. Perhaps ventilation grilles at low level might have been tampered with, so the air outlets are designed into column features on either side of the doors, disguised as elements on

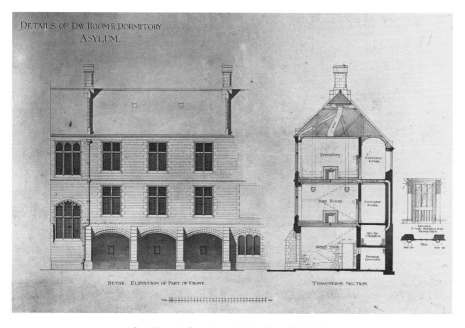

*The Riccartsbar Lunatic Asylum in Paisley
stood where the Royal Alexandra Hospital is now sited.*

the column capitals. Windows would have been secured shut, so extract ventilation was taken via grilles on the side walls or in the ceiling up through the roof. A basement tramway corridor allowed clothes and bedlinen to be transported from the laundry and airing sheds around the hospital without coming into contact with the patients. The hot-air chambers were located to provide warmth to both the airing rooms and the patient accommodation.

Riccartsbar Hospital was inherited by Dykebar and Associated Hospitals in 1948 under the NHS, and in 1968 it passed to Paisley and District Hospitals which demolished the buildings to make way for the Royal Alexandra Hospital.

While with James Sellars, John Keppie had worked on the design of the Victoria Infirmary in Glasgow. His partner Campbell Douglas had not allowed such an important project to be taken from his office when Sellars died, but Keppie must have kept in touch with the hospital authorities, for in 1899 he received the commission for the Victoria's Bellahouston Dispensary.

Like today, there was no shortage of people requiring hospital treatment, and the governors of the Victoria had to develop a system for screening potential patients before admission, as well as dealing with them afterwards if they still required medication. As today, where the Royal Infirmary of Edinburgh (1997–2003) had to be located on the outer edge of the city to obtain enough space, the Victoria in Glasgow was at the edge of its catchment area, and what we would now call ambulatory care and diagnostic centres were required closer to the River Clyde where most of the population lived. The first opened in Tradeston in July 1892, and in 1896 John Keppie was approached to design the Bellahouston Dispensary at the corner of Morrison Street and Dundas Street (later Laidlaw Street). There was some debate as to whether the second facility should be built, as in a time of regular bouts of tuberculosis and typhoid the wisdom of allowing unwell people to congregate in crowded waiting areas was questioned, and would have made today's hospital-acquired infections seem a minor issue. The clinicians also took some time to decide what they wanted (some things never change). £6,000 had been raised for the project in 1894, and between January and May 1897 Keppie prepared three different proposals, none of which found favour. The 'approved' scheme in July was subsequently altered to provide an extra floor for the hospital secretariat, the caretaker and the collector (fund-raiser).

The building was finally opened on 28 June 1899. It contained clinics for dermatology, gynaecology, ophthalmology, laryngology and otology. The last two, associated with the throat and ear, were still separate disciplines whereas nowadays ear, nose and throat specialisms are combined. The dispensary was also a proving ground for other specialisms. However, mindful of funding limits, the new X-ray technology, pioneered by Rontgen in 1895, was not adopted. Compulsory registration for dentists did not begin until after the First World War and there were many 'quacks' around. Treatment at the Bellahouston or Tradeston dispensaries ensured patients of a properly trained dentist.

The Bellahouston Dispensary was a busy place for many years. The day after the Glasgow Fair holiday in 1930, a visiting governor noted that by 2.30 p.m. 350 patients had been treated. The workload included minor surgery, such as the snaring of nasal polyps using cocaine as a local anaesthetic. In 1941 the building was bombed, but was repaired and was still being used as a funeral parlour in the early 1990s. Its site has since been developed for new housing.

It was not until 1925 that the practice received its first major acute hospital project, the David Elder Infirmary (see chapter 1).

The National Health Service

The National Health Service came into being on 5 July 1948, following Aneurin Bevan's NHS Act of 1946, and the opportunity presented itself for the practice to develop a new specialism.

Whilst incidences of heart disease, cancer and strokes had significantly increased since the 1920s, strides were being made against infectious and respiratory diseases, especially those which afflicted children. Typhus was transmitted by infected body lice, but improved hygiene had virtually eradicated it by 1925. In 1940, diphtheria struck over 5,000 people in Glasgow, with 226 dying. However, with the introduction of immunisation it had practically disappeared by 1955. Scarlet fever, which had been a killer in the nineteenth century, developed a milder strain in the twentieth with outbreaks rarely causing death. The introduction of vaccines for whooping cough and measles in the 1950s also kept these diseases under control. This left tuberculosis and poliomyelitis. The former had killed three of Honeyman's family.

These 1957 posters were designed to promote the use of X-ray screening in detecting and treating TB.

The fight against TB made good progress in the first half of the twentieth century. By the late 1920s X-rays were being used in its diagnosis, and TB testing of cattle herds gradually reduced the bovine infection that was passed on through milk. The death rate from pulmonary TB in Glasgow had dropped from 136 per 100,000 in the 1920s to 86 by 1939. However, the war disrupted the TB programme and cases increased again.

It was not until the introduction of the drug streptomycin in 1947, and the BCG vaccine in 1950, that the situation could improve – but only if those infected could be identified. The Western Regional Hospital Board had taken over the various TB hospitals and sanatoria in the Glasgow area in 1947, and it organised a mass screening programme. 714,915 people were X-rayed, with around 8,000 testing positive, 2,000 of whom were actively suffering from the disease. The average weekly throughput for each clinic was 4,760. 31,000 people were recalled for a further X-ray. John Keppie and Henderson's first recorded healthcare project after the war was a TB unit at Stirling in 1952. The following year one was built at the Southern General Hospital in Glasgow.

Poliomyelitis attacked the nervous system and crippled children. The afflicted had to use calipers and crutches. The virus was discovered in 1909, with 103 cases in Glasgow in 1928, 92 of these resulting in paralysis. By 1947 the number of cases had tripled. An outbreak in 1954 led to Keppie Henderson being appointed to convert Nightingale wards for polio treatment at the fever hospitals of Belvidere and Ruchill. These hospitals also treated measles, scarlet fever and diphtheria. Opened on 26 October 1956, the polio unit at Ruchill contained laboratories for the study of viruses and an 'animal house' for experimentation. Great strides were made by medical staff and the Department of Bacteriology of the University of Glasgow, and contraptions such as the 'iron lung', which helped breathing, became a thing of the past.

By 1954, suitable vaccines had been prepared in Canada and the USA. There was an initial setback when a manufacturing defect in one batch tragically caused paralysis and death to those who were administered it. As a result it was not until May 1956 that immunisation started in Britain. It became easier to administer than the dreaded school BCG injections as the vaccination drops could be taken orally in sugar cubes.

In 1949 the practice had changed its name to John Keppie and Henderson and J.L. Gleave. Whilst a student in 1931, Joseph Lea Gleave (1907–1964) had won an international competition for the Columbus Memorial in the Dominican Republic (although it was not completed until 1992). From 1935 to 1950 he lectured at, and was latterly head of, Edinburgh College of Art. He married the daughter of Sir William Kininmonth (1905–1988), an architect who had been a partner of Basil Spence in Rowand Anderson, Kininmonth and Spence. Gleave is reputed to have given ideas to Kininmonth for the design of the Renfrew Airport Terminal (1953/54), although project architect Michael Laird may have contested this.

Gleave became an authority on hospital design. With little hospital building since Victorian times, the subject was somewhat theoretical, inspiration being taken from Sweden where ideas had continued to develop while the Second World War ravaged the rest of Europe. Hugh Llewelyn-Davies was another expert, pioneering ideas and looking for projects to test them on.

Graham Henderson headhunted Joe Gleave, who moved to Glasgow and bought Henderson's house, Lincluden, at 14 Dalziel Drive in Pollokshields, which he had occupied since 1925. In 1952 Gleave got his chance to turn theory into practice with the first large commission being Vale of Leven Hospital in Balloch. Some of the ideas were more successful than others. The external walls were formed with three-foot-wide modular panels which could be dismantled for future extensions and alterations, but this facility was little used. In fact, it was as much a stylistic device as a practical one, being seen later in other buildings – such as Littlewoods stores, the Queen Mother's Maternity Hospital in Glasgow and Lightburn School, Glasgow – the last designed by Gleave's assistant, Geoff Wimpenny, after Gleave had left the practice.

Vale of Leven Hospital was located in a valley, and was to be no more than three storeys high so that the blast from a nuclear bomb dropped on Glasgow would pass over the top. Injured people in Glasgow could then be transferred out for treatment. No one at the time could have predicted that atomic weapons would become so powerful and prolific. The nearby Clyde bases for British and American nuclear submarines would become a greater target and the concept of 'nuclear winter', exterminating most of the life forms on the planet, had still to be born.

However, other concepts of modern hospital design were born at Vale of Leven, including nurse stations and hospital streets. The basement corridors were used for servicing, ground floor ones for the public, and first floor ones for staff. Many hospitals at the beginning of the twenty-first century still do not have this segregation, with visitors, patients, staff, supplies, refuse and the deceased often sharing the same corridors. Vale of Leven was completed in 1955 by the builder Angus MacDougall at a

Vale of Leven Hospital,
the first NHS district hospital.

272

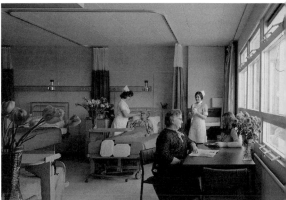

Clackmannan County Hospital in Alloa opened in 1899, and the ward on the left was typical of the type named after Florence Nightingale (the 'Nightingale ward'). Keppie Henderson added an extension to the hospital in 1954. On the right is a typical NHS ward featuring four beds and a day space at the window.

cost of £343,005. The next major new hospital scheme in the UK was Altnegelvin in Northern Ireland, completed in 1960 to a design by YRM Architects. Others then followed in England, many based on Llewelyn-Davies's 1955 report *Studies in Functions and Design of Hospitals*.

Other work by the practice in the 1950s involved new wards, outpatients departments and extensions to Law Hospital, the Southern General in Glasgow, Clackmannan County Hospital in Alloa, and Stirling Royal Infirmary. An artificial limb centre at Belvidere Hospital in Glasgow was converted from existing buildings to take advantage of advances in prosthetic limb technology, largely for those who had been injured in the war.

By 1958 Joe Gleave was no longer part of the practice. He fell out with the other partners, his academic approach contrasting with the more pragmatic, hard-edged commercial one of Henderson and Smellie. There were also younger partners looking for responsibility – Dick De'Ath, Tom Scott and Geoff Wimpenny. The next generation of Stan Carrie, Matt Neilson, Jim Cuthbertson and Ian Plenderleith was also appearing. Joe Gleave was not very popular among the staff he had working all night to meet deadlines, especially when he came in from his home at 4.00 a.m. to review their work. Graham Henderson had a vision of the practice as being a team of talented individuals under a corporate banner, with innovative management ideas like multidisciplinary design teams, critical path production methods and manuals of corporate procedures. This was in contrast to Joe Gleave who was seen as more of a prima donna. He won the commission for the Queen Mother's Hospital in Glasgow using his own name while still a partner of the practice.

As Matt Neilson was finishing his two years of national service as a lieutenant in the Royal Engineers in November 1959, Gleave wrote to him offering him a job in his new practice. Geoff Wimpenny also wrote to him and Neilson chose to stay with Keppie Henderson and Partners (he worked in the practice for almost 50 years). Only Ivor Dorward went with Gleave, and they took the Queen Mother's Hospital and Prestwick Airport to establish their practice. When Gleave died of cancer in 1963 his practice was renamed Dorward Matheson Gleave and Partners, then in 1987 it became Matheson Gleave before it was purchased by Young and Gault.

The Falkirk Ward, illustrated here, was an experimental unit which went on to form the core of the post-war Falkirk Royal Infirmary.

Keppie Henderson was a proving ground for a number of people who went on to work in, or become partners in, other practices. Ian Plenderleith joined Baxter Clark and Paul (he married Clark's sister) and helped design Yorkhill Children's Hospital, Paisley Maternity, Raigmore in Inverness, and the Royal Alexandra in Paisley. Geoff Jarvis, John Boys and Jim Cuthbertson; Bill Greenock and Ian Will; and Alastair Fletcher and John McNeece also set up their own practices. In all of these cases the departures were cordial. Jarvis and Boys moved next door to Keppie Henderson at 19 Woodside Place, in 1960 and 1961 respectively, to form Lothian Barclay Jarvis and Boys. Jim Cuthbertson joined them later, and when Boys retired in 1993 the practice became known as James G. Cuthbertson Architects. With Gleave the separation had been conducted in a colder, more businesslike fashion.

The 1960s saw further experimentation in healthcare design. Following Llewelyn-Davies's experimental ward at Larkfield, Greenock, Keppie Henderson created the Falkirk Ward (the hospital has since been developed round it), working directly for the Scottish Home and Health Department. It had 120 beds and a four-theatre operating suite, and informed later designs for hospitals in Scotland and Ireland.

Patient accommodation in one-, four- or six-bed wards contrasted with the old Nightingale wards of up to eighteen beds, designed by Florence Nightingale so that a single nurse could view as many patients as possible from her desk. The psychology behind bed numbers in a ward was that two-bed wards might lead to two people who did not get on with each other being located together. A three-bed ward might have two patients on good terms to the exclusion of the other, leaving single bedrooms and four-bed wards as the standard. Six-bed rooms became less desirable in case the two central-bed occupants felt more exposed than the four outside ones.

The desire for nurse visibility of patients led to vision panels being introduced to ward doors. In many other countries this has not happened as nurses (or, worse still, visitors) peering into rooms as they walk down the corridor is seen as intrusive and detrimental to patient dignity. They regard it as more patient-friendly for nurses to spend less time at their bases and more time observing patients close up and speaking to them in their beds. This is more practical in a country like France, which has twice as many nurses as the UK per head of population.

Toilets and showers at the Falkirk Ward were en suite, thereafter a standard feature in Scottish and Irish hospitals, whereas patients in most English hospitals had to endure the indignity of walking down a corridor to visit the loo or have a shower or bath, sometimes in mixed-sex wards. Durham Hospital, completed in 2001, still did not have en suite toilets. The 'Consumerism Agenda', launched in England in 2000, sought to address a number of issues like this and make hospitals more patient-friendly, rather than be designed to suit the system, with the patient somewhere further down the list of priorities. Other features included increased space around beds for relatives to sit, a higher proportion of single beds and the introduction of women-only day rooms.

Those hospitals that can afford the extra 12 per cent average cost of such measures will experience the first major changes to ward planning since the early 1960s.

Having tackled infectious diseases, another post-war target for the NHS was to reduce the infant mortality rate by providing specialist maternity units. Previously, most babies were born at home or in private nursing homes. Improved housing conditions had reduced the mortality rate from 16 per cent to 10 per cent in the 50 years to 1921, but little further improvement was made until after the Second World War. By 1960, the rate had dropped to 3 per cent.

Keppie Henderson's Stirling and Glasgow Southern General maternity units had the added security of the back-up facilities of a larger hospital on the same site. The old Stirling maternity facility had been in the grounds of what was planned to be the University of Stirling, so it had to be replaced anyway. Some maternity units of the time, not designed by Keppie

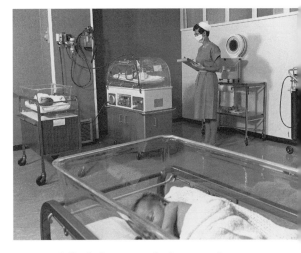

Specialist baby-care units in maternity hospitals, such as this one at the Southern General, helped improve the outcomes for premature and sickly babies.

In this aerial view the first phase of the Western Infirmary in Glasgow is complete, including staff accommodation on University Avenue. Although the Victorian buildings were demolished, a second phase was never built.

Henderson, were built separately, for example at Bellshill and Rutherglen, and the practice was involved in later option-appraisal exercises to relocate these respectively to Wishaw and the Glasgow Royal Infirmary, and to resite Ayr's maternity unit to Crosshouse Hospital at Kilmarnock. In 2004 Keppie Design was appointed to design the last of these.

During the planning of the Southern General maternity unit, the designers were sent to look at the Duchess of Kent maternity wing of Hillingdon Hospital, where John Frankenberg had invented the 'Continuous-Process Delivery System'. This allowed the super-efficient delivery of 3,000 babies per year. The production line had the most modern of equipment, which concluded with 'almost all the secretions, excretions, and solutions, together with the swabs and pads, passing down the sleeve into the disposable receptacle'.

The 1960s and early 1970s saw a number of extensions at Stirling Royal (including another experimental ward) and the Southern General, Glasgow, but demand for modern accommodation required the construction or complete redevelopment of whole hospitals. Keppie Henderson received commissions for the Western and Gartnavel in Glasgow, and for Airdrie District General Hospital (Monklands).

Wylie Shanks had been the previous architects working at the Western. Tom Scott's mother was a friend of Fred Wylie's wife and he had worked for this practice during the summers when he was a student. Wylie Shanks did not have a place for him when he qualified, so he walked along the road and knocked on Graham Henderson's door. Henderson had been a friend of Fred's uncle, Edward Grigg Wylie (c.1885–1954), and had obtained Scottish Industrial Estates work through him. Up to the 1960s, prior to competitive interviews and much later competitive fee tendering, architects were usually invited to take on commissions on the basis of their reputations and track record. Appointment conditions and fee levels were set by professional bodies.

In 1950, the practice had twelve staff at 196 West Regent Street. In 1952, 21 Woodside Place was purchased for £5,000 and the next year number 20 was bought for £2,500. With the workload mushrooming, and with

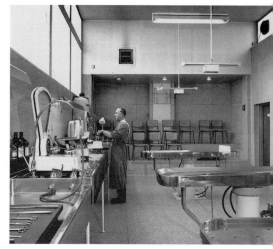

A man happy at his work in the bright, new mortuary at the Southern General Hospital.

Key Keppie Henderson staff who worked on Airdrie Hospital photographed outside the office at Woodside Place. **Left to right:** *Hector McKenzie, Robin Greer, Alister Newal, Colin Thom, Fred Seaton, Les Adams, Richard Wood, Jim Barr, Roy Elliot, David Ray.*

temporary premises at Lynedoch Street and at the Glasgow Western site, the staff complement rose to 120. The temporary wooden building at the Western is still being used today by the hospital. In it was based a multidisciplinary team of architects, engineers and other specialists, working closely with the building contractor. Client representatives Dr Ken Fraser and administrator Fiona Brough were also based in the site office, facilitating quick decision-making. John Henderson, managing director of builder John Laing, agreed to carry out the works for £5 million, the promise as much a 'gentleman's agreement', according to Tom Scott, as a commercial contract. It was delivered.

The briefing of phase two of the Western did not progress so well, with the 52 hospital committees unable to agree a consensus on their requirements. The Scottish Home and Health Department briefed the new hospital at Gartnavel themselves and phase two of the Western never transpired. Keppie Henderson was appointed for Gartnavel and a contract negotiated with John Laing for £3.5 million. Again the contractor delivered to budget.

Airdrie District General Hospital was completed in 1975 at a cost of £7.2 million and opened by Jim Callaghan. The site had mine workings underneath it, and it took a long time to find the best part to build on. In the event large quantities of concrete had to be poured into cavities in the ground to consolidate it. An infectious diseases unit was built at the same time, linked to the main hospital by a covered walkway.

At a lower level in the healthcare scale community facilities were required. With the Scottish Home and Health Department and local doctors, Woodside Health Centre in Glasgow was developed as a prototype in 1971 to provide GP, dentistry and other local health services for a population of 30,000. Health centres followed in Airdrie in 1974 (to serve 44,000 patients) and Port Glasgow in 1977. Airdrie and Port Glasgow adopted a prefabricated panel system called CLASP, developed by the Consortium of Local Authorities and Trent Concrete, with the structural frame by Beardmore. This system was more often used on schools, although when I worked at Baxter Clark and Paul in Glasgow it was being adapted for use on the Royal Alexandra Hospital in Paisley.

There was a small private healthcare sector and around 1975 Keppie Henderson was approached by Mr Wilcox, the chief architect of the Nuffield Hospital in the West End of Glasgow, to design an extension on the basis of his sketches. His son was Desmond Wilcox, the television producer, who married television presenter Esther Rantzen.

Ireland and abroad

While the practice had occasionally worked outside Scotland, it was healthcare expertise that launched expansion to deliver projects in England, Ireland and abroad. One Monday in 1968, Tom Ridley of Ove Arup engineers asked Tom Scott if he had noticed an advert in the previous day's *Observer* newspaper for the design of a new teaching hospital in Cork. That evening he asked his wife if she still had the paper, but it had to be rescued from the bin so that the advert could be responded to. 114 others also applied. One of these was the famous American architect Walter Gropius.

Tom Scott attended the first interview as a shortlisted candidate. Dick De'Ath was to be the project architect but missed the plane. Flying from Glasgow via London, Tom Scott hired a taxi at Cork airport and asked the driver if he knew the way to the local

Cork University Hospital. In 2004 a new maternity unit by Keppie Design was under construction on the grassed area in front of the ward block.

hospital. 'You must be going to be interviewed to design the new hospital. You're the eighteenth person this week' was the reply. The odds did not look good. The nineteen interviewees were shortlisted to four for a second interview, three from London plus Keppie Henderson. Dick De'Ath made it this time. The Keppie Henderson approach was modest and extremely businesslike, concentrating on experience gained in Scotland and on project process management. The practice is still working at the hospital in 2004 where a maternity unit extension is under construction, and an oncology extension was completed in 2002.

The *Irish Build* magazine of April 1968 reported the appointment of Mr R.R.C. De'Ath of the firm of Keppie, Henderson and Partners for the £7 million regional hospital. It did not approve:

> British hospital design in post-war years has not attained any remarkable heights of excellence . . . . Without wishing to be narrowly chauvinistic on this issue, we consider the Board were dangerously *flaithuil* in a way the British would not be; most of their competitions are closed to nationals of this country . . . . When it comes to chauvinism there is no one quite so good as the British themselves . . . . With imports again racing upwards the Cork Hospital Board have agreed not only that fees in excess of four hundred thousand pounds will sail down the Lee, but it may well not stop there. A cross-channel architect is likely to select the things he knows; cross-channel materials, cross-channel sub-contractors.

Ireland did not have established procedures for briefing and designing hospital projects. Previously, large hospitals had been run by the Church. St Vincent's Hospital in Dublin was the only hospital built since the war, but it had been based on pre-war thinking, and had Nightingale wards. For the next year Keppie Henderson and the rest of the design team wrote the medical, engineering, furniture and equipment specifications.

The building contract was based on the drawings and these specifications. One contractor suggested that he could build the hospital cheaper if he was given five years to construct it rather than the four specified, and for the first time penalty clauses were introduced to a construction contract in Ireland to ensure that it did not take any longer than five years. In the event, due to the raging inflation of the time, the construction cost rose from £IR5.5 million to £IR12.75 million. The foundation stone was laid on 27 January 1973 by Taoiseach Jack Lynch, and he was back on 7 May 1979 to officially open it. The people of Munster had long waited for their new regional hospital, since the land at Wilton was originally purchased in the mid-1930s. The first patients were admitted on 30 November 1978. A dental hospital was added in 1980, and various alterations have taken place since.

Cork led to other work in Ireland, the copyright for the design of the pathology block having been sold for use at other hospitals. Charles Haughey, then Minister of Health, opened one of these, and was intrigued by the good sense of standardising a design to make delivery of a building quicker: but why stop at a bit of a hospital he asked? Why not replicate the design of a whole hospital?

Haughey was a flamboyant politician who loved the limelight and attained most of

The design of Beaumont Hospital in Dublin was based on that of Cork University Hospital.

279

the high offices in Irish government. As Minister for Justice from 1961–64 one of his key aims was to crush the IRA's border campaign. By 1966 he was Minister for Finance at a time when Ireland's economy was extremely healthy. At the start of the 'Troubles' in 1969 it was decided to use some government money to support nationalists in Northern Ireland who were suffering severe hardship, distress and persecution. Haughey was caught up in controversy when £50,000 was alleged to have found its way via the Irish Red Cross to the IRA for the purchase of guns from Germany. Haughey had given instructions for the cargo arriving in Dublin on 19 March 1970 to be cleared through customs without being inspected. However, British intelligence had already thwarted the scheme.

Haughey was brought to trial in September 1970 and was found not guilty, but the controversy lost him his office. However, he returned in 1977 as Minister for Health and Social Welfare. While his predecessors had planned new hospital projects, Haughey made them happen, at Beaumont in Dublin, and at Mullingar, Sligo and Tralee. His plan for Beaumont was to replicate the Keppie Henderson design for Cork. Showman that he was, he hired a train, filled it with doctors and nurses from north Dublin, took them to Cork and offered them the same, shiny new hospital.

Keppie Henderson teamed up with Dublin architectural practice Tyndall Hogan Hurley for the project. There was initial reluctance from them as it was made clear that they would have to resign from a smaller hospital project at Cavan so that work could

The Mater Private Hospital, Dublin.

be shared around other architects. This hesitation annoyed Haughey, who, according to his secretary, had ordered that the architects be dismissed altogether and the copyright for the Cork design purchased instead. Humble apologies ensued, and Tyndall Hogan Hurley resigned from Cavan. Haughey's secretary phoned on Glasgow Fair Friday to say that the appointment was confirmed, subject to the project starting on site by the end of the year. 'Of course it could' was the practice's reply.

Discussions on the clinical make-up of the hospital took place with the Royal College of Surgeons during August. The design for Cork could not merely be replicated, not just because of a different brief requiring a second ward block, but because the Beaumont site was relatively flat while the Cork one was sloping. Nevertheless, tender documents were issued in September and the contract awarded in December to G. and T. Crampton. The design team included services engineers Varming Mulcahy Reilly, structural engineers Ove Arup, and quantity surveyors O'Reilly, who worked through the night on several occasions to meet deadlines. Charles Haughey cut the first sod of ground in February 1978, and the building was completed in record time. Unfortunately, the funding and procurement of the medical equipment lagged behind, and the hospital lay mothballed for a year.

Other projects in Ireland followed after Beaumont. Since the nineteenth century, the Sisters of Mercy had been providing healthcare at the Mater Misericordae Hospital in Eccles Street, Dublin. They visited Beaumont and were sufficiently impressed to commission Tyndall Hogan Hurley and Keppie Henderson to design the 148-bed Mater Private Hospital in Dublin. Construction commenced in March 1984 and the first patients were admitted in May 1986. The Sisters of Mercy were astute businesswomen in addition to being caring nuns. They asked for the installation of the first magnetic resonance imaging (MRI) equipment in Ireland.

Devotees of James Joyce did not appreciate the construction of the Mater Hospital, as it involved the demolition of 7 Eccles Street, home of Leopold Bloom, hero of the epic novel *Ulysses*. The novel was set on 16 June 1904, the day of Joyce's first date with his future wife Nora Barnacle, and every anniversary, on 'Bloomsday', hundreds of James Joyce pilgrims retrace Bloom's day-long walk around Dublin. Unfortunately, a hospital now stands where his house once was, although the front door was salvaged and is to be seen at a museum in Joyce's old home in North Great George Street.

The next project was a masterplan for St Patrick's Psychiatric Hospital in Dublin. By the 1980s developers were becoming interested in delivering hospital projects. American Medical International (AMI) had offered to build and run the Mater Private Hospital for a share of the profits, but the Sisters reckoned they could run it better and more efficiently themselves. Courtaulds Engineering of Coventry construction-managed the St Patrick's project, providing a single point of responsibility with a design and build package using Keppie Henderson as architects and Crampton as builders. They provided a guaranteed maximum price for doing this, possibly the first time this had been done on an Irish or British hospital project, where costs usually increase as projects are developed. Courtaulds were also involved, but this time only as engineers, in the conversion of a mansion house at St Edmundsbury, Lucan, for psychiatric accommodation for alcoholics.

When Sean Mulcahy of Varming Mulcahy Reilly mechanical engineers introduced Keppie Henderson to their Irish partner Tyndall Hogan Hurley, strong personal relationships formed. Dick Hurley and Dick De'Ath got on well, and Brian Hogan and Tom Scott came up with the idea of using the joint-venture organisation to obtain work abroad. The Architects Planning Export Consortium (APEC) was born and a marketing brochure was prepared in February 1975. Foreign work sounds glamorous, but the reality is less so. APEC and Keppie Henderson obtained work in the ostensibly rich OPEC oil-producing states of Libya, Iraq and Nigeria. The hike in oil prices in 1974 caused havoc with western economies and recession became inevitable in Britain and Ireland, so seeking work abroad seemed particularly attractive.

Maternity and paediatric hospitals were designed for Tripoli (500 beds) and Benghazi (350 beds). Travel to Libya was via Dublin. Irish doctors on exchange visits were also on the plane, and with the IRA campaign in Ulster and the British mainland in full swing, and Colonel Muammar al Gaddafi in power in Libya, the Keppie Henderson architects wondered about the business of other passengers. It took several hours to clear passport control and Europeans were not allowed to move about the country freely. Eventually the political environment became too risky and the practice baled out before the hospitals were built. The Tripoli project had been won by Swedish builder Skanska, but they were no more keen to continue.

Design for the
Anambra Teaching Hospital in Nigeria.

A similar situation occurred when a neuro-psychiatric hospital in Nigeria was commissioned. A military coup took place, and anyone associated with the old regime was in mortal danger. Stan Carrie of Keppie Henderson was asked if he would mind going back to negotiate outstanding fees, but he declined.

The Iran/Iraq War started in 1980 when a hospital was being designed by the practice in Baghdad. Thereafter, air transport was only available to neighbouring Jordan and a long bus ride across the desert from Amman to Baghdad was necessary to get to site. The bus did not have air-conditioning. One evening Peter Scott and client representative John Thomas had been out for drinks with friends and got lost trying to get home in the blacked-out city. Uninhibited due to the refreshments he had partaken of, John approached an armed soldier and asked for a lift home in his jeep. Overwhelmed by the audacity of the Brit abroad, and obviously being a decent chap, the soldier duly obliged.

Once again the practice retreated from a foreign country before construction started, and it was assumed that work never got underway. However, at the end of 1990, prior to Operation Desert Storm and the First Gulf War, our offices in Glasgow were 'raided' by MOD personnel seeking plans of the hospital. These were probably of less interest than Scott Brownrigg and Turner's drawings of the airport in Baghdad, which they found in their head office in Guildford.

England

It was probably safer looking for work in England. Ex-Keppie Henderson man Ian Plenderleith, subsequently at Baxter Clark and Paul, won the commission for a masterplan at Leeds, and Dick De'Ath and Matt Neilson were successfully interviewed for the design of a 1,500 bed hospital at Bradford Royal Infirmary. This would have been the largest hospital in Britain, and the drawings for phase one had been completed when the Labour Party came to power in 1974. Barbara Castle was appointed Minister of Health and Social Security in local Huddersfield lad Harold Wilson's third government. She declared that a hospital with more than 500 beds was too large and impersonal, and she cancelled the project. Once an opportunity has passed, it takes time to revive it, and only in 2003 was the project launched again. Unfortunately, so many minor extensions had been added as funding became available in dribs and drabs that there was no room on the site for a proper rationalisation of the hospital buildings, and in April 2004 the project failed again and was withdrawn from the PFI initiative.

Although an outline design had been drawn up for Lynford Mount Psychiatric Hospital in Bradford, Staincliffe Hospital in Dewsbury was seen as the replacement project for Keppie Henderson. A district general hospital, it was to be designed using a standard planning system called 'Nucleus'. The Department of Health had been experimenting with standardisation for many years in an attempt to reduce costs and the length of design programmes. The predecessor of Nucleus was called 'Harness', and today neither is held in much regard. Various types of hospital accommodation were pre-planned into kits of parts in cruciform shapes, which could be fitted together endlessly to form a hospital. In Scotland and Ireland, Keppie Henderson had been used to designing bespoke hospitals in close collaboration with clinical staff. With options restricted, Nucleus reduced the need to talk to doctors and nurses, and while it might have saved time it did not gain many friends. Nevertheless, Keppie Design is still working with the same hospital trust today at Pinderfields Hospital, Wakefield and Pontefract Hospital, and they seem happy with what was designed in Dewsbury.

The period 1979–2004

The public spending of the 1960s and 70s was a major contributory factor in the decline of the British economy, and the curtailing of this spending was a key part of Margaret Thatcher's strategy to convert the country from a dependency culture to an entrepreneurial one. Hospital projects have been a valuable workload for the Keppie practice because they span recessions. Large projects are committed to in times when money is available and the guaranteed stream of fee income lasts for several years. The large Scottish hospitals helped the practice survive the ups and downs of the 1960s and early 1970s. Cork evened out some of the effects of the oil crisis in 1974, and Beaumont and Dewsbury provided income during the recession at the beginning of the 1980s.

However, there was little hospital work in Scotland in the first half of the 1980s and only one whole hospital development in the second half of the decade, Ayr Hospital, the last publicly funded hospital the practice has designed. In an attempt to reduce the costs and timescales for delivering hospital projects, the Scottish Office experimented with different procurement methods on three hospitals. On the Western Isles Hospital at Stornoway a contractor-managed route was chosen. At West Fife, now called Queen Margaret's Dunfermline, design and build was used. Defects after construction could be blamed on bad design (designer responsibility) or bad workmanship (contractor responsibility), with the hospital authorities unable to apportion blame and picking up the bill. With

Ayr Hospital.

design and build the contractor employs the designers and acts as a single point of responsibility for anything that goes wrong.

Ayr Hospital was advanced using a traditional accelerated method. Previously, with a traditional method, every detail of the design would be completed, and using this contractors provided competitive tenders. It takes several years to fully design a hospital, giving lots of opportunity for clinical consultants to change their minds about what they want, and consequently delay the process. They will also seek changes during the construction period (wanting the most up-to-date medical equipment installed), giving the contractor the possibility to claim delays and extra costs.

At Ayr, the accelerated route allowed the design team to obtain prices for early stages of the construction works to get a contractor on site quickly. The design could be completed while the foundations were being laid and the structural frame erected, the contractor obtaining tenders for more detailed work which was built later, sums that he reported to the hospital to demonstrate value for money. There was a risk in having the design and construction work overlapping, and everyone had to be competent and efficient in their tasks. Key to the process was a good client decision-making structure. A team of three people coordinated decision-making: Ken Rankin from the hospital estates department, Eric Howie representing the hospital board to ensure financial stringency, and Stan Carrie from Keppie Henderson representing the designers. The hospital, from start of design to occupation, was delivered in just over four years. Some changes had been required during the process to meet current medical practice, but the cost had only risen from £21 million to £22 million.

Ayr is one of the few hospital sites where the practice has had plenty of space to design a building. Most projects involve redevelopment of existing sites or cramming too much accommodation onto the site available. The rural location overlooking the Heads of Ayr allowed the plan to be arranged in such a way that all departments had room for expansion, and this facility has been well used in subsequent years. Imaging has been extended to install the latest MRI (magnetic resonance imaging) equipment. 30 extra beds were added for a geriatric assessment unit, and when keyhole surgery and other day surgery techniques came into effect the theatre block was extended

Healthcare International Hospital at Clydebank
is now the Golden Jubilee National Hospital.

and given a dedicated entrance off the hospital ring road. The one thing I have never understood is why a hospital only a few miles from Alloway does not have a Burns Unit!

Another large project was Healthcare International at Clydebank. Two American doctors, Professors Raphael Levey and Angelo Eraklis, had a plan to build three specialist, world-class, private hospitals, one in Boston where they were based, one to serve Europe and the Middle East, and one to serve the Far East. Keen to encourage inward investment, and with the possibility of developing an advanced medical research facility at Clydebank in an area of high unemployment, the Conservative government provided incentives to clear the ex-industrial site beside the Clyde and get the project underway.

The design was based on the hospital under construction in America, so there is a little bit of Boston in Clydebank. US company The Architects Collaborative prepared the concept design and Keppie Henderson (soon to become SBT Keppie) applied UK medical and building standards. The American descendent of Walter Gropius was collaborating with the British descendent of Charles Rennie Mackintosh.

John Laing negotiated the £80 million contract and put together a team from various parts of the country to build the hospital. It went well until near the end of the project when the world economy refused to recover from the financial crisis of 1989. The practice knew something was going wrong when fees began to be paid in shares in the hospital instead of money. We were in the business of designing hospitals, not owning them, a prudent course of action we remind ourselves of when we are asked to take equity in PFI projects today. Three months after the hospital opened, Healthcare International went into receivership and the hospital was put up for sale. After some time, the Abu Dhabi Investment Authority purchased it (and SBT Keppie's shares), although only about 50 beds were occupied at any time. The most successful part of the development was the four-star hotel, originally intended for families of patients and for recuperation, but now operating independently from the hospital. A 'royal suite' was created for visitors from Abu Dhabi.

Despite being an underused – but highly specialised and well-equipped facility – it was politically unacceptable for Scottish NHS patients to be treated in it. With the scandal of public money going to the original private developer, it would have been unpalatable for services to be bought from it, and there was a concern that NHS staff might be poached to operate it. However, many English hospitals had no qualms about reducing their waiting lists by using its services.

Eventually the Scottish Executive saw sense by purchasing the building in 2002, renaming it the Golden Jubilee National Hospital with the aim of reducing waiting lists in Scotland. Keppie Design had already carried out feasibility studies to convert sections of it for NHS use as Abu Dhabi tried to persuade the government to use it, and a programme of adaptations is in progress. Orthopaedic theatres were completed in 2003.

With public funds becoming rare, new healthcare projects in the mid-1990s were restricted to alteration works at Yorkhill Hospital and the health centres at Knightswood and Possilpark in Glasgow, followed by a major design-and-build extension project at Ninewells Hospital in Dundee with Miller Construction.

Despite the lack of public funding, public infrastructure was still badly in need of renewal. The government was keen not to return to the public spending crises of earlier years, with the consequences of high public borrowing, taxation and inflation. It was also concerned that public bodies were not efficient at spending money on large projects. In the early 1990s the Conservative government invented the Private Funding Initiative, where money would be borrowed from the private sector to design, build and operate public facilities. This would keep large capital projects off the balance sheet and treat them as services instead, with monthly rentals paid to private sector operators. A simplistic way of looking at it was that if one had £100 million to spend each year for ten years, one could build one hospital a year, or pay £10 million a year for ten hospitals over ten years, and have the benefits of new, efficient hospitals earlier.

While it costs more for the private sector to borrow money than the public sector, the efficiencies that the private sector would bring to the process, and the risks it would take away from the public sector, would prove better value for money. In hospitals and schools, where it is politically unacceptable for doctors, nurses and teachers to be privatised, the economies are difficult to quantify, although in PFI prisons, where all services have to be carried out by prison staff in a secure status, the warders are employed by the private sector. In these prisons, costs have been shown to be half those in publicly procured ones (Scottish Executive *Consultation on the Future of the Scottish Prison Estate* 2002).

The big advantage of PFI projects (or 'Public Private Partnerships' as they have been better-termed) is the integration of design, construction, maintenance, and services, such as cleaning, catering and laundry. Before PPP, designers only had some input as to how buildings would be built and maintained, but with the builder and facilities manager available at design stage, and the service provider subject to penalty payments for poor performance, much more robust design solutions are required.

For example, at the Royal Infirmary of Edinburgh and University of Edinburgh Medical School, more expensive, higher-quality finishes are used where they reduce maintenance costs over the 30-year contract period. The additional costs of providing basement service distribution tunnels and extra access lifts are paid for by the enhanced efficiencies in the movement of materials and waste about the building when costed over 30 years. Toilets were prefabricated in a factory to a higher quality than they would have been on the building site, also saving time in installation. The higher quality factory finish should make them easier to clean.

The hospital had been waiting 50 years for new premises, with the public funds of the 1970s only managing phase one of the redevelopment of the Laurieston Place infirmary before they ran out. Now with PPP, a major hospital had been designed, built and handed over within seven years in phases from early 2002 to early 2003. This is very quick for such a large, complex building. The original Ninewells Hospital at Dundee took fifteen years to design and build. Unlike HCI at Clydebank, the hospital is being used as a catalyst to develop a

The Royal Infirmary of Edinburgh and University of Edinburgh Medical School.

Medical Research Park, Keppie Design obtaining outline planning approval for this in 2003. The University of Edinburgh Medical School building, opened on 12 August 2002 and called the Chancellor's Building, carries out research into reproductive physiology and human fertility.

With PPP, the capital cost is less critical for project creation, and funds can flow to initiate major renewal of public facilities. The initiative has been such a success that there are more schools and hospital projects than the design and construction market can cope with. In its success lies its greatest danger of failure, as demand outstrips supply.

As architects, we have left behind the world where standard NHS solutions were the inevitable consequence of tight budgets, and now regularly visit America and Europe (the latter cheaply with budget flights) to learn the best of world hospital design. Instead of one or a few projects at a time, and then a famine, there is a constant supply of new hospitals throughout the UK where lessons learned in conjunction with clinicians, builders and facilities managers can be applied. Breaking through the bureaucracy and conservatism of the NHS, one of the largest employers in the world, is not easy, but if we do not make the best of this golden age future generations will condemn us.

The Royal Infirmary of Edinburgh, February 2003.

The Eagle Building in Bothwell Street, Glasgow. On the right is the former Britoil Building (the state oil company formed in the 1970s), which was fitted out for Abbey National by SBT Keppie when Britoil was denationalised.

CHAPTER 25

The practice from 1980 to 2004

There have been a number of key events and dates in the history of the practice: 1889 when it went from a sole practitioner to a partnership; the First and Second World Wars; and, in the post-war period, in terms of change to the country's economy and direction and the effects it had on architecture, the year 1979 is significant as it was then that Margaret Thatcher's government came to power. Before that, the country had been driven by public sector borrowing to feed public-sector led development. In 1979 the free trade principles of Adam Smith came back into fashion, with the disbanding of vast public sector bureaucracies and subsidies as public spending was brought under control. Nationalised companies were denationalised and provision of public services was put out to tender.

The architectural profession changed forever, although old-style public sector projects could not be halted overnight. During the transition the business community became used to the highs and lows of boom and bust cycles, with unemployment reaching a post-war high by the early 1980s. However, the main change was to the status of architects as professionals. The mandatory fee scale set up by architecture's professional institute was deemed uncompetitive and illegal, and the way was set for competitive fee tendering. With the influx of professionals into the private sector as local authority in-house design departments were disbanded, fees for tendered work quickly dropped to a fraction of previous levels, and remained low into the twenty-first century for those unfortunate enough to obtain work in this way. The professional code of conduct was also changed. Advertising, speculative work and involvement in many commercial property ventures was deemed unsatisfactory by the professional institutes in the 1970s, and would have led to censure. In the 1980s architects had to enter the big, bad commercial world. On 1 December 1982, the practice became a limited company, reducing the personal liabilities which the partners, and their widows after their deaths, could endure.

Client organisations were also becoming frustrated by the traditional way projects were procured. With increased competition, builders got into the habit of bidding cheaper than they could carry the work out, and relied on securing extras once the project had been secured and was underway. To do this they had to claim increased costs or delays caused by the client or his designers. In return, architects used their role as administrators of the building contract to assess claims, as if they had an independent position. Clients were often left with design or construction defects at the end of a project, with the completion of defects resolutions and final accounts taking months or even years.

Britannia Court in Bothwell Street, Glasgow, was reputed to be the largest retained facade project in Europe.

Delta House in West Nile Street, Glasgow.

Architects were removed from their privileged position at the head of the design and construction process, and contractors, project managers and cost consultants rushed in to fill the gap. The result did not produce any better buildings, because with the contractor in charge buildability and cost-saving became the priority, while with the recessions at the beginning of the 1980s and 1990s the trade did not invest enough in training. It was not until Sir John Egan's *Rethinking Construction* report came out in 1998 that the gross inefficiencies of the construction industry were fully defined, and the report made recommendations, including integrated supply chains of designers, builders and suppliers, working together with their clients' interests to the fore. Six years later we are still trying to apply these, and the old conflict culture, in which no one wins, is slowly being lost.

In the 30 years since the Second World War the practice had been built around a public-sector workload. While it had worked with some developers like Ravenstone, the mood switched in the 1980s towards private investment, encouraging people to use their own initiative. Developers were encouraged to seek opportunities to recreate the consumer economy first seen in the 1960s, and every city-centre redevelopment opportunity or potential out-of-town retail site was explored. This meant a lot of speculative design by architects to prove development potential, and one had to pick one's developer runners carefully if one was not to lose a lot of money. Some of the individual developer representatives were already part of respectable organisations, some sought respectability, others did not bother. Many feasibility studies were carried out, but few resulted in completed buildings.

The buildings at 206–228 St Vincent Street were redeveloped for Scottish Provident, 36–62 Bothwell Street for Next Properties (becoming the headquarters for Britannia Life) and Delta House, West Nile Street, for Royal London Mutual Insurance. Given the gestation time projects like this take to prove their viability and obtain funding, construction work on all of these was delayed to the end of the 1980s. Better fortunes were found with retail chains that were expanding from the beginning of the 1980s. General George was a cut-price carpet warehouse operator which opened outlets at Birkenshaw, Renfrew, Prestwick and Dundee. Granada service stations were built at Kinross, Stirling and Musselburgh, and expansion into England, firstly at Southwaite, Tamworth and Washington, allowed Keppie Henderson to open a small office in Leicester. McDonalds restaurants appeared in the second half of the 1980s, and after the first one in Argyle Street in Glasgow high street restaurants and 'drive-thru' freestanders were built all over Scotland. These were not prestigious projects, but, particularly with McDonalds over a ten-year period, they gave a steady stream of income.

The Granada Lodge in Leicester was one of a number built on the UK motorway network.

Ravenstone was the development arm of the Reo Stakis organisation. When work was about to start on a shopping centre in Londonderry they decided to pull out of property development. The government stepped in to salvage the project, and Reo Stakis and his manager, Joe Friel, at a meeting at Stormont, asked if Keppie Henderson could be retained on the project. The Richmond Shopping Centre in Derry led to a Keppie Henderson office in Belfast, which did not survive the 1980s when further work in the province failed to materialise.

The Richmond Centre, Londonderry.

In 1989 Keppie Henderson merged with Scott Brownrigg and Turner (called Scott Brownrigg in 2004). SBT did not have a significant public sector pedigree and concentrated more on commercial projects. Jim Fisher had set up their Scottish office in Glasgow in 1968, and he had built it up from a few people to over twenty when the merger with Keppie Henderson took place in 1989. He gained a reputation as perhaps Glasgow's shrewdest commercial architect, the office able to maximise the development potential of even the tightest city centre site. After being appointed by the Reo Stakis organisation for small alterations to their hotels, he worked with their development arm, Ravenstone Securities. The supermarket at Grosvenor Lane, Byres Road, Glasgow was the result of this. Findlay House at 10–24 West Nile Street was developed for James Findlay and Co. (1977), Moncrieff House at 69 West Nile Street for Sheraton Caltrust (1985/86), Waring and Gillow's store at 247–251 Sauchiehall Street, shops at 1–11 Argyle Street (1986–87), the Argyle Street/

Parkhead Forge Shopping Centre was part of the government's Glasgow East Area Redevelopment (GEAR) strategy to tackle the problems of the decline in heavy industry in the area. The Beardmore forge had previously been on the site.

Queen Street corner for Taylor Woodrow, 61–69 West Regent Street for Marcton, the Ca'd'Oro Building for the Co-operative Insurance Society, and 159–175 St Vincent Street for Coats Patons as their new headquarters. I joined Scott Brownrigg and Turner in 1984 to work on the new Paisley Shopping Centre for Bredero, but another opportunity, Parkhead Forge Shopping Centre, for Arlington, moved forward first and I was transferred to it. It had silver/white wall panels and blue-tinted glass in red frames, but it was honestly not intentional that a red, white and blue colour scheme was chosen for a building directly opposite Celtic Park!

Negotiations with the planning department on commercial projects were often fraught, as the developer wished to gain as much out of the site as possible. At 241–243 West George Street, developer Bett Brothers decided not to seek approval for a modern design to replace the tasteless post-war NCR-occupied building, but to build a traditional stone one which fitted in with the surrounding buildings.

In a place like Glasgow, the historic links between two practices are probably inevitable. By coincidence, the SBT West George Street site had originally been occupied by a John Honeyman building from 1876; the Ca'd'Oro had been designed by Honeyman; the Argyle Street/Queen Street corner had been refurbished for the Kenilworth Hotel by John Keppie and Henderson in 1933; and Jim Fisher lived in Windyhill, Kilmacolm, designed by Mackintosh. I first met Peter Scott, current chairman of Keppie Design, and John Miller of Keppie Henderson when they were trying to persuade me that they could design a McDonalds freestander to fit sensitively into the Parkhead Forge car park, for which I was project architect.

A retail development on the corner of Argyle Street and Queen Street
replaced the Kenilworth Hotel, which the practice had refurbished in the 1930s.

The merger between the two practices made sense in a lot of ways. Jim Fisher, Tom Scott, Dick De'Ath, Stan Carrie, Matt Neilson and Ronnie Kennedy were due to retire within the next five years or so; many of the commercial clients were common to both; and Scott Brownrigg and Turner would gain access to public sector project skills. In effect it was a takeover, since in 1989 Scott Brownrigg and Turner had 350 staff against Keppie Henderson's 65. This disparity was not to last long with the recession biting at the beginning of the 1990s. The south-east of England had not experienced the effects of a recession to the extent of this one – in the same way that areas with traditional heavy industries had – and lacked the resilience to fight it. The southern staff dropped to about 50 whereas the SBT Keppie complement levelled out at 40.

The merger also saw a move back into the city centre to 158–160 West Regent Street. Scott Brownrigg and Turner had identified the John Ross Memorial Church (designed by Norman A. Dick of Sir John Burnet, Son and Dick and completed in 1931) at number 160 as a new home, and, in conjunction with developer Pat Kelly of London and Clydeside redesigned it as a design studio. Luckily, the rest of the redundant Deaf and Dumb Institute premises were being converted into offices by another developer, and were more than big enough for the enlarged SBT Keppie practice.

The momentum gained in Glasgow by the merger and a few large, ongoing public and commercial projects meant that only one year recorded a loss at a time when several architectural competitors went out of business. The refurbishment of the McLellan Galleries was completed in time for Glasgow's Year of Culture in 1990, despite the dome on the corner of the building having to be rebuilt after a fire. The

The John Ross Memorial Church in West
Regent Street, Glasgow, before conversion.

293

The Keppie Design offices in West Regent Street
were converted from the John Ross Memorial Church and opened in 1989.

Loreburne Shopping Centre in Dumfries wavered for some time as the economy declined, but it was completed in 1991, albeit with few shops occupied at first. At one end of Bothwell Street Britannia Life was moving into its new headquarters, doubling the size of the developer project, which was the largest retained facade project (knocking down everything except the outer walls) in Europe. At the other end of the street the Eagle Building was being erected, both SBT and Keppie Henderson having tried for many years to find a scheme that worked and which retained the existing listed building on the site. The solution was to rebuild the best-preserved sections of it as features in the entrance hall. Britannia Life helped to fund Glasgow Caledonian University's Britannia Building, a project won in a limited design competition.

The masterplanning of Hillington Industrial Estate for private-sector purchaser Caledonian Land yielded a few low-cost building projects, Rank Xerox and a small retail centre. A Tesco supermarket in Greenock was built for Callender Land. Condor won a design-and-build contract for an ice rink at Dumfries. Ventureline and Tulloch developed the Queensgate project in Inverness. Legal and General advanced their office and retail redevelopment on Buchanan Street/Mitchell Lane, and when they came into the office they were amazed that we could pull out a copy of the original 1890s drawings of the building from our archives. They had not appreciated that we

Redevelopment of the Eagle Building site was delayed for many years as the city planners insisted that the historic building facade was kept. The solution they eventually accepted was for the best bits to be reconstructed in the entrance hall.

had been the architects for the old *Glasgow Herald* offices. A small office project was completed at 19 Blythswood Square for Sheraton Caltrust just before they went into liquidation. Fisher House at 80 Bath Street, Sainsbury's at Darnley and business units at Hillington were finished before developer London and Clydeside was wound up. The office block at the corner of Bath Street and Hope Street was not originally called Fisher House, but, one year before he was due to retire, Jim Fisher died of cancer, and it was fitting that the last building he designed was named after him. Unfortunately, a new occupant has recently renamed it.

295

Sainsbury's superstore, Darnley, Glasgow.

Had SBT Keppie won the redevelopment of Glasgow Airport in the 1990s (Edinburgh Airport followed for the successful architect) they might have survived what was possibly the deepest post-war recession without any reduction in size, but Scott Brownrigg and Turner's masterplan was over-elaborate and too expensive. SBT had just designed Heathrow Terminal 4 and Manchester Terminal 2, and compared to these the international terminal at Glasgow as finally proposed was regarded by some in SBT as little more than a bus shelter for air passengers. The client's aspirations as expressed in their brief may have been to blame, but the fee proposal for the redevelopment work by both BDP (Building Design Partnership) and SBT Keppie was vastly undercut by Parr architects.

The inability as SBT Keppie saw it of the part of the business based in south-east England to adapt to prevailing economic conditions made them question the southern link. SBT's financial position was also weak, the partners who retired at the end of the 1980s having, in retrospect, overvalued their share of the business and not taken account of the workload grinding to a halt immediately after – or many clients going bust before they had paid fees. They seemed to have taken money out before it had been fully secured. After months of sleepless nights in 1995, frustrated by their inability to affect the overall SBT business, the four Scottish directors of SBT Keppie, David Collin, Peter Sassoon, Peter Scott and David Stark, offered to buy Keppie back out to reduce the company debt. Keppie Design Ltd. was born.

The nine years since then have been the most economically stable that any living person can remember, and have provided an ideal climate in which to prosper. The thing that impressed me most about Scott Brownrigg and Turner when I joined them was their professionalism and organisation. They were taking professional project managers on and proving that architects could be trusted with practical issues. An extensive database of technical knowledge was ensuring that the errors in construction details and materials of the 1960s and 1970s would not be repeated. Being a 'safe pair of hands' is important to clients spending millions of pounds. However, with this goes a reputation of playing safe and not always designing exciting buildings. Being careful means being the second person to employ an innovation, not the first. However, with the confidence of a stable economy, the capabilities of the practice have been extended.

One of the major changes in working practice has been the introduction of computers and electronic communication. Keppie Henderson had been one of the first to invest in computers, setting up Keppie Computer Graphics Ltd. in 1982, partly to market its services outside the practice and help pay for the enormous costs of the technology. Computers helped the complicated hospital specification and production information process, but the lack of sophistication in the systems of the time probably contributed to less than inspiring designs where they were employed, such as the riverside housing at Kingston Dock on the south side of the Clyde, east of the Kingston Bridge, for Laing Homes. McGurn Logan Duncan and Opfer did use the system to benefit with the setting out of the curved walls in their twentieth-century tenement at Stratford Street in Maryhill (1984–88). A laptop in 2004 has much more computer power than the mainframe machine that took up a whole room at Woodside Place, and colour presentations, more complex geometries and 3D computer modelling are now taken for granted. A BBC producer who used the Keppie offices for filming an episode of a drama in 2000 was disconcerted that there were no drawing boards visible, just computer screens, and in case his audience did not realise that it was an architect's office had drawing boards brought in for the shoot.

Since 1995 a large number of projects have been carried out, both independently and in joint venture with Seymour Harris in England. Seymour Harris Keppie has been seeking PPP school and hospital projects in England and Wales since it was set up in 1999. It has been very successful to date. The projects mentioned in this chapter have mainly been commercial ones, as other chapters have covered schools and hospitals. With the Conservative government's Private Finance Initiative being continued by Labour successors (although now usually referred to as Public Private Parnerships), the door has been opened to an enormous pool of work, more than the industry can handle in the timescales set by politicians.

Parkhead Forge Shopping Centre.

SBT Keppie refurbished the McLellan Galleries in 1989/90.

The Overgate Centre in Dundee is almost unique in comprising a single-sided shopping mall providing views across the town from the shops within it.

CHAPTER 26

Selected projects since 1995

It would take too long to describe all the major projects since 1995, and without the perspective of time having passed might sound like a sales pitch. A sample of them has therefore been picked out to illustrate various aspects of work. Three are described below.

Perth Council Offices, 2000

The council offices in Perth were opened in 2000, the project being a redevelopment of the former Pullars of Perth works in Mill Street. Pullars had been a major employer in the area for over 150 years, and had also commissioned buildings from Honeyman Keppie and Mackintosh at the beginning of the twentieth century. In 1902 a row of cottages was designed at Tulloch, Perth, and alterations to the Pullars' offices at 202 Bath Street in Glasgow were carried out. John Honeyman probably obtained the work from Laurence Pullar, a neighbour in Bridge of Allan. The cottages are modest by today's standards, but at a time when workers in the big cities lived in tenements with whole families in a single room and with outdoor toilets, the employees at the Tulloch works should have been very happy with their lot. However, industrial relations were not good at Pullars, and the employer paternalism of the nineteenth century began to turn into the employer/trade union confrontation of the twentieth century.

Pullars' southern rivals, Eastman and Johnson Brothers, started to cut their prices and in 1907 old Sir Robert badly handled a wage demand. His son Rufus took over management of the business, but further loss of trade took place in 1912 when a national miners and railway strike cut off Pullars' connections with their southern market. By 1914 shop stewards were demanding a minimum wage and suffragettes sought equal pay. In 1917, with living costs soaring because of the war, the

Houses designed in 1902 for Pullars staff at Tulloch, near Perth.

Pullar House
provides modern office accommodation
behind a retained stone facade.

Many features of the old Pullar House
building were retained, including roof
trusses and stone flooring.

works were besieged by a mob of 2,000. Mounted police were called in and the 'Battle of the Gates' ensued. Rufus had a nervous breakdown and died in September that year. Rivals Eastman and Sons purchased the works but retained the Pullars name. In turn, they were acquired by the Johnson Group in 1938, their Scottish headquarters remaining in Perth. However, all cleaning operations in the city ceased in the 1990s and the Mill Street premises were vacated. The resultant site redevelopment offered an opportunity for the new Keppie Design office, which was located in George Street, a few hundred metres from the Mill Street building.

Having effected a management buyout from Scott Brownrigg and Turner in 1995, the directors of Keppie Design were approached by struggling architect David Davies the following year to see if they would be interested in purchasing his Scottish office in Perth. In the event D.Y. Davies went out of business soon after, and the liquidator was happy to settle on a low price for a quick deal. Davies had purchased the practice of Hugh Wilson and Lewis Womersley in 1989. In the mid-1980s this practice had 22 staff working in offices in London, Middlesborough, Manchester and Perth. Sir Hugh Wilson and W.M. Armstrong were two of the partners at this time, the latter coming out of retirement in 1997 to become the project manager for the Scottish Parliament Building. Bill resigned when he could no longer put up with the failings of the process, failings which were well-known in the building industry at the time but which only the Fraser Report has finally chronicled. Hugh Wilson had been chief architect at Cumbernauld new town and Lewis Womersley chief architect of Sheffield City Council, the former setting up his own practice in 1962 and going into partnership with the latter in 1964.

The Keppie Design Perth office had prepared plans for a local developer to centralise local authority offices in Perth to the Mill Street site, close to the bus station, from thirteen disparate locations. A multi-storey car park would provide parking for staff during the week and for shoppers at the weekend. The business case demonstrated the efficiencies that the council would obtain, while the public would have access to all local authority services at one location.

When the council applied for funding to carry out the works they were informed that all capital projects had to be tested under the new government Private Finance Initiative. Having prepared a design which satisfied the council's requirements, and having thus expected an appointment to carry out the works, Keppie had to align itself with an organisation which could fund, build and maintain the building for the contract period of 25 years. Other PFI bidders were in competition, but the knowledge Keppie had of the council requirements was undoubtedly a key part of the successful Morrison Construction bid.

This was the first project completed by Keppie under PFI, and demonstrated the

The multi-storey car park at the rear of Pullar House serves the council offices and Perth shoppers. There is also ample room to park bicycles.

benefits of the initiative. Since Morrison would not earn any money from the project until it was available to the council to occupy, they went about their business efficiently and delivered the project on time, essential to ensure the coordination of the migration of council employees from the thirteen other sites. The person acting for the council could not believe how easy the process was, being more used to constant arguments with building contractors about delays and increased costs.

There would have been plenty of opportunity for conflict. The development extended over the old city wall and time had to be allowed for archaeological investigations. Various finds were made. Ground contamination had been left from the Pullars' activities, but could not be defined in advance of excavations. With a normal building contract there would have been ample room for extensions of time and consequent cost increases.

An old stream runs under the site, and this was used to provide cooling for the building in summer. Since the builder was also responsible for maintaining the development, it was in his interests to spend more money installing the necessary equipment for this at the beginning of the project to allow energy savings to be made over the next 25 years. A similar balance was required on the specification of all parts of the building, since cost-cutting could be counterproductive if maintenance costs were increased in the future, or elements failed before the 25-year contract was complete.

The memory of Pullars is retained, with the old stone facade kept and cast iron roof trusses designed into the internal public space. Stone paving slabs were also carefully reused. The project was awarded an 'excellent' environmental standard under the relevant UK government scheme.

The Overgate Centre, Dundee, 1996–2000

In the 1960s, the old street pattern of the Overgate was destroyed with the construction of a shopping centre. A few right-of-way pedestrian routes had been retained, but by 1996 when Keppie Design was approached by developer TBI, the centre was not offering shop tenants the quality of environment expected of the era, and the retail hub of the city centre had shifted further east.

While it is a large building, the Overgate Centre complements the setting of St Mary's Steeple and its church.

The previous developers were originally planning a £2 million refurbishment, but TBI came to the conclusion that a brightened up 1960s centre was still a 1960s centre, and that something more radical would be necessary to change its fortunes. Over a few days, Keppie produced some concept ideas that were enough to secure the commission. An unwritten condition of the appointment was that Keppie ensure that Stirling architects, Prentice Kennedy, who were in place for the smaller refurbishment, but who did not have the resources to take on a multi-million pound redevelopment, did not lose out. Keppie involved them in other work so that they did not suffer financially.

Before TBI could implement the proposals, Australian developer Lend Lease identified the project as a good investment and purchased it. Keppie were retained, but Lend Lease's modus operandi was to appoint a concept architect in addition to the executive architect, the latter detailing and delivering the design. Lend Lease's executive architect on the Bluewater Valley Centre in Kent, Benoy, became the concept architect on Overgate. Bovis won the construction contract and before the project was complete Lend Lease had also purchased them.

The approach of having separate concept and executive architects was introduced from America and presumably works on the assumption that some architects will be better at producing innovative ideas, while others will be more

Detail of the Overgate Centre.

practical and better able to deliver the design – or at least the separation of the two will allow the concept architect not to be over-constrained by practicalities in his initial thinking. While this contention is debatable, its success depends on two architects being able to work well together, and a large part of Keppie's work in the twenty-first century involves joint ventures and collaborations with other architectural practices. With an enormous workload available, there is not the cut-throat competition between practices that there had been in some earlier eras, and most architects respect each others' skills and collaborate well. It nonetheless takes time to develop an understanding of each other's design culture and designers, and the trust that follows.

The Angus Hotel was part of the original Overgate Centre when it opened in 1964, and was demolished in 2000 to make way for the new centre.

The Benoy collaboration worked well on Overgate, as did Ocean Terminal at Leith with Conran, again with Bovis Lend Lease as builders. The fresh eye of Benoy on Overgate and the dynamism of Lend Lease took the design a stage further than it had reached previously. Most shopping centres are, by their very nature, introverted, looking into a mall with the rear of shop units facing outwards to the rest of the town. Overgate is one of only a few modern shopping centres which is single-sided, one entire wall being glazed and facing onto the City Churches (three congregations used the one building) which anchors a very attractive civic space. This respect for an existing urban fabric was often missing from 1960s and 1970s centres. These displayed a 'brave new world' philosophy, and comprehensively swept away much of what appeared drab and outdated at the time, but which had qualities that are difficult to replace today.

One of the elements of the shopping centre redevelopment was the restoration of St Mary's Steeple, part of the church dating from around the year 1500, and its conversion into an interpretative centre. It survived occupation and looting by English troops in 1548, and a three-day siege by Cromwell's forces in 1651. From the top there are panoramic views of the Tay estuary and the two Tay bridges. The mechanisms that operate the clock and the bells are on public display, the latter being installed in 1872. The antiques room contains carved stones rescued from historic Dundee buildings, many of which were demolished in the nineteenth century.

Springvale Campus, Belfast

In 1997 Keppie was asked by a project manager if it would take part in a design competition for a university building in Belfast. The limited competition had four entrants, but one pulled out a week before submission and there was a spare place. Although the chances of success were slim, there was the possibility of impressing a new client

Overleaf: *Leith's Ocean Terminal was designed so that the Royal Yacht* Britannia *could be accessed through the shopping and leisure centre.*

The University of Ulster's Belfast Outreach Centre sought to bring two divided communities together.

who was offering a good workload and a design was prepared over a weekend. The Keppie scheme won.

The concept was to build a university outreach centre between Catholic and Protestant communities as the first step in the creation of the new Belfast City Campus for the University of Ulster, which would be a catalyst for regeneration of the area and a vital contribution to the peace process. Northern Ireland has the highest percentage of students that leave their area of residence to pursue further education, and most do not return. One of Keppie's first tasks was to prepare a masterplan for the area. During the design stage Professor Wallace Ewart spent four months in America raising money. Half of the funds came from this source, and half from the British Lottery Fund, many projects at this time being termed Millennium Projects.

Although work was not ready to commence for several months, a visit by Bill Clinton in 1998 to encourage the peace process was too good an opportunity to miss, and he performed a ceremonial first-spade sod cut on the site. Martin McGuinness was the Minister for Education and gave his sanction to the project.

The launching of the Belfast Outreach Centre focused the attention of politicians who were keen to get the peace process back on track.

There were plenty of sceptics as to the scheme's viability. The site had been picked because it was a no man's land between the Catholic and Protestant communities. It had one road in but four footpaths out, ideal for gangs of both religious persuasions carrying out beatings around Springfield Road to flee from the police, abandon and torch their getaway cars and run off in various directions. The site was also bounded by the infamous Mackie's factory, often the starting point for loyalist marches in July. The RUC were consulted about security and their crime prevention officer recommended that the building should have a minimal number of windows in case they were vandalised, no light-coloured walls in case they were spray painted, and that there should be an electric fence around the site, with enough current to stun, but not enough to kill, you understand. The architectural consequence would hardly have afforded the desired welcoming ambience.

The external walls of the Belfast Outreach Centre are robust but attractive.

In such circumstances, a positive and attractive architectural approach, which gains community buy-in to the project, allied to good and proactive facilities management attending to any damage or deterioration quickly, achieves much better results. When we started designing Parkhead Forge Shopping Centre in the East End of Glasgow we were confronted with the same merchants of doom. However, large areas of glass at entrances, and external walls that slope down to the

Britannia Life helped to fund Glasgow Caledonian University's Britannia Building.

ground have not been abused, and the car parks are some of the safest places in the city to leave a car.

At one point the site agent fell out with boys playing football against the site fence and for several weeks thereafter there were bouts of vandalism and arson. Being in Gerry Adams' constituency, he was asked to help. Soon after, a big man in a string vest came on to the site and announced that he was the new security agent. He was never seen again, but neither were the vandals.

Like the earlier Britannia Building at Glasgow Caledonian University, the client was single-minded, had a clear vision for the project, and could drive it through. The result is a building design of which the architect and the community can be proud. It appears to have been a success and is still standing. A second building on the campus was awarded to a local Northern Ireland practice, although the initiative has sadly been shelved.

Offices and laboratories for East of Scotland Water at Riccarton.

Central Exchange, a new office block at the corner of Waterloo Street and Wellington Street in Glasgow, was opened in the autumn of 2004.

Opposite: Offices under construction in 2004 at Admiral Park, St Peter Port, Guernsey, forming part of a larger retail, office and residential development.

Designs for the conversion of old industrial premises for IT use at Seabraes Mill, Dundee, are underway in 2004.

Conclusion

Obviously, one cannot write retrospectively about Keppie Design in 2004. One can only say that the practice is the busiest it has ever been, and the thrust of optimism is currently exhausting. It would also be impossible to describe in the same detail as the pre-1939 periods the hundreds of projects and services carried out over the last ten years. In our electronic world, the writer of the 200th anniversary book could have enormous quantities of data to pore over, or perhaps electronic information will be as easy to lose as hard copy, deleted in an instant from a computer, lost in an endless row of uncatalogued compact discs, or inaccessible in an obsolete software package.

Will future architects still be infuriated by bureaucracy, as every architect over the last 150 years has been? Will they still struggle to prove their financial worth as John Honeyman did when he was arguing for paid competition design? Will they still have to fight for that little bit of extra money to make a great building out of an average one? Some contend that architects will become obsolete as computers take over and translate a virtual world into reality. We have overtaken such 1984 concepts before and found that the human spirit and imagination has conquered.

Having a tradition such as Keppie Design's makes one wish to sustain it through a culture that encourages younger talent to emerge, and with a succession strategy that allows the older custodians of the practice to retire without damaging the business. Particularly in the last 50 years, the building design process has normally been a team response, and the best individual talent must play within a team structure. Architects need to remember that they are working in a commercial business world, and sustained success will only be possible if a profit is consistently made. To do this, design must satisfy the needs of clients and building users, not pander to the passing trends of architectural fashion, dogma and celebrity. Most of all, there is an imperative to continually assess social, economic and political change, and respond to it, so that the design skills that society demands are at its disposal. It is impossible to predict the future, but I would expect that the tradition which was strong in the 1860s to 1870s, 1890s to 1900s, 1960s to 1980s and from 1995 to 2004 will still be strong in 2054.

Reception, oncology suite,
Belfast City Hospital.

Opposite: The entrance atrium of 200
Broomielaw, Glasgow, a waterfront office
building completed in 2003.

*In October 2004 the practice was commissioned to design a
headquarters building for Scottish Natural Heritage in Inverness.*

Further reading

Anderson, R.D.: *Scottish Education Since the Reformation*, Economic and Social History Society of Scotland, 1988

Bailey, Rebecca M.: *Scottish Architects' Papers, A Source Book*, The Rutland Press, Edinburgh, 1996

Beauly, Iona: *John Honeyman: a Catalogue of Work*, Department of Architecture and Building Science, University of Strathclyde, Master of Philosophy thesis, 1998

Billcliffe, Roger: *The Glasgow Boys: The Glasgow School of Painting 1875-1895*, John Murray, London, 1985

Billcliffe, Roger: 'The Mackintosh Circle: James Herbert MacNair (1868-1955)', *Charles Rennie Mackintosh Society Newsletter*, No. 33, 1982

Billcliffe, Roger (compiler): *The Royal Glasgow Institute of the Fine Arts 1861-1989*, The Woodend Press, Glasgow, 1991

Brown, A.L., and Moss, Michael: *The University of Glasgow: 1451-1996*, Edinburgh University Press, 1996

Buchanan, William: 'The Mackintosh Circle: Mackintosh, John and Jessie Keppie', *Charles Rennie Mackintosh Society Newsletter*, No. 32, 1982

Buchanan, William (ed.): *Mackintosh's Masterwork, the Glasgow School of Art*, Richard Drew Publishing, Glasgow, 1989 (first edition) and 2004 (second edition)

Burkhauser, Jude (ed.): *The Glasgow Girls: Women in Art and Design, 1880-1920*, Canongate, Edinburgh, 1990

Cairns, George M.: 'The Glasgow School of Art: an Architectural Totality', thesis presented to the University of Glasgow, February 1992

Cairns, Robert O.: 'The Vale of Leven Hospital, Alexandria', *Scottish Medical Journal*, 1961 6:485

Cameron, Thomas (ed.): *Glasgow Chamber of Commerce and Manufacturers Year Book 1915*, Bermrose & Sons, Derby, 1915

Charnley, Bob: *Iona and Staffa via Oban*, Clan Books, Doune, 1994

Christie, Guy: *Crieff Hydro 1868-1968*, Oliver & Boyd, Edinburgh and London, 1967

Collin, David: *Kirkcudbright: An Alphabetical Guide to its History*, The Stewartry Museum, Kirkcudbright, 2003

Cotton, Vere E.: *Liverpool Cathedral: the Official Handbook*, Littlebury Bros., Liverpool, 1932

Coupar, Robert: *The Parish Church of St Michael of Linlithgow*, Oliver and Boyd, Edinburgh, 1938

Crawford, Kenneth N. and Roberts, Alison: *Around Helensburgh*, Tempus Publishing, Stroud, 1999

Dalziel, Nigel:	*Glasgow in Old Photographs*, Sutton Publishing, Stroud, 2002
Davidson, Peter Wylie:	'Memories of Mackintosh', extract from unpublished autobiography, *Charles Rennie Mackintosh Society Newsletter*, No. 22, 1979
Davies, John McG.:	*Social and Labour Relations at Pullars of Perth 1882-1924*, Centre for Tayside and Fife Studies, 1993
Donnely, Michael:	'Charles Rennie Mackintosh and The Glasgow Herald', *Charles Rennie Mackintosh Society Newsletter*, No. 34, 1983
Dow, Derek A.:	*Redlands House: Hospital, Hostel and Home*
Dunbar, John G. and Fisher, Ian:	*Iona: A Guide to the Monuments*, HMSO, Edinburgh, 1995
Dunlop, A.D.:	*Hutchesons' Grammar: The History of a Glasgow School*, Glasgow, 1992
Dwyer, T. Ryle:	*Short Fellow, A Biography of Charles J. Haughey*, Marino Books, Dublin, 1999
Edwards, Brian:	'John Honeyman, Victorian Architect and Restorer and Partner of Charles Rennie Mackintosh', *Charles Rennie Mackintosh Society Newsletter*, No. 36, 1984
Emmerson, Roger:	*Winners and Losers: Scotland and the Architectural Competition*, RIAS, 1991
Eunson, Eric:	*The Gorbals: An Illustrated History*, Stenlake Publishing, Ayrshire, 1996
Eyre Todd, G.(ed.):	*The Book of Glasgow Cathedral*, Glasgow, 1898
Fawcett, Richard:	*Scottish Cathedrals*, Historic Scotland/B.T. Batsford, London, 1997
Ferguson, Hugh:	*Glasgow School of Art: The History*, The Foulis Press of Glasgow School of Art, Glasgow, 1995
Foreman, Carol:	*Lost Glasgow*, Birlinn, Edinburgh, 2002
Frankenberg, John, MRCS, MRCOG:	'The Continuous-Process Delivery System', The *Lancet*, 14 October 1961
Galbraith, Iain B.:	*A Village Heritage: The Parish of Rhu 1648-1980*, Rhu and Shandon Kirk Session, 1981
Geddes, Jane:	*Deeside and the Mearns: an Illustrated Architectural Guide*, The Rutland Press, Edinburgh, 2001
Gifford, John and Walker, Frank Arneil:	*The Buildings of Scotland: Stirling and Central Scotland*, Yale University Press, New Haven and London, 2002
Gilmour, Sir John:	*The Story of Largo Kirk*, Levenmouth Printers, Leven, 1990
Glendinning, Miles (ed.):	*Rebuilding Scotland: The Postwar Vision 1945-1975*, Tuckwell Press, East Linton, 1997
Graham, Angus:	*Skipness: Memories of a Highland Estate*, Canongate, Edinburgh, 1993
Hall, Keith:	*Old Garelochhead and the Rosneath Peninsula*, Stenlake Publishing, Ayrshire, 1999
Hall, Robert:	*The History of Galashiels*, Alexander Walker & Son, Galashiels, 1898
Harding, Albert W.:	*Pullars of Perth*, Perth and Kinross District Libraries, Perth, 1991
Harrison, Margaret M. (ed.) and Marker Willis B. (ed.):	*Teaching the Teachers: The History of Jordanhill College of Education 1828-1993*, John Donald, Edinburgh, 1996
Hood, John:	*Old Helensburgh, Rhu and Shandon*, Stenlake Publishing, Ayrshire, 1999
Hume, John R.:	*The Industrial Archaeology of Glasgow*, Blackie, Glasgow and London, 1974
Jamieson, Bruce:	*The Church of St Michael of Linlithgow*
Jaques, Richard and McKean, Charles:	*West Lothian: An Illustrated Architectural Guide*, The Rutland Press, Edinburgh, 1994

Jarvis, Geoffrey:	'518 Sauchiehall Street', *Charles Rennie Mackintosh Society Newsletter*, No. 60, 1992
Jones, D.:	*Looking at Scottish Furniture: A Documented Anthology 1570-1900*, Crawford Arts Centre, St Andrews, 1987
Kinchin, Perilla and Kinchin, Juliet:	*Glasgow's Great Exhibitions: 1888, 1901, 1911, 1938, 1988*, White Cockade, Wendlebury, 1988
Kinchin, Perilla:	*Tea and Taste, the Glasgow Tea Rooms 1875-1975*, White Cockade, Oxford, 1991
Lambie, Brian:	'Plans for a Country Manse (Biggar)', *Charles Rennie Mackintosh Society Newsletter*, No. 21, 1979
Lamont, Alan:	*The Life and Works of John Honeyman*, dissertation, 2002
Lawson, Margaret:	*Forgotten Families of Galashiels*, M. Lawson, 1997
Macartney, William Newton:	*Skelmorlie and Wemyss Bay South Church: One Hundred Years*, 1956
MacArthur, E. Mairi:	*Columba's Island: Iona from Past to Present*, Edinburgh University Press, 1995
MacArthur, E. Mairi:	*Iona Celtic Art: The Work of Alexander and Euphemia Ritchie*, The New Iona Press, Iona, 2003
Macaulay, James:	'Mackintosh, Keppie and the Glasgow Art Club', *Charles Rennie Mackintosh Society Newsletter*, No. 81, 2001
MacCulloch, J.A.:	*R.L. Stevenson and the Bridge of Allan*, John Smith, Glasgow, 1927
MacLean, A. (ed.):	*Handbook on the Local Industries of Glasgow and the West of Scotland*, British Association for the Advancement of Science, 1901
Maclean, Ella:	*Bridge of Allan, the Rise of a Village*, Burgh of Bridge of Allan, 1970
Maclean, Magnus (ed.):	*Archaeology, Education, Medical and Charitable Institutions of Glasgow*, Glasgow, 1901
Malcolm, Donald:	*Yesterday's Paisley*, Stenlake Publishing, Ayrshire, 1991
Marriott, Charles:	*Modern English Architecture*, Chapman and Hall, London, 1924
McAlpine, C. Joan:	*The Lady of Claremont House: Isabella Elder, Pioneer and Philanthropist*, Argyll Publishing, Glendaruel, 1997
McCarroll, James:	*Glasgow Victoriana: Classic Photographs by Thomas Annan*, Fort Publishing, Ayr
McGhie, Nevin:	*Killermont: The Home of Glasgow Golf Club*, Glasgow Golf Club, 2003
McGill, Jack:	*Investing in Scotland: An Account of The Fifth International Forum, November 1974*, Collins, Glasgow, 1975
McKean, Charles; Walker, David; and Walker, Frank:	*Central Glasgow: An Illustrated Architectural Guide*, The Rutland Press, Edinburgh, 1999
McKean, Charles:	*The Scottish Thirties: An Architectural Introduction*, Scottish Academic Press, Edinburgh, 1987
McKenzie, Ray:	*Public Sculpture of Glasgow*, Liverpool University Press, Liverpool, 2002
Melville, Lawrence:	*Errol: Its Legends, Lands and People*, Thomas Hunter, Perth, 1935
Melville, Lawrence:	*The Fair Land of Gowrie*, William Culross & Son, Coupar Angus, 1939
Moss, Michael:	*Range and Vision: The first 100 years of Barr and Stroud*, Mainstream, Edinburgh, 1988
Pearson, Eric:	*Trends in School Design: British Primary Schools Today*, Macmillan, 1972

Pease, Matthew:	'Mack at Muckhart?', AHSS Magazine, Summer 1998
Phillips, Alastair:	*Glasgow's Herald 1783-1983*, Richard Drew Publishing, Glasgow, 1982
Pinkerton, Andrew:	'Keppie Henderson Archives: An Important Source for Mackintosh Research', *Charles Rennie Mackintosh Society Newsletter*, No. 45, 1987
Pratt, George:	*School Life in Old Scotland*, The Educational Institute of Scotland, 1925
Rawson, George:	'Mackintosh, Jessie Keppie and the Immortals', *Charles Rennie Mackintosh Society Newsletter*, No. 62, 1993
Rodger, Johnny:	*Contemporary Glasgow: The Architecture of the 1990s*, The Rutland Press, Edinburgh, 1999
Rowand, David:	*Pictorial History of Paisley*, Alloway Publishing, Darvel, 1993
Roxburgh, James M.:	*The School Board of Glasgow, 1873-1919*, University of London Press, 1971
Ruthven, Ianthe:	*The Scottish House*, Collins & Brown, London, 2000
Saville, Richard (ed.):	*The Economic Development of Modern Scotland 1950 to 1980*, John Donald, Edinburgh, 1985
Schotz, Benno:	*Bronze in my Blood: The Memoirs of Benno Schotz*, Gordon Wright Publishing, Edinburgh, 1981
Shaw, J. Berend:	*The Glasgow Battalion of the Boys' Brigade 1883-1983*, St Andrew Press, Edinburgh, 1983
Sillar, W.:	'The Accident and Orthopaedic Department at the Southern General Hospital', *Scottish Medical Journal*, 1964 9:76
Sinclair, Fiona:	'North, South, East and West: A Process of Banking Patronage', *Charles Rennie Mackintosh Society Newsletter*, No. 44, 1986
Sinclair, Fiona J.:	'Some Observations on No. 40 Sinclair Street, Helensburgh', *Charles Rennie Mackintosh Society Newsletter*, No. 59, 1992
Slater, S.D., and Dow, D.A. (ed.):	*The Victoria Infirmary of Glasgow: 1890-1990: A Centenary History*
Slaven, Anthony, and Checkland, Sydney (ed.):	*Dictionary of Scottish Business Biography 1860-1960*, Aberdeen University Press, Aberdeen, 1986
Small, Robert and Small, David M.:	*History of the Congregations of the United Presbyterian Church, 1733-1900*, Edinburgh, 1904
Smart, W.:	*Skelmorlie: The Story of the Parish Consisting of Skelmorlie and Wemyss Bay*, Glasgow, 1968
Stark, David:	'Mackintosh Models Exhibition', *Charles Rennie Mackintosh Society Newsletter*, No. 85, 2003
Stark, David:	'Milwaukee Greek Orthodox Church', *Charles Rennie Mackintosh Society Newsletter*, No. 85, 2003
Stewart, Averil:	*'Alicella', A Memoir of Alice King Stewart and Ella Christie*, John Murray, London, 1955
Twaddle, Graham:	*Old Bute*, Stenlake Publishing, Ayrshire, 2000
Twombly, Robert C.:	*Frank Lloyd Wright: His Life and Architecture*, John Wiley and Sons, New York, 1979
Urquhart, Gordon R.:	*Along Great Western Road: An Illustrated History of Glasgow's West End*, Stenlake Publishing, Ayrshire, 2000
Walker, David:	'The Honeymans', *Charles Rennie Mackintosh Society Newsletter*, Nos. 62, 63 and 64, 1993/94
Walker, Frank Arneil:	*Argyll and the Islands: An Illustrated Architectural Guide*, The Rutland Press, Edinburgh, 2003
Walker, Frank Arneil:	*The Buildings of Scotland: Argyll and Bute*, Penguin Books, London, 2000
Wemyss, Robert:	*The Church in the Square: a Brief History of the United West Free Church Helensburgh*, 1925

Williamson, Elizabeth; Riches, Anne; and Higgs, Malcolm:	*The Buildings of Scotland: Glasgow*, Penguin Books, London, 1990
Wimpenny, Geoffrey:	'Reconstructing the Willow', *Charles Rennie Mackintosh Society Newsletter*, No. 24, 1979
Wimpenny, Geoffrey G.:	'Renovation and Restoration of the Glasgow School of Art', *Charles Rennie Mackintosh Society Newsletter*, No. 13, 1976
Worsdall, Frank:	*The City That Disappeared: Glasgow's Demolished Architecture*, Molendinar Press, Glasgow, 1981

Archaeologia Aeliana, 4th series, 1957

The *Architect*

The *Builder*

The Journal of the Architectural Heritage Society of Scotland

Scottish Country Life, article on the Apex Motor Engineering Company, June 1916

100 Years of Education in the City of Glasgow 1872-1972, Corporation of Glasgow Education Department

'A Happie and Golden Tyme': Education in Scotland since the Fourteenth Century, The National Archives of Scotland

The Lord Provosts of Glasgow, Gowans and Gray, Glasgow, 1902

Factsheets, Heatherbank Museum of Social Work, Glasgow

Minutes and reports of the Glasgow Magdalene Society, the Mitchell Library, Glasgow

Report on the Educational Requirements of Glasgow Education (Scotland) Act 1918, Education Authority of Glasgow, 1920

The Hill House, National Trust for Scotland booklet

Broughton House and Garden, National Trust for Scotland booklet

Transactions of the Glasgow Archaeological Society, 1881 to 1891

The First Hundred Years, booklet on the history of Park Church, Helensburgh

Corporation of Glasgow Handbook on the Municipal Enterprises (for the Sanitary Institute Congress), Glasgow, 1904

Reports and letters by John Honeyman on the Glasgow Municipal Buildings Competition

Minutes of the Corporation of Glasgow 1903/04, Libraries Committee

House for an Art Lover, Glasgow City Council brochure, Randak Design Consultants/The Fraser Press, Glasgow

The Book of Glasgow 1931: Glasgow Civic and Empire Week, The Corporation of the City of Glasgow, 1931

The Trades House of Glasgow: A Short Tour Guide, leaflet for visitors

Interview with ex-employee of Pilkington Electro-Optic, Ian Murray

New Primary and Secondary Schools, Study Group Report, The Corporation of Glasgow Education Department, 1967

New Secondary Schools, Study Group Report, The Corporation of Glasgow Education Department, 1971

Building Seminar on Primary School Design 1976, Department of Education, Strathclyde Regional Council, Glasgow

Educational building notes (various from the 1960s), Scottish Education Department, HMSO

Quality Indicators in the Design of Schools, The Royal Incorporation of Architects in Scotland, Edinburgh, 2002

'50 Years of Health Building', supplement to *Hospital Development* magazine, Wilmington Publishing, Dartford, 1998

'Report to the Governors and Accounts Session 1967 to 1972', H.J. Barnes, Glasgow School of Art

'Every Amenity at Stirling's New Maternity Unit', *Construction Technology*, November 1969

Brochures prepared by the practice and others to mark the opening of hospital and school projects, plus various press cuttings

'Know Your Perth - Tulloch, Pullars Housing', *Perth Advertiser*, 19 November 1989

Information on various buildings was received from the Royal Commission on the Ancient and Historical Monuments of Scotland, Edinburgh

Charles Rennie Mackintosh

Asensio, Paco (ed.):   *Charles Rennie Mackintosh*, teNeues, LOFT Publications, Barcelona, 2002. **Nicely compiled summary of the major projects with commentary in English, German, French and Italian.**

Billcliffe, Roger: *The Art and Design of Charles Rennie Mackintosh: a Book of Postcards*, Pomegranate Europe, Fullbridge Maldon, Essex, 1995. **Attractive postcards in book form illustrating Mackintosh paintings and photographs of his furniture.**

Billcliffe, Roger: *Charles Rennie Mackintosh: Textile Designs*, Pomegranate Artbooks, San Francisco, 1993. **An interesting and well-illustrated study on a facet of Mackintosh not previously covered.**

Billcliffe, Roger: *Charles Rennie Mackintosh: the Complete Furniture, Furniture Drawings and Interior Designs*, Lutterworth Press, Guildford and London, 1979. **This encyclopaedic reference book is unique and would merit being updated.**

Billcliffe, Roger: *Mackintosh Furniture*, Lutterworth Press, Cambridge, 1984/ Cameron and Hollis, Moffat 1990. **An up-to-date and fresh perspective.**

Brett, David: *C.R. Mackintosh: The Poetics of Workmanship*, Reaktion Books, London, 1992. **An interpretation of Mackintosh's work rather than a chronological summary of it.**

Cairney, John: *The Quest for Charles Rennie Mackintosh*, Luath Press, Edinburgh, 2004. **Cairney has used his imagination to fill various gaps in our knowledge about Mackintosh, creating a controversial work that is potentially misleading.**

Cooper, Jackie (ed.):   *Mackintosh Architecture: The Complete Buildings and Selected Projects*, Academy Editions, London, 1977, 1984. **The title describes the contents, although it is debatable whether a 'complete' guide is possible.**

Crawford, Alan: *Charles Rennie Mackintosh*, Thames and Hudson, London, 1995. **Despite the publishers persuading a reluctant Crawford to take on the task of writing Mackintosh's biography, if one needs only one reference book on him, this is it. He challenges some of the myths which have surrounded Mackintosh to try to reach the truth.**

Davidson, Fiona: *Charles Rennie Mackintosh*, Pitkin Guides, Andover, 1998. **A brief introduction to Mackintosh.**

Grogan, Elaine: *Beginnings: Charles Rennie Mackintosh's Early Sketches*, Architectural Press, Oxford, 2002. **Extracts from sketchbooks that came to light in Dublin in 1991, along with commentaries.**

Howarth, Thomas: *Charles Rennie Mackintosh and the Modern Movement*, Routledge, London, 1977. **Out of print, this is the original biography. Still a great reference book, despite more modern studies. Only Pevsner in his *Pioneers of Modern Design* had given Mackintosh a prominent position before.**

Kaplan, Wendy (ed.): *Charles Rennie Mackintosh*, Abbeville Press, New York, 1996. **Published to coincide with a Mackintosh exhibition touring Glasgow, New York, Chicago and Los Angeles during 1996 and 1997, this is an interesting collection of essays on various parts of Mackintosh's work, representing much of the established wisdom on the subject. It is also a useful source of illustrations.**

Macleod, Robert: *Charles Rennie Mackintosh: Architect and Artist*, Collins, London and Glasgow, 1983. **For its time, a good guide to Mackintosh and his work.**

McKean, John, and Baxter, Colin: *Charles Rennie Mackintosh: Architect, Artist, Icon*, Lomond Books, Edinburgh, 2000. **McKean's text is entertaining and Baxter's photographs are wonderful.**

McKean, John, and Baxter, Colin: *Charles Rennie Mackintosh Pocket Guide*, Colin Baxter, Grantown-on-Spey, Moray, 1998. **An interesting summary, but serious Mackintosh students should get a bigger pocket.**

Miller, A, and Opfer, J.: *Charles Rennie Mackintosh: Scotland Street School: A New Survey*, Glasgow Print Studio Gallery, 1980. **Catalogue from an exhibition of drawings prepared by the Mackintosh School of Architecture.**

Moffat, Alastair: *Remembering Charles Rennie Mackintosh: An Illustrated Biography*, Colin Baxter Photography, Lanark, 1989. **An interesting selection of reminiscences of Mackintosh from letters and quotes.**

Neat, Timothy, and McDermott, Gillian: *Closing the Circle: Thomas Howarth and the Modern Movement*, ITNX Publishing, Aberdour, Fife, 2002. **This biography of Thomas Howarth gives the Mackintosh scholar insight into the research Howarth carried out in the preparation of his 1952 book.**

Robertson, Pamela: *Charles Rennie Mackintosh: Art is the Flower*, Pavilion Books, London, 1995. **Collection of paintings and sketches of flowers by Mackintosh with an interesting commentary.**

Robertson, Pamela (ed.): *Charles Rennie Mackintosh: The Architectural Papers*, White Cockade, Wendlebury, 1990. **This contains the only known writings by Mackintosh, along with a commentary on them.**

Robertson, Pamela (ed.): *The Chronycle: the Letters of Charles Rennie Mackintosh to Margaret Macdonald Mackintosh 1927*, Hunterian Art Gallery, Glasgow, 2001. **The long-awaited publication containing letters that the University of Glasgow received in 1972.**

Robertson, Pamela: *The Mackintosh House*, Hunterian Art Gallery, Glasgow. **A stylish catalogue for the recreated home of Charles and Margaret at the Hunterian Art Gallery, of the type that should be available for all Mackintosh buildings that are open to the public. Only Hill House has anything approaching this.**

Steele, James: *Charles Rennie Mackintosh: Synthesis in Form*, Academy Editions, London, 1994. **Most notable for Eric Thorburn's fine illustrations.**

Tames, Richard: *Charles Rennie Mackintosh*, Heinemann Library, Oxford, 2001. **A straightforward summary of Mackintosh's work.**

Wilhide, Elizabeth: *The Mackintosh Style: Decor and Design*, Pavilion Books, London, 1995. **Compact review of Mackintosh's work in context.**

Charles Rennie Mackintosh (1868-1928): Architecture, Design and Painting. **This catalogue from an exhibition at the 1968 Edinburgh Festival provides an interesting source of information on the 350 exhibits.**

Charles Rennie Mackintosh Society Newsletters, 1973 to date. **Two issues are usually produced each year covering a variety of Mackintosh-related subjects.**

C.R. Mackintosh, Corona Books (other details in Japanese). **Purchased at the Glasgow School of Art, this book is written in Japanese, and contains illustrations of various Mackintosh buildings.**

C.R. Mackintosh: The Chelsea Years, Hunterian Art Gallery, University of Glasgow, 1994. **Catalogue for an exhibition held at the Hunterian Art Gallery and the Royal Institute of British Architects in London in 1994.**

Mackintosh at the Hunterian: Guidelines to the National Curriculum and The Mackintosh House, Hunterian Museum and Art Gallery, Glasgow. **Intended for young students, this is a useful summary of Mackintosh and his work, with particular attention given to the Mackintosh House.**

Mackintosh Flower Drawings, Hunterian Art Gallery, Glasgow, 1988, 1993. **Pamela Robertson's forerunner to her 1995 book on the same subject.**

An early design for the redevelopment of Glasgow Cross.

Index

This index details key projects and locations associated with the practice, but does not include references to John Honeyman, John Keppie and Charles Rennie Mackintosh due to the frequency of their appearance in the text.

For full details of all books currently available from Stenlake Publishing, and to order copies, please visit www.stenlake.co.uk. (If you would prefer a printed list and order form please phone or write to us.) All orders to UK addresses are **post-free**, and books can be despatched worldwide for a small flat-rate charge.

Stenlake Publishing Ltd.,
54–58 Mill Square, Catrine, Ayrshire, Scotland, KA5 6RD.
phone +44 (0)1290 551122
www.stenlake.co.uk